THE
WINNING
CONVERSATION

UNLOCKING RESULTS FROM THE INSIDE-OUT

GARETH MORGAN

THE
WINNING
CONVERSATION

UNLOCKING RESULTS FROM THE INSIDE-OUT

The Winning Conversation
Unlocking Results from the Inside-Out

Copyright © 2015 Gareth Morgan / Personal Revolution Ltd.

Published using KWS services: www.kingdomwritingsolutions.org

ISBN: 978-1518737411

Contents

The Conversation that makes you MORE

Introduction

Do you have that ache inside—that deep longing that there must be MORE to your life than what you are experiencing right now? Do you hit those moments of frustration when your actions fall short of your best intentions and wonder if you can ever get past the point to which you keep returning?

This is a very common experience yet so many people feel as if they cannot talk about or even admit to having such feelings. In the western world we are encouraged to suppress them through consumerist choices that act like an anaesthetic, numbing the ache. Often it takes a crisis to remind us of the stark reality that we are missing out on something significant.

In this book I want us to face and pinpoint this problem together. But I also want us to see the potential that lies behind the problem.

I believe that inside every person there is a desire to win in life —a longing to make MORE of life and to connect with something bigger than ourselves.

To dig deep into that treasure within, I want to start a conversation:

- a conversation with you
- a conversation designed to heighten your awareness of the conversation you have with yourself
- a conversation that acts as a catalyst to help you have life-changing conversations with other people.

There is a proverb that has become the driving force for everything I do which says: *The purposes of a man's heart are like deep waters, but a man of understanding draws them out.*

In the pages that follow I want to dive with you into the deep waters of your 'being' to discover the purposes and potential that should be shaping your 'doing.' As we explore the deep ocean trenches of your life we will not only discover the astonishing possibilities that are tied into your potential but also some of the toxic dump from your negative life experiences that is poisoning the waters and preventing your desires from growing into realities. I will direct a strong beam of light onto your life so you can take a good honest look at what is really happening in you.

I want to connect to the innate aspiration inside you that wants to win in life. That aspiration may be like a strong flame that just needs more fuel or it may be a dying ember that needs fanning into life. Whatever the case, this conversation will challenge you to remove the beliefs that are extinguishing the fire within and reinforce the beliefs that fuel an inner inferno. You can discover a future greater than you could ever have imagined. My task is to ask the questions that will lead to clarity on the WHY of your life and to talk you through taking control of the key areas of your life that will unlock the results you desire.

The Winning Conversation will challenge you to keep your conversation going with a community of like-minded people who will cheer you on towards the life you always wanted.

To do this, I will help you to establish three building blocks in your life:

i) The Winning Conversation. This is about creating self-awareness and building an impenetrable self-belief.

ii) The Winning Goal. This will be your life map designed to help you establish clear personal goals and a means to staying on course.

iii) The Winning Team. This is the group of like-minded people to which you need to be accountable if you are going to remain committed to your goals.

Each chapter is designed to take approximately twenty minutes each day over the course of 66 days. As you read I am going to encourage you to create your own immersive experience—one essential for bringing lasting change. You can also connect into our online conversations taking place throughout social media. Head to www.garethmorgan.tv and get involved.

This book will be the start of your journey and lead to unprecedented opportunity and conversations with people.

I will begin with a parable that will introduce you to the framework of our conversation...

A Parable

LIFE Incorporated is a long established business running in New York. For over 25 years they have been a market leader in producing lifestyle goods that encourage people to live life in a positive and motivated way. They produce clothing, household items and even games that inspire people to look at their lives in a different way. They have steadily grown to the point where they now employ over 150 staff members. The owner, Jim Burns, has been the life and soul of the company and an ever-present figure. Five years ago, however, he decided to take more of a back seat.

Jim had a very clear goal for *LIFE Inc.* He wanted to produce products that inspired people to become MORE in their world: MORE

i) Valuable
ii) Prominent
iii) Resilient
iv) Influential
v) Memorable
vi) Expansive

He empowered six directors to be his voice and manage the business.

However, since Jim withdrew, the life that had once run through the company had slowly ebbed away. The business had fallen into the habitual pattern of simply creating what they knew worked. There was no proactive consideration for changes in the market or future events. The directors lacked the stimulus to rethink their approach or reflect how they could do things differently. There was a mood of complacency.

Jim knew that the business had the potential to do far more than it is was accomplishing but without much challenge from competitors and with the company still producing a healthy profit he put off doing anything. While they were still leading competitors in the lifestyle market there was no sense of urgency. It would take a crisis to create any need for a change.

The Crisis

A day finally came when the business had to sit up and take notice. This was not an internal but an external crisis. The American economy had taken a catastrophic hit. Being in the non-essential goods market, the lifestyle sector was severely affected as people stopped spending on what they really did not need. Sales dropped. Demand from wholesalers for lower prices increased. The Eastern markets became a real threat; they were producing similar products in quantities and at prices with which *LIFE Inc* could not compete.

Jim Burns relinquished his back seat to get to grips with the company that had been the love of his life. The more Jim focussed on the financial situation through dialogue with the directors the more he became frustrated. Jim knew that his current conversation with the directors was not producing any way forward so he looked outside the company for new input.

He came across a consultancy firm called *Quick Fix Solutions Inc* (QF). They were specialists at going into challenging work environments and quickly identifying WHAT the owner/leaders could do to rectify the situation. Jim called QF and arranged for a meeting. QF was in great demand as innumerable businesses were being negatively influenced by the downturn. QF seemed to be one of the few companies experiencing real growth at this challenging time.

Jim met with a consultant called Max Whyte. Max was a hugely positive character who immediately impressed him. His charisma and ability to put Jim at ease gave Jim a strong feeling that he had made the right call.

Max was shown around *LIFE Inc* and given access to the

company for a week to look into HOW it was working with its systems and methods, and into WHAT they were producing for the current market.

Max Whyte unpacked his findings in the boardroom:

'Jim, I've got some good news and some not so good news.' Max leaned forward in his chair. 'The good news is that I think you have the ingredients to get out of this hole. Taking the existing strengths but introducing new approaches and products I think in a short period of time we can get this ship turned around. The not so good news is that you are going to have to throw some significant money at new systems and approaches in order to reduce the time it takes to produce your goods. We need to develop additional product lines so that you can appeal to more people. If you can create a new way in HOW you approach the production line and WHAT it is that you produce then I really feel you can survive this storm and position yourself for a greater future.'

Jim sighed with relief. 'That doesn't seem so desperate to me. In fact it makes perfect sense. After all it's the speed of our competitors and their greater range of goods that is making us a poor competitor in the current market. How long do you think it will take before we see different results?'

'I would say three months from the moment the investment is actioned. I will have my team pull together my report and suggested options to bring a quick fix to this great company.'

Jim's reply was filled with a renewed sense of belief. 'I'll get the directors together and we'll implement your suggestions.'

Jim thanked Max and had his PA arrange an emergency director's meeting.

The Changes

Jim sat down with the six directors and went through the report. Each of the directors had an area to focus on and a budget to throw at the problems identified by QF. They agreed to meet weekly during the three months that Max estimated would be needed to get the company back to its former glory days. The directors were invigorated by the proposals as they loved systems and processes. The freshness that came with the new product lines captured everyone's imagination. They were ready to focus intensely on HOW and WHAT they were doing in order to produce different results.

Three months later a two-day review was held and each of the directors gave a report.

The facts and feedback were not what the group had been expecting. They certainly weren't what Jim had been hoping for. The reports contained feedback based on financials and market research. Some of the conclusions were devastating:

'The market no longer understands the identity of *LIFE Inc* and therefore the positioning of the brand is suffering.'

'The new products have had minimal exposure on the shelf and have failed to be noticed. Promotional products have failed to become memorable to the users and so failed to create brand loyalty.'

'The quality of the products has suffered with the increase in production. MORE busyness in the factory has created a fragile product.'

'The financials show a sharp drop in overall sales along with poor performance of new products. The company is diminishing.'

The accountant concluded that the overall worth of the company had now reduced and was in fact significantly in debt as it had tried to change its future by changing HOW it operated and WHAT it produced.

Jim had started the first day of the meetings with renewed hope but as the day of reporting and discussion came to a close he sat alone in the empty boardroom. With deep sadness he realised that what had once been a vibrant organisation was now on a life-support machine. With little remaining in the bank the situation seemed hopeless.

That night Jim had the worst night's sleep he could remember. His mind was full of decisions he had made being replayed over and over again. He spent much of the night pacing up and down the floorboards of his home while his wife lay asleep. He had come to the conclusion that if he could not come up with a solution on day two then there was only one option—to close down the company.

The Conversation

On day two the 150 staff members at *LIFE Inc* were blissfully unaware of the desperate state of the company. Some had been with the company since the very beginning. Others had come in at the junior apprentice level as part of their college course in order to acquire industry experience. The company had been committed to bringing younger people in, largely because they were a cost-efficient way of getting some of the more menial jobs done. Some of these had become key members of staff over the years.

One of them was a young man in his early 20's called Jo Styles. Jo had been taken on in a full-time capacity after he completed his college course. He had started to take on more responsibility once he had a fuller understanding of how the company operated. He was full of life and had aspirations to see *LIFE Inc* become all it could be. However, he had also recently become very frustrated as he realised that not everyone carried that same desire to grow and excel. He was committed to the future of the company so he hung in.

It was 10:30am on day two of the director's review meeting and along with his normal daily duties Jo was to be on hand that day to make sure the boardroom had food, drinks and a clean environment.

Jo went up to the door of the boardroom and listened in to see if now would be an appropriate time to go in. He knocked.

'Come in,' Jim said.

Jo walked into a very depressed atmosphere.

'Excuse me, gentlemen,' Jim said as he made his way to use the

17

washroom.

As Jo was clearing away he could not help catch the various conversations at the boardroom table. He realised that something serious was happening. He heard two directors speak negatively about Jim. One of the directors just sat despondently, looking at his mobile phone. The other three seemed to be reeling off a list of excuses why they the company was performing badly. He heard them question the integrity of the managers, the commitment of the staff members, the methods implemented by the product teams and even the president of the US and his policies. Those at the helm of the company were consumed by negativity, blame and excuses.

Jo cleared up and started to make his way out, just as Jim came back in.

'Thank you...' Jim stuttered as he looked for Jo's ID on his lanyard.

'Jo, sir. My name is Jo Styles. It's a pleasure to meet you.' Jo shook Jim's hand.

'Well thank you, Jo.'

Jo suddenly realised he was staring so he closed the door. He then continued to sort out his trolley and as he did listen to Jim's voice through the keyhole.

'Well, gentlemen, all I have heard today and yesterday is tremendously disappointing. It really is. I was awake most of the night. This is a very dark situation for us as a company.'

Jo was leaning in heavily now.

'Time is of the essence and I am proposing that we call it a day. We only have two months worth of operating costs left and I think we need to action a process of winding this company up.'

Jo quickly pulled away in shock. As he returned the trolley to the kitchens his mind was awash with fear and a strange excitement. Jo was afraid that the company was about to be closed but excited about the dreams he had for change.

At lunchtime Jo was pacing around the factory floor when he saw Jim Burns over at the vending machine fetching a bottle of cola.

'Sir, could I have a minute?'

Jim turned round. 'Ah, John isn't it?'

'No it's Jo, sir … Jo Styles.'

'Ah yes, Jo. What can I do for you?'

'I hope you don't mind but when I came in to clear up earlier I could sense that it was a difficult meeting you were having and well… to be totally honest I overheard that the company is on the brink of closure.'

Jim frowned.

Jo continued. 'I was wondering if I could make one observation before you decide to close the company or not.'

Jim looked quizzically at Jo before smiling. 'Come with me, Jo. You have two minutes before I have to go back.'

The two of them stepped into a vacant office.

'I'm all ears.'

Jo cleared his throat. 'I have been in the company for five years, I came through the graduate scheme and I have gotten to understand how things are around here. When I was in the boardroom this morning it was a light bulb moment. I understood what the source of the challenge is and therefore I believe we have the potential to find a solution.'

Jo took a deep breath. 'It is going to sound so simple but it's one word—'conversation'. The conversations in that boardroom are the problem. And if you, like me, want to see this company turned around then the conversations need to change. When you walked out of the room I could hear the comments. They were from people who did not have the right beliefs to produce the LIFE that this company needs. Those conversations set the environment for the factory floor, the managers, the team members and every member of staff. Those conversations are setting the culture and atmosphere. They are the unseen driving force behind the visible results. It is those conversations first of all that need to change if we are to be good enough for the market we are serving in the current economic climate.'

Jim stood in silence as Jo finished.

'Jo, I want you to meet me at 5pm in the boardroom,' he said after a pause. 'I think you and me need to carry on this conversation.'

Jo went to the board room at 5pm just as the other directors were leaving. He received strange looks from the men as they walked past him.

'Come in Jo,' Jim called out. 'Take a seat. Those were some pretty bold words you gave me earlier. It must have taken some courage.'

'I care about this company and my job,' Jo replied. 'I felt a personal responsibility to do something.'

'I could tell that. You are the first person to actually take responsibility for the situation. I am sick and tired of excuses. You stood out today because even though you don't have the position to do so, you spoke because you care. I was going to make the call to close the company today but your words have pulled me back from the brink for now.'

'I certainly would be willing to do whatever it takes,' Jo said.

'Good. Be here tomorrow at 10am and we will carry this on.'

The Coach

The next day Jo was at the boardroom for 10:00AM on the dot. He knocked on the door and entered. Jim was sat with a lady Jo did not recognise.

'Jo, let me introduce you to Creatia. Creatia is going to help us fully understand your observations.'

'Hi Jo, it's a pleasure to meet you,' said the very smart and efficient looking woman.

'I met Creatia last year,' Jim said. 'She has a great gift for helping to present peoples' ideas in a creative and meaningful way. I thought she would be the perfect person to help you over the next seven days to unpack your thoughts ready to present to me a week tomorrow. I do not want to put pressure on you, Jo, as this is a wild punt, a last gasp attempt to change what I fear may be an unchangeable and inevitable situation. But even at very least if it develops you and helps me to know we have exhausted all opportunities then it will be worth the time. I'll leave you to get on.'

With that Jim left the room.

Jo smiled. 'I can't quite believe I'm here to be honest.'

'Well Jo', said Creatia. 'Jim saw something in you yesterday. I am here to simply ask the right questions to unpack your thoughts.'

'Great,' said Jo. 'I'll be here at 9am to get started!'

The next day Jo was in the boardroom at ten to nine and in walked Creatia.

'Are you ready then?' she asked.

'Oh yes!'

'Well, the best place to start is by asking what we want the end goal to be,' Creatia said.

Jo took a deep breath. 'Jim wants to see us produce goods that are:

i)   Valuable in the eyes of the customer
ii) Prominent in the market place
iii) Resilient in durability
iv) Influential in their reach within the world
v)   Memorable to the user
vi) Expansive in terms of how they can develop and grow

In order to achieve this, the people in this factory need to have these same qualities. The more they display these qualities the more the products will carry the same level of distinction. I don't believe you can separate the product from the person. The fruit a tree produces comes from the root of the tree.'

'That makes sense,' Creatia said. 'How do you propose to do this?'

'I've been thinking about this and what is obvious to me and what that I do not think is necessarily obvious to everyone else is the tone and content of the conversations between company employees. The challenging economic climate has created a negative conversation in the workplace which has created a negative conversation in the employees. *LIFE Inc* may be our badge but *Death Inc* is what we have become. The company drains life rather than produces it! We need to create employees who hold positive and energising conversations that instil a winning mood in the workplace and then create a winning product and winning results for the company. If *LIFE Inc* works hard on producing winning employees then they will produce winning products.'

'I have heard it said,' Creatia interjected, 'that a person's output will never surpass their personal investment. So if we invest in the people, the products will increase in quality and quantity. This means we are looking for a change from employees working according to an OUTSIDE-IN conversation, defined by the environment, to an INSIDE-OUT one in which beliefs drive actions.'

'You've got it!' Jo exclaimed.

'We will pick this up tomorrow,' Creatia said. 'I'll leave you to use the rest of today to think this through.'

Creatia packed her belongings away and left while Jo sat down with blocks of sticky notes and began to jot down his ideas.

The Custodians

'Good morning, Jo,' Creatia said as she walked into the boardroom the next day.

'It is a good morning, isn't it?' Jo said, looking up from his notes.

Cretia looked surprised. 'It's good to hear that you are so positive. Do you have a breakthrough?'

'I believe I have. When I talked with Jim I said that the problem came down to the conversations taking place in this boardroom between the directors. They were negative and destructive. I realised that what was in them had filtered through the entire company. If we want to turn this company round the people we have directing from now on have to embody the qualities of the products. The people Jim brings in as directors going forwards have to be custodians of the qualities.'

'If they are going to produce winning results,' Creatia added, 'they will have to hold to winning beliefs!'

'Yes, that's right.'

With that Jo and Creatia began to discuss and write out the six values that were represented by the current board and then the six opposing values that that would unlock the winning results in the employees.

After hours researching and discussing they settled on the six that would create the right belief system in the boardroom, as well as the six that Jo had witnessed in what he now refers to as the 'losing conversation.'

LOSING Voices behind a LOSING conversation	WINNING Voices behind a WINNING conversation
Lethargy	Passion
Irrelevant	Relevant
Exclusive	Inclusive
Predictable	Creative
Mediocre	Excellent
Apathetic	Devotion

'If a winning conversation is to be developed in this company, then these are the voices that need to be heard in the boardroom,' Jo concluded.

'I like it!' Creatia smiled. 'I like it a lot! People can remember that and we could even put up pictures in the boardroom of the six voices that speak of WHO we are.'

Both left the boardroom on day two buzzing about what they called 'the winning conversation.'

The Clarity

Jo worked into the night. He jotted down some thoughts about the colleagues he had seen move on from *LIFE Inc.*

'WHY HAVE PEOPLE LEFT?

These were good people who never wanted to leave. However what was in them seemed to have become incompatible and at odds with what the company started to represent.

They were strong in self-belief and high in aspiration, focus and commitment. These attributes stood in stark contrast to those I encountered that day in the boardroom. The directors were low in self-belief, aspiration, focus and commitment. The directors have become consumed by a losing conversation that in turn was responsible for the results of the company.'

The next morning Creatia opened. 'Having a winning conversation in the boardroom of belief is one thing but this is just one room hidden in the centre of this building. How do we get the conversation to spread throughout the floors of the factory? We know that people often view their job as a means to an end and so will not have the same awareness and ownership the directors have. How do we get that awareness and ownership throughout the rest of the workforce in order for the winning conversation to really take effect?'

'That's a good point. As someone who has spent much of the last few years across most of the floors it always amazed me how much the mood of the people affects what we do and what we produce. Great mood equals great results. Negative mood equals negative results. We need to create a winning mood, a winning feeling.'

'I know what you mean,' said Creatia. 'It's like we all have these appetites that need feeding and when they are starved we cannot function effectively.'

'That is a great way of putting it. My Mum used to always say, "Jo, don't go out on an empty stomach" in the mornings. I would love to see managers bringing their teams together every morning or at the start of each shift and for a few minutes set the tone of the conversation.'

'For this to work,' Creatia interrupted, 'It is vital that the leaders in the boardroom spend time with the managers. In fact for the sake of our diagram let's call it the 'office floor of feelings'. The managers are first and foremost 'mood managers'. Each manager needs to actively cultivate a particular 'feeling'. So we need to identify and list these feelings and identify the role of the director/leader in the conversation.'

Creatia stepped up to the white board to act as scribe.

'Well,' Jo replied. 'During the remainder of yesterday I got the go ahead from Jim to observe the workforce and I listened closely to the conversation and observed the mood of the place. In those producing a good mood in the workplace I could see that their internal needs were being met. For instance those who felt like they had a voice in what was taking place carried a sense of ownership and they became more helpful to the managers and leaders. Likewise, those who felt unappreciated produced less than satisfactory results.'

'So the managers who created the right mood were those who understood the needs of the workers and worked hard to feed their internal appetites,' Creatia said.

'That's right. It's like when you are physically hungry you are more likely to be in a bad mood which in turn affects your results. And the same is true for our soul appetites. We need to discern what these appetites are.'

The two now worked out what appetites needed to be fed in order for the right mood to be created. They also identified the results of these appetites not being fed and the subsequent moods that would ensue.

WINNING CONVERSATION	EXPANSIVE CONVERSATION	INFLUENTIAL CONVERSATION	VALUABLE CONVERSATION	RESILIENT CONVERSATION	MEMORABLE CONVERSATION	PROMINENT CONVERSATION
VALUE (Director)	Creative	Inclusive	Excellent	Passionate	Relevant	Devoted
APPETITE	Achievement	Acceptance	Appreciation	Assurance	Authority	Affection
MOOD (Manager)	Enthusiastic	Curious	Grateful	Optimistic	Helpful	Expectant

LOSING CONVERSATION	DIMINISHING CONVERSATION	INFERIOR CONVERSATION	WORTHLESS CONVERSATION	FRAGILE CONVERSATION	FORGETTABLE CONVERSATION	UNNOTICED CONVERSATION
VALUE (Director)	Predictable	Exclusive	Mediocre	Lethargic	Irrelevant	Apathetic
APPETITE	Underachieved	Un-Accepted	Unappreciated	Unassured	Unauthorised	Undervalued
MOOD (Manager)	Unenthusiastic	Uninterested	Ungrateful	Pessimistic	Unhelpful	Unexpectant

The next day Creatia was in the boardroom getting ready for the day ahead and looked at the clock. Jo was late.

A few minutes later Jo rushed in through the door. 'I'm so sorry, Creatia. I hate being late but something caught my attention at reception. I think it's going to help us.'

'What is it?'

'Last night I was unable to sleep because I was aware we needed a framework to communicate what we are unpacking. I remembered that at reception we have this large plan of this building containing instructions how people are to evacuate the building in case of a fire. The factory building is effectively made up of four oval layers. When I drew it on my notepad I realised we could communicate our findings in the form of the building layout.'

Jo proceeded to draw four concentric circles.

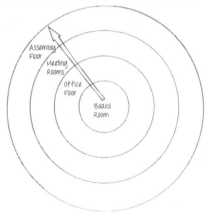

'The boardroom sits at the centre. We have agreed this is where the BELIEFS, VALUES, IDENTITY and the HEART of the company are. Then we have the next layer, the office floors of management which is where the FEELINGS, DESIRE, DRIVE and SOUL of the company are. I then saw a pattern forming. The next layer in the building is the meeting rooms where the managers meet team leaders to formulate plans and rotas—they are the MIND of operations. Anything that gets actioned is decided here. It's where the THOUGHTS are determined and from where the PRACTICE and the MIND of the company operate. Finally, you have the assembly floor where the products are made and leave the factory to go out to the customer.'

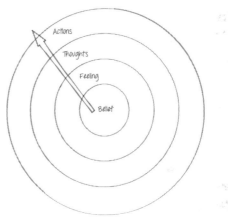

Jo put the pen down and turned to Creatia.

'So far we have looked at the winning beliefs from the boardroom and the winning mood on the office floors but now we have to understand how the conversation moves into the meeting rooms where the mindsets are established and the plans for action are in place. This is the HOW of the factory.'

'I can see the pattern,' Creatia commented. 'The problem is that because of weak leadership in the boardroom the external and poor results ultimately defined the belief of the company. The actions, thoughts, feelings and ultimately beliefs have been shaped from the OUTSIDE-IN.'

'Yes!' Jo cried. 'That is right, exactly right.'

'So how do we keep the conversation flowing through all layers of the building?' asked Creatia. 'What does the conversation need to sound like?'

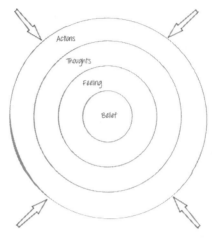

'The relationship between the manager's team room and the assembly floor is essential. The manager's team can come up with all the plans they want but if there's a disconnect in relationship between them and the assembly floor then the plans are useless, just as intention without action is meaningless. What use is a plan in the team room if it does not make it onto the assembly floor? The THINKING and FOCUS of the team room need to inform the CHOICES and COMMITMENT of the assembly room to activate the RESULTS we want to see.'

Jo quickly drew on the board the flow of conversation that needed to happen:

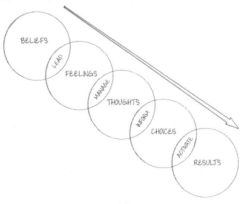

'You can see from this diagram that if the directors effectively outline and embody the values and beliefs of the company working closely with the managers who will set the mood of the floor it is then down to the team leaders to develop 'a winning mindset' that becomes the mentality of the company. Each manager has a team leader and they come together in the meeting rooms to help them manage their area and key team members. Here they train their workers with the action plans for their area of the production process.

A mindset as you know is an accepted attitude. Our attitude influences our approach to everything we do; it informs our choices. We need six THOUGHTS and ATTITUDES that form the MINDSETS in order to progress a consistent conversation from the leader to the manager and from the manager to the team leader.'

'That looks like our job for today then,' said Creatia.

Both Creatia and Jo got to work for the rest of the day. They made a list of the mindsets that naturally flow from the winning conversation and then identified the losing mindsets of the losing conversation. By the end of the day they had clarity on their findings.

LOSING CONVERSATION	DIMINISHING CONVERSATION	INFERIOR CONVERSATION	WORTHLESS CONVERSATION	FRAGILE CONVERSATION	FORGETTABLE CONVERSATION	UNNOTICED CONVERSATION
BELIEF	Predictable	Exclusive	Mediocre	Lethargic	Irrelevant	Apathy
MOOD	Unenthusiastic	Uninterested	Ungrateful	Pessimistic	Unhelpful	Unexpectant
MINDSET	Maintenance	Unconfident	Careless	Unwilling	Insincere	Undetermined

WINNING CONVERSATION	EXPANSIVE CONVERSATION	INFLUENTIAL CONVERSATION	VALUABLE CONVERSATION	RESILIENT CONVERSATION	MEMORABLE CONVERSATION	PROMINENT CONVERSATION
BELIEF	Creativity	Inclusive	Excellence	Passion	Relevant	Devotion
MOOD	Enthusiastic	Curious	Grateful	Otimistic	Helpful	Expectant
MINDSET	Progressive	Confident	Diligent	Perseverance	Sincerity	Determinined

The Cause

The next morning Creatia was going to be late into the factory and this gave Jo some time to think through how the winning conversation was going to work its way from the team room of thoughts onto the assembly floor of action.

Jo often found it useful to journal his thoughts and ideas so he took out his computer and began to talk with himself.

'In my experience this has always been a real weakness in the factory. A real division has existed between the MEETING ROOM of team leaders and the ASSEMBLY FLOOR. Because of this many of the plans in the team room were never actioned. Sometimes you will get a team who are CAN DO people but then assembly workers who won't action the plan. This is like the MINDSET having a clear and positive intention but the BODY not putting the intention into action. What use is a positive mindset with no action? Therefore the only way to get these two to work together is to have a clear goal that is burning inside of them that produces the results we are looking for. I suggest goal setting, and accountability to those goals, should become part of the working relationship between these two areas. If there is agreement between them and shared ownership of the goal then the goal will be the unifying driver. The more I think about this the more I realise that this is same for my life. Many of my intentions have never made it through to action which has left me feeling frustrated because the belief, the feeling and thoughts have been there but for some reason the process breaks down more than it works.'

Time had flown by when Creatia came into the boardroom.

'Hey Jo, are you winning?'

'At first I wasn't but I am now.' Jo went on to explain what he had been journaling.

'That is so true in business and life,' said Creatia. 'Goal setting is powerful and when it is not present a team lacks passion. So what picture do you think could generate the life back into this company again?'

'We have to create conversations in our team meetings that encourage individuals to share their personal goals. We then have to find the link between the personal goal and the goal of the company. Our people need to see that this is more than a job; it is about their development as people and the unlocking of their potential.

This will influence every area of their lives!' Jo concluded. 'When we get a unified vision then this pulls us past any disagreement or disconnect that may exist because the CAUSE is bigger than a personality.'

'So if you can get agreement on a goal,' Creatia added, 'this galvanises each layer of *Life Inc* to cultivate the conversation that will lead to results in both the business and the employee's lives. So let's come up with the six behaviours that reveal a person hosting the winning conversation!'

The two now set out to list six actions for each corresponding conversation:

LOSING CONVERSATION	DIMINISHING CONVERSATION	INFERIOR CONVERSATION	WORTHLESS CONVERSATION	FRAGILE CONVERSATION	FORGETTABLE CONVERSATION	UNNOTICED CONVERSATION
BELIEF I AM	Predictable	Exclusive	Mediocre	Lethargic	Irrelevant	Apathy
MOOD I AM IN	Unenthusiastic	Uninterested	Ungrateful	Pessimistic	Unhelpful	Unexpectant
MINDSET I HAVE	Maintenance	Uncertain	Careless	Unwilling	Insincere	Undetermined
ACTION I WILL	Duplicate	Disconnect	Disregard	Drop out	Distance	Disengage

WINNING CONVERSATION	EXPANSIVE CONVERSATION	INFLUENTIAL CONVERSATION	VALUABLE CONVERSATION	RESILIENT CONVERSATION	MEMORABLE CONVERSATION	PROMINENT CONVERSATION
BELIEF I AM	Creative	Inclusive	Excellent	Passionate	Relevant	Devoted
MOOD I AM IN	Enthusiastic	Curious	Grateful	Optimistic	Helpful	Expectant
MINDSET I HAVE	Progressive	Confident	Diligent	Perseverance	Sincerity	Determined
ACTION I WILL	Construct	Connect	Compete	Complete	Contribute	Commit

The Convergence

There was one more part of the pattern that needed to be discovered. How was Jo going to present the conversations so that the results could be tracked and measured?

He then remembered something Creatia had said in conversation about the workers actually being the products that they are selling. It felt like an 'Aha' moment. Here they were making and distributing LIFE products but most did not have any interaction with the products or principles they were selling. They were selling a message they weren't embodying. What if Jo could create a programme through which the workers could use the products, learn the principles and relate the winning conversation of the factory to their own lives?

'Creatia, I've got something to show you.'

'Sounds intriguing,' replied Creatia. Jo explained the idea of the employees using the products they were creating.

'What if each employee at *Life Inc* developed a LIFE map? It would be based around goals they have for their lives beyond their employment. If we showed we were committed to their personal development, to the whole person, I know that the productivity levels in this place would more than double in due course.'

'So what does a LIFE map look like? And how would the worker interact with it?'

'I have something that I use to help me,' said Jo as he pulled out his journal. 'I start with the most important conversations I will have with people at the end of my life. I allow the ultimate conversations of my life to shape my immediate conversations. Then I ask myself what is the legacy that I want to leave, the one thing that I feel my life is about and I create different plot points and set goals.'

'That is really good,' said Creatia. 'I am guessing that is why you are in the position you are right now. You have worked on your personal development in every area and it has prepared you for promotion.'

'Maybe,' Jo blushed. 'But what excites me is the potential of every person in *Life Inc* to contribute to the success of the company by the company focussing on the success of the individual. In most areas of life people are looking to consume what others bring.'

'Which is outside-in,' added Creatia.

'Exactly, but what if we flipped that and said we were about unlocking the potential of our people first? I believe the results will be unrecognisable. Stress levels would be down, absenteeism reduced, job satisfaction up, targets smashed and this workplace would become the place where people want to work. I even think we would get people offering themselves as volunteers just to get in the door!'

'I am beginning to feel like I want to work for the company,' Creatia laughed.

Jo spent the rest of the day walking the pattern through with Creatia and they came up with the finished matrix for what *Life Inc* should look like and also a very clear picture of what *Death Inc* looks like.

The Completion

It was the final day before Jo had to report back. Creatia and Jo sat down for the final time.

'What a week it has been Jo. I feel like I've been working with you forever!'

Jo smiled. 'I've loved it, Creatia, and I can't thank you enough for the partnership. Now we've just got to complete the pattern today!'

'I was thinking about that,' said Creatia. 'Do you think formal conversations are going to be the only environment where you keep the winning conversation going? You know supervisions, appraisals etc?'

'That's a great question. I think we can organise conversations through our formal lines of communication and this is important. However, for this to really take effect it ultimately has to be organic. People prioritise what they prefer to talk about rather than what is prescribed. So we have to connect what we want to see more of to what people are already passionate about. If we can list the things that people truly value and help them connect the results of these areas to the conversations then they are more likely to take up the conversations organically and therefore feed the culture we want at *Life Inc.*'

Creatia and Jo now set about listing a number of ways the

winning conversation would affect a person's life:

The Winning Conversation…changes how you feel…shapes your experiences…unleashes your passion…builds a strong family life… unlocks your ideas…defeats your fears.

Jo summed up. 'The more we connect the winning conversation to what people value in life the more I believe we will cultivate natural conversations. So I suggest we demonstrate this through powerful imagery around the factory. I've also come up with a very simple way of keeping it in front of people using a dice.'

'Dice?'

Jo went on to unpack his ideas as they put the finishing touches to the presentation.

The Culmination

Jo spent a lot of time over the weekend diligently polishing up on his presentation. He woke up Monday morning early and prepped himself before heading into the factory. He arrived at the boardroom—unchartered territory only a week ago—a place which in the past week he had spent more time in than his own home.

As he walked in expecting to find Jim and the directors, he saw Jim, Creatia and five new faces.

Jim spoke. 'Jo let me introduce to you my friends Reeva, Dev, Ince, Paz and Xavier.'

Jo gasped.

'You may be wondering why the other directors are not here. Well, on the back of what you said to me last week I realised that my confusion and inability to see a way past the problem was in large part down to the people surrounding me in my conversations. I had to shut those conversations down and so asked the directors to step down. Over the past five days Creatia has been keeping me up to date with how you have been getting on and while she has not disclosed anything of your presentation, she was hugely impressed. I have been having conversations with my business friends who are here today potentially interested in investing and therefore becoming the new directors along with Creatia ... should your presentation stimulate enough interest.'

Jim now handed proceedings over to Jo.

'Thank you, ladies and gentlemen, for giving me the opportunity to share my thoughts and findings with you. Since joining *Life Inc* I have come to understand that our goal and privilege was to serve the wider public with a life-inspiring message that would aim to unlock the potential inside every person who bought into our product. Our messages essentially communicate 'you are a winner'. They inspire and promote that champion spirit. Our vision is that when people put on our clothing, hang up that inspirational message or are given one of our gifts that they are reminded WHO they are and WHAT they can become.'

Jo took a sip of water. 'That vision requires there to be a *resilience* in this factory greater than the financial crisis happening right now. If we say you are a winner and yet cultivate a losing environment then our product does not match our practice. I also believe it shows that our practice does not match our potential.'

Several of the audience smiled.

'With so much running through my mind over the last number of days I was struggling to have a framework through which I could communicate to you exactly what I feel is the problem and therefore the solution. However it was late on the second day of working on this that I looked at the staff notice board with our fire procedure and an outline drawing of this building, highlighting the exit points. The more I looked at the drawing of the building the more I realised that right in front of me was the framework. As I looked at the four layers to the building and the activity that takes place in the different areas I realised there was a pattern.'

Jo then drew four concentric circles on the white board.

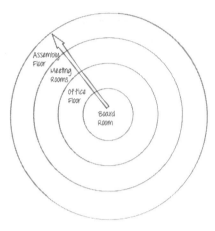

'Essentially the building is circular and has four areas of activity. There is the boardroom at the centre, the office floor, the managers' rooms and then assembly floor. Each of these spaces can be associated with a different action:

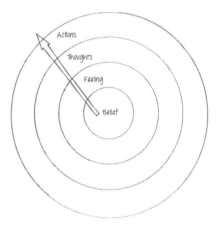

Up to now it is my belief that the current climate has revealed that our current beliefs, drive, plans and actions are weaker than the external environment.

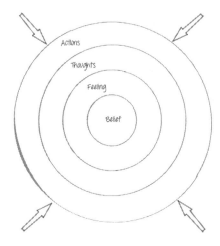

The conversations that have been voiced from this boardroom have indicated that this is essentially the case. Therefore the losing conversation we have been having has been the undercurrent to a winning life we are promoting. This duplicity has created an identity crisis. If we were called *Death Inc* it would better explain our reality.

Rather than creating products that are:

i)   Valuable
ii)   Prominent
iii)   Resilient
iv)   Influential
v)   Memorable
vi)   Expansive

Death Inc has created products that are:

i)   Worthless
ii)   Unnoticed
iii)   Fragile
iv)   Inferior
v)   Forgettable
vi)   Diminishing

While it was a natural reaction to bring in Quick Fix Solutions it was in fact the wrong decision.'

Jo had gone past the point of no return now.

'As a worker on the office floor during this three month period I witnessed time, energy and effort being poured into HOW we do things and WHAT we produced. However, this is like dealing with a dying tree by simply changing how it looks and the shape it takes. The source of the problem went deeper. It was in the WHO. This brings me to the boardroom. When you start from the boardroom you are starting with the root of the tree.'

Jo took another sip of water.

'As a worker who has experienced life on the various floors over the past five years I saw that I never had a direct conversation with any of the directors. My conversations were between me and my manager. I suddenly realised that the conversations quite literally flow from the central room that we are sat in now and make their way outward to the factory floor, then into the managers' development rooms. Conversations are POWERFUL! They shape our lives. The words we speak and the words we choose to listen to have impact.

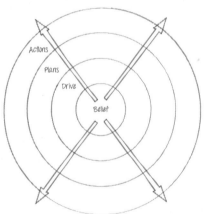

Therefore my presentation is based around the principle and framework that we do not want to be shaped by outside forces, what I would label an 'outside-in' pattern, but we want an 'inside-out' pattern. We want what is on the inside of this company to be the belief and driving force of our plans and actions. Therefore our product is not just WHAT we sell but it is a reflection of WHO we really are.

I want to present to you my plan called 'the winning conversation.'

Jo handed out notes and proceeded to tell the story of the seven day process of discovering and developing the WINNING CONVERSATION with Creatia.

'This concludes my presentation, ladies and gentlemen.'

The Consequences

There was a moment of silence. Then there was a round of applause led by Jim, who was smiling as he spoke.

'Jo, that was a profound presentation of what needs to happen in this organisation. As I explained to you earlier, I want and need the backing of these potential directors to turn this from what you have rightly called *Death Inc* back to *Life Inc*. While there's still lots of work to be done in applying what you have said I wonder if there are any questions from the group?'

Reeva put her hand up. 'Jo, what ideas do you have to start creating this 'winning conversation' as you call it?'

'The pattern of 'the winning conversation' is taught through creating an immersive experience. How did the previous regime, unintentionally, create the results they did? By hosting a constant conversation based upon beliefs that were self-focussed, self-serving and self-destructive. They immersed the culture of this company in that conversation. This led to people unconsciously behaving parallel to their beliefs. In order for us to establish a new culture there has to be a fresh immersion in the winning ethos through both organised and organic conversations.'

'Can you explain what those look like?' Reeva asked.

'I'll start with organized conversations. In every leader's and manager's team meeting I am encouraging them to use the 'winning dice.' Every game uses a dice and the dice is the key to winning. On each side of the dice there is a statement that communicates what we accept and what we reject, what we want to celebrate and what we will not tolerate. This helps to create a very clear distinction. It means that in every conversation there is a reference point that keeps a level of accountability amongst workers. Should you invest and become directors you will each own one of the conversations and in the manager you lead and the product development area you oversee you will guard and protect and proliferate that conversation.'

'And what about organic conversations?' Reeva asked.

'Creatia and I also discussed the importance of creating an immersive environment through ad hoc and unplanned conversations. We can celebrate winning stories of staff members who have made progress, sharing stories via our social media accounts.'

Jo started to show images on the projection screen in the boardroom.

'Images are powerful and if we can communicate that the winning conversation changes how you feel, shapes your experiences, unleashes your passion, builds a strong family life, unlocks your ideas and defeats your fears, this creates greater self-awareness and increases aspiration.'

'I like it, I really do,' Reeva said.

Jim turned to the group. 'There's lots to be done but what I want to know at this point is are you in? Will you invest the necessary time, effort and money to put *Life Inc* back on the map and release the potential of this company?'

A man called Ince raised his hand. 'I have been very happy with what I have heard but there is one condition to my investment?'

There was a pause.

'I will only invest if Jo accepts the job of becoming the CEO of *Life Inc*.'

All eyes moved to Jim and then swiftly to Jo.

Jim spoke first. 'I think that is absolutely the right call. Is everyone in agreement?'

Everyone except Jo nodded.

'Well Jo?'

'I am in!' Jo cried. 'If you as directors will accept your responsibility to guard the winning conversation then let's start having the right conversations and producing the right results.'

And with that a new era began.

Day 1: The Winning Order

'An incorrect order in our lives is like trying to pull a door that says PUSH!'

Have you ever tried pushing a door open despite the fact that the sign says 'PULL'? Embarrassing isn't it? We can often feel like this in life. We try to push past a certain point but our progress is halted because we fail to read the sign. We either try to break the door down or we stop our advance.

Just about every person at some point feels as if they are going about life the wrong way, as if something is not quite right, as if they are missing something that could release potential and purpose?

I have always been notoriously poor at putting together any product that requires any level of construction. In fact anything that requires a manual is an unattractive prospect. I will usually skim the instructions, gauge a rough idea of how things work and then start building. Within a few steps I realize my folly.

As a child I was no good at Lego because I would become frustrated with instructions and how they related to what appeared to be millions of little pieces. My son Reuben however is very different; he loves Lego and enjoys the process of following instructions in order to bring to reality the picture on the front of the box.

My natural inclination is to build using the right pieces but according to how I think it should go together. This is usually in the wrong order, resulting in frustration. When I take the right pieces but bypass the correct order it makes even the right pieces the wrong pieces.

The right things + the right order = the right results.

The right things + the wrong order = the wrong results.

The Winning Conversation is about understanding the right order that unlocks the results that we all deeply desire.

Pursuing the Prize

When I make my life about the pursuit of results I set myself up for a rollercoaster journey. When I pay careful attention to doing the right things in the right order I position myself to unlock my potential and achieve results that are beyond my expectations.

In life generally we often continue to make things up as we go along because there are no instruction manuals. The good news is that you do not have to continue this way. You can win in life and it's simpler than you think. It is within the ability and control of every person to win. In fact I will go as far as to say you were designed to win.

The key is to be aware of the parts required to make the final picture complete and then put them together in the right order. I am naturally a compulsive person and will try and figure how the pieces correlate to each other and just get on with it. If I managed my natural inclinations then I would achieve more and enjoy more. This is where the Winning Conversation has become so important to me. *The Winning Conversation is a set of guiding principles founded in the Bible, an instruction manual full of timeless, ancient wisdom that can help people of faith or no faith.*

How would you answer the question, 'What is the prize you are looking for in life?' My guess is that, like me, you would think of the things you want to possess, the person you would like to meet or marry, the places you would like to go and the profits you would like to achieve. This is the natural starting point for every human being. It's where babies begin when they cry out for WHAT they want, a cry that continues through adolescence into adulthood. This is much like me wanting to avoid the correct process for building a product or completing a puzzle.

Let me show you what happens when we make the WHAT our starting point, ignoring the HOW.

The Losing Order to Life

We are naturally **prize**-driven beings; we see **WHAT** we want and we go after it. How successful in turn shapes our belief in **WHO** we are.

Whether we are conscious about this drive or not, this creates an internal conversation in which we ask, 'How do I possess the prize?' Let me be clear from the start. There is nothing wrong with pursuing a prize; you are designed this way. However, many of us want to gain our goal as quickly as possible. My passion for the prize bypasses the process to the prize. I value the prize before the process. However, the key to unlocking our personal potential is to prize the process!

Make the process your prize!

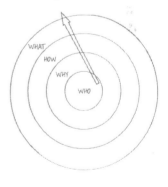

When we are prize-driven we naturally allow the prize to be the leader. This defines the pattern of choices we make, the habits we form. These patterns determine our feelings concerning why we are alive—in other words, our purpose. Because we rely upon something we have not yet attained to fulfil our need for purpose we become like a hungry person watching a cooking show, able to see but unable to taste. This then activates our belief concerning who we are. Who we are as a person is defined by what we have or have not attained in terms of what we prize in life.

When our lives are led by the prize and not the process we are working back to front. In fact the instructions I rely on ask me first to lay out all the pieces so I can clearly have in mind the constituent parts I am dealing with. Then step-by-step I am encouraged to work through the correct order to achieve the prize, which is the end-product.

When I value the prize over the process I end up losing time, losing enjoyment and losing patience. This is the losing approach and in life I call it the losing conversation. When we believe that this is the right approach it influences our internal conversation and shapes everything.

The Winning Order to Life

The winning approach does not start with WHAT you are trying to possess but WHO you are, the person you are determined to be. You will never lose WHO you are but you could lose WHAT you try and possess. Therefore it makes sense to invest in what is more permanent—yourself.

WHO you are unlocks WHAT you possess in life. Even though it is not exciting to start the process like this and can at times feel like you are wasting time, the reality is that this is a process connected to how you are wired; you cannot bypass your design.

As the story at the beginning of this book reminds us, we are the product of our conversations. What we become determines our impact and influence on this world. We all want to matter and we all can matter when we seek to unlock our potential through the correct conversation. That conversation has to start with a daily focus on the person I am becoming. When I invest in this I can start to get clarity on my purpose, which then manages my priorities. I make better quality choices when I am being true to WHO I want to become rather than allow WHAT I do to define me. This then produces my pattern of behaviour and what I repeatedly do determines the prize I reap in life.

There are no limits in life other than those we place on ourselves. In fact to believe that our potential is limited is to allow our perception of a reduced prize to make us feel a smaller person. You are not the size of the prize you have achieved; you are the size of your potential and that is a goldmine worthy of deep exploration.

Throughout our conversation together, we will take your life apart, understand the constituent parts and learn how to order it correctly. We will start to discover practical ways of outworking this winning conversation every day. We will learn the importance of involving others on the journey of unlocking the real you.

The concentric circles used in this book form the pattern that helps you to unlock your potential in life. While the words inside will change, they all help us follow the correct order for the conversation we should be having with ourselves in life.

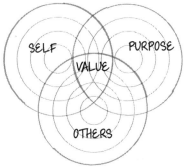

The winning conversation always starts in the middle and works to the outside. Our natural disposition is to start from the outside and then get stuck the further we make our way to the middle, just like constructing the product in the wrong order.

As we will see, there is a much better way than this—a winning way.

Day 2: The Winning Circles

My potential resides in unlocking my personal value and worth

The results of my life are determined by how much value I place on my future, other people and myself. The more I centre my life on valuing any of these areas, the more potential I unlock. Potential is personal value. If each of us carries extraordinary potential, we have to accept that we carry extraordinary value. My value is equal to my potential.

These three areas are interdependent and any increase in a single circle will bring increase to all three. For example, the more I value others, the more value I actually place on myself and my future. When I value others, I sense something happen deep inside of me. I am unlocking my purpose to create value for others. This in turn causes me to think more of my future. In addition, the more I value others, the greater level of self-esteem I have; I feel a sense of value within myself.

Unlocking potential in a person is about getting clarity on the three circles and allowing an increased sense of personal value to

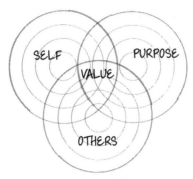

grow in them. Our perspective on how we see ourselves, how we view our future and how we view others reveals much about where we are but can also plot where we will end up in life should our perspectives in these areas not change.

Throughout this book I will help you see how the circles reveal the pattern that unlocks our potential.

From the Root to the Fruit

Our personal sense of value plays the same role as the soil in which a tree is planted. If the roots of a tree are like the values and beliefs of a person then the quality of what feeds these values is of ultimate importance. If the soil is good then the tree can grow. If the soil is contaminated then this will impact the growth of the tree and ultimately the fruit it produces. What is in the soil will course through every root, branch and fruit of the tree.

Poor choices follow a lack of personal value, just as bad fruit comes from bad soil.

Let me introduce you today to an overview of the three circles before going into more detail as to how they operate in a persons' life.

The Concentric Circles

Each of the three value circles breaks down into four concentric circles. The concentric circles reveal an order that provides the key to unlocking human potential.

There are four parts to each of us. Each part of you has a

distinct function and your integrity and togetherness as a person is determined by how well you get these working together as one. The quality of a person's internal conversation will be determined by the clarity of these parts and how they are empowered to contribute to your conversation.

THE SPIRIT

The Spirit is the place where your identity is formed—your beliefs about **WHO** you actually are. This is the deepest level of a person's life; it is the warp core that determines the size and strength of the life that you build.

THE SOUL

The Soul is the part of you where your feelings are formed. It is where your motivation for what you do resides. It is the **WHY** of your life. This is the part of you that is moved emotionally. Our instincts and gut feelings are products of the soul. It is this part of you that determines whether you change the atmosphere positively or negatively.

THE MIND

The mind is the control-centre for all your thoughts. This is where you plan and construct **HOW** you are going to do something in life.

THE BODY

The body is where the inspiration of the soul and information in the mind is earthed in actions that bring about a change in what can be seen. People see the invisible reality of WHAT you believe, feel and think through the visible reality of your actions.

Unlocking the Interlocking Circles that Produce the Winning Conversation

Based on this pattern let me now give you an overview of the three sets of concentric circles that are driven by our personal sense of internal value.

The Winning Goal: 'I value my purpose'

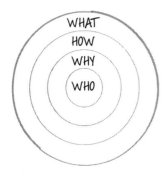

The level to which I value who I am will determine the level to which I value my purpose in life. The more I invest in my purpose the more my personal sense of value increases. I will unpack this more in Days 4 and 5.

When I value my purpose, I believe that I will win in life and leave the world better than when I arrived. I have called this circle the winning goal.

The Winning Conversation: 'I value my self'

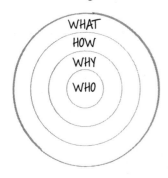

Valuing yourself is about having a correct and balanced perspective on your personal worth. A warped perspective can create one of two extremes. If a person undervalues themselves they will become self-consumed in a toxic way and if a person over-inflates their sense of value they will become ego-centric. From Days 6-14 I will look at how we develop what I have called *the Winning Conversation*. The winning conversation is the major focus of this book; this is often the one that we struggle with most.

When I value myself I believe that I will host a winning conversation. That is why I have named this circle *the winning conversation.*

The Winning Team: 'I value people'

The way we avoid the extremes of poor self-appraisal is through having a correct and healthy perspective about other people. When a person realises that valuing others is a key to unlocking personal potential then they understand the power of valuing other people. I will unpack this on Days 15 -18.

To win in life is to help others win. Therefore the extent to which I value other people will affect how much of my potential I unlock.

Day 3: The Winning You

You are the product of My Life Inc.

My Results, my Responsibility

Imagine yourself watching the news. There is a report of a factory closing in your vicinity. The owner of the factory is being interviewed about the reasons for the closure. 'We are closing because the products our employees produced were not good enough. I am annoyed about that because the economy is a major contributing factor and it is not fair. Our employees did not perform and our managers were incompetent which did not help. Our team leaders did not communicate to our administrators who in turn lacked any influence on our dispatch room. Those guys rarely completed putting the orders together to get them out of the factory. It is unfair and I feel hard done by!'

If you heard this, then like me you would question the owner. Why did he not take responsibility for making the decisions to correct what was happening in his four walls? Why did he blame everyone and everything else? What he gave are excuses rather than valid reasons. He is delusional.

Our lives are like the factory in the parable you read at the start of this book. What the factory produces is the responsibility of the factory owner. Likewise, the results of our lives are our responsibility and no one else's. While there may be many external factors that

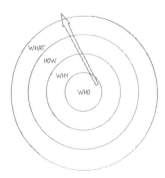

influence our lives, we have the potential not only to ride the challenges but allow them to and start taking responsibility. The word responsibility even suggests that we have the ability to make the correct response in life. It literally means, *the ability to respond.*

Every Result Starts in an Unseen Place

My son asked me one night before going to bed, 'Daddy how was I born? Where did I come from?'

Despite my attempts to pass the conversation on to my wife, he persisted. 'How are dogs born and what about chickens?'

I was glad he moved so quickly away from where humans came from.

I tried to come up with an answer that would apply to all the questions. 'Reuben, everything that you can see starts as something so small you cannot see it.'

That was as good as I could manage!

As humans we are part of an eco-system that works according to this timeless principle. Everything that is seen starts as something unseen.

It is the same with human potential. The elements are all already there but there has to be conception—a belief that they can come together over a process of time and a time of process until they are birthed and are then able to be seen.

The winning conversation starts from an unseen place of unlocking WHO we are and WHY we are alive. There is often little or no evidence in what we see around us that anything has changed and yet when we believe, we trigger a process through which everything can change.

Becoming the winner you were born to be is not going to happen overnight and is not going to happen without a fight. This is a fight for a revolution involving a change of leadership in your life. No longer are you going to be led by ordinary beliefs but by extraordinary beliefs. It is the fight of a lifetime, in every sense.

The Creative Power of your Conversation

While we may think that we are always fully aware of our decision-making process, the truth is that we are often unaware of the biggest influence in our choice-making. Where do you think the decision-making process starts in your life? Your answer is likely to be 'in the mind.' We know that our choices are incubated in our conscious minds. However, there is a deeper place inside every person called the spirit. You are more than just a physical being. *Even if you cut me open and went searching for what makes me who I am you would not find me because I am first and foremost a spiritual being. My spirit life is translated and filtered through my physical life.*

Everything external is merely a reflection of what happens internally. 3D printers can now produce an identical replica of the image given to the computer. The image on the screen is brought to life through the printer. The intangible becomes tangible. In the same way, my outer world is formed by my inner world.

I remember walking around a brand new facility we had built in my home town of Newark-on-Trent. It had been a three-year hard slog to get it to fruition but on the day I was given the keys I walked around and as I did I sensed these words: 'all you see around you started inside of you…so don't get caught up in what you see because what is seen starts in the unseen place.'

Who can forget the global economic downturn of 2008? People lost businesses and homes. Some even ended their lives because of the pressure. Where did it all start? Many will say it was the sub-prime market that collapsed in the US and they would be right to a degree. But there is something deeper than that; it started with greed—with people borrowing more than they could afford to repay because of a deep-rooted dissatisfaction with who they were. Greed is an internal choice based on a lack of self-worth. People tried to change their outside 'ordinariness' through external means, only to find that it all came crashing down. This is the natural choice for every one of us; we try to deal with external issues through external means and bypass the laws of the world in which we live. Let me say it again, 'everything seen is driven by what is unseen.'

The Results of my Losing Conversation

When your life is incorrectly ordered, from the outside-in, you find your life becomes the home for all kinds of toxic beliefs—beliefs that form feelings, mindsets and actions that produce six kinds of results. You feel

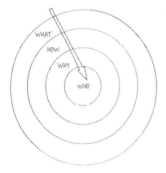

i)   WORTHLESS in the eyes of others
ii) UNNOTICED in your world
iii) FRAGILE through challenge
iv) INFERIOR in your appeal
v)   FORGETTABLE to the people you meet
vi) DIMINISHING in your growth

The Results of my Winning Conversation

However, if you immerse yourself in the winning conversation and operate from the inside-out, the results begin to change. The unseen beliefs that come from a life-giving source start to create winning feelings, a winning mindset and winning actions that over time produce MORE out of you than you could ever think

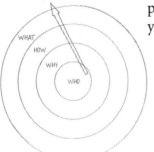

possible. The winning conversation means you become

i)   VALUABLE in the eyes of others
ii) PROMINENT in your world
iii) RESILIENT through challenge
iv) INFLUENTIAL in your appeal
v)   MEMORABLE to the people you meet
vi) EXPANSIVE in your growth

An Ordinary Day that Changed my Life

It was in 2006 I became acutely aware of a new conversation that was taking place inside of me. It was the 'Aha' moment that would shape my life forever. It was as if a light bulb had switched on inside of me.

I remember sitting in my small house, reading about the first Christians. I was reading about a group of ordinary, unschooled men. These men were no one's first choice for anything but somehow they made a world-defining impact, causing others to sit up and take notice as they went about their daily lives doing extraordinary things. As I was meditating on the story two words came to mind—two words that appear at odds with one another and seem like they should not exist in the same sentence: the words 'everyday' and 'champion.'

People were taking notice of these people because they knew they were not defined by their past, by their social status, credit rating, education or achievements. Their external activity was being driven by a deep-seated belief.

So what was my big revelation, my 'Aha' moment?

At the time I had no problem seeing myself as an everyday person. Very few people need convincing of their normality. However this light bulb moment created a deep shift inside me; I believed that alongside the 'everyday' Gareth is a champion.

This brought no overnight transformation but it started a process that has led to me being and doing more than I ever thought possible. It created the conversation that has resulted in this book. For someone who never voluntarily read a full book until the age of eighteen and disliked reading anything other than comics, that is no small feat!

The conversation initially created an inner conflict. How could I be a winner when I lived in such 'ordinariness'? My guess is you live in this place too. The word means *no special or distinctive features.*[1]

1. ordinary. Oxford Dictionaries. Oxford University Press, n.d. Web. 23 September 2015.

The problem with 'ordinary'

The problem with 'ordinary' is that, well, it's ordinary. So what is the problem with ordinary? Well the problem is that when you start to understand the way we are wired as human beings you soon realise that we were never designed to stay in a place called 'ordinary.' We were designed to be connected to the extraordinary.

When we read words like this we immediately start making the assumption that we are talking about something external—the house we live in, the people we mix with or the job we do. This highlights our natural 'outside-in' thinking. While I believe that this book will cause many people to make decisions that influence the external areas of our lives, this is not what I am talking about. I am talking about belief and that is an internal reality.

The famous sculptor and artist Michael Angelo famously said, *'Every block of stone has a statue inside it and it is the task of the sculptor to discover it.'*

This is a great example of what I am talking about. The stone that Michael Angelo worked with would have been walked past and unnoticed by most because they believed the stone was ordinary. Michael Angelo however had an extraordinary belief. He believed that an everyday stone could be formed into an outstanding masterpiece. He could see what it could become—his timeless statue of King David, arguably the most famous statue of all time.

Don't Despise Ordinariness: Harness it

I need you to understand that there is nothing wrong with ordinariness. It's how you use it that determines whether your life remains ordinary. Unless you are willing to face the 'stone' and embrace the process of chipping away at it, the extraordinary will never be released in your life. Winning results start with winning beliefs. Michael Angelo did not despise the ordinariness of the stone. Every extraordinary event, person or entity has been born out of ordinariness. The key is what you do with it.

The revelation I had was this: 'I am extraordinary therefore I will treat the ordinary with extraordinary belief and will in time reap extraordinary results.' Since 2006 I have seen the results unfold in my life and the lives of many others who have applied this principle. For this to happen, however, we must confront the counter-intuitive nature of the transformation. In a world that craves instant results at the expense of embracing process, we must come to understand that true results take time because the process first requires a change of conversation.

The challenge comes when we do not see the results and we start to feel like giving up. Becoming a champion in life is a long haul process; it involves persevering with extraordinary belief regardless of how difficult the journey becomes.

Chip away at the Ordinary to Reveal the Extraordinary

When Michelangelo was asked how he went about making this incredible statue he is reported to have said, 'It is easy. You just chip away the stone that doesn't look like David.'

It took Michelangelo over two years of constant work and effort to finish his statue. What I need you to grasp very early on is the power that lies in the small and insignificant. Our lives on this day are the result of millions of tiny, apparently insignificant decisions. The only way to shape your future is through an increased awareness of the small 'insignificant' choices you make and to make them with extraordinary belief.

Revelation has great Internal Significance but very little Outward Significance...at First!

The revelation I had that day was that while many people would walk past me not taking any notice, not attributing any value to my life, I have been designed to live in a place called the 'extraordinary' and to hold fast to a belief that I am extraordinary. In other words, I am a champion.

In that moment nothing outwardly changed. And here lies the problem. I have long been immersed in the world's philosophy that 'seeing is believing.' In other words because all I see is ordinary, I must therefore be ordinary. We must nail this lie right from the very start. You will be tempted time and time again to believe that the outward ordinariness of your life is a reflection of your benign and bland influence on this world. However, it is vital that you stay the course until your belief shifts from ordinary to extraordinary.

If I hold an acorn up in the air and say 'I am holding a forest', while what is seen may not fit the description, the principle is true. While the process of that acorn becoming a forest would not be witnessed by one generation, this truth does not diminish.

That day in 2006 I had a deep rooted shift in how I saw myself. I embraced my new ordinary called the extraordinary. I embraced the belief that I am a champion.

Today is time to plant the acorn, the seed of the belief that while I might be an everyday person I am indeed extraordinary.

I am a champion.

Section 1: The Winning Purpose

Day 4: The Winning Legacy

My belief about my future has a significant impact on unlocking my potential. If I do not believe that my future can be better than my present then what motivation do I have to deal with the other key areas of my internal conversation and the community I connect to? If I carry no sense of aspiration or ambition then I will allow circumstances and the aspirations of others to determine these things for my life.

Taking personal responsibility for your potential starts with you taking responsibility for your future. The greater clarity you can get on your purpose the greater desire you unlock to sort out your internal conversation and the relationships in your life.

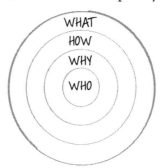

The concentric circles are designed to get clarity and create order for our winning purpose:

WHO—Who stands for the **PEOPLE** you ultimately live for that are informing your immediate choices and will be the main beneficiaries of your purpose.

WHY—Why are you alive? What impact and effect are you wired to bring? Every film has a story line and so does your life. Having clarity on the plot of your story is about your **PURPOSE**. Establishing a timeline for how that story unfolds is essential. This is the purpose of your life.

HOW—How do I use the resources that are available to me and build them around the WHO and WHY? How do I align the four areas of my life around the core people and purpose? What are my **PRIORITIES?**

WHAT—What do my current choices look like in the light of the clarity I now have? Unless I get clarity on what I am actually doing as opposed to what I feel I am doing then I will not be able to successfully plot my way forward. I will have no clear grasp of what **PRACTICES** I need to cultivate.

The core circles are about building your life around a legacy. The winning purpose is cultivated when we build it around what we seek to leave behind us. When we have clarity on our legacy we are able to allow that ultimate picture to bring perspective and definition to our immediate choices and decisions.

You may have realised by now that I like to use acrostics as a learning tool. The word 'legacy' reminds me to

Let
Eternity
Guide
All the
Choices
You make.'

THE WHO—The heart of my PURPOSE is WHO I am living for

"Clarity and perspective comes when we allow our ultimate conversations to shape our immediate conversations"

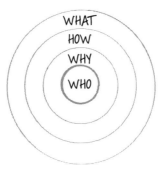

The winning conversation always starts with WHO. When creating a vision for your life the starting point should be the most important people in your life. WHAT you do in life has to be built around WHO. There is no greater focus, motivation or enjoyment than building your life around people who you value and who value you.

For me the WHO starts with God, my wife and my children. I will build towards my legacy around those I value most. My legacy is the influence that lasts beyond me. When it comes to creating goals we must learn to pull back and see what ultimately counts. We have finite lives but our legacy can become infinite. Our legacy will not only carry on beyond our lifetime but our impact can potentially increase in its influence and reach as it ripples throughout generations.

A Picture that Moves is a Picture with a Soul

Pictures of people have the potential to move us more than a picture of a building or landscape. Inanimate objects have no soul or spirit and so we cannot connect to them with our whole being.

Unlocking the more that is in you requires an image that triggers your belief, a picture that gives you the deep conviction to raise the intensity of your desire to meet the need connected to that person. If your cause is to influence a people-group in a certain socio-economic demographic, imagine that person receiving your help and the change of expression on their faces.

As an example I imagine people from every continent reading this book and a look of hope beginning to appear on their faces. I want this book to help lift people from poverty, whether poverty of mindset or poverty of circumstance. That image stirs me and creates a certain desire inside that I must do whatever it takes to accomplish the legacy that I have.

You can be creative and even put together a montage of pictures of even a short film that you can watch to keep the images alive.

Create Clarity through Tension

Over the course of my life and leadership I have been able to make courageous decisions because I have become convinced of a 'not yet' picture. This is a picture that I could see in my mind but had not yet seen come to reality yet. Having clarity on your 'not yet' goal causes you to start pulling the future into the now. Throughout the book I will use a phrase called 'holding the rope.' This is to indicate the fact that in life all things grow through tension. This is the ability to hold on to two apparently contradicting beliefs, realising that when both are held in tension something positive will result.

Many people stop thinking about the 'not yet' because it highlights what they lack in the 'now.' It feels more comfortable for them to keep a distance from what highlights their lack and the pain of what they do not yet possess. This is because they do not understand the law of tension. NOW is not bad and neither is NOT YET. When one is overemphasised it brings an imbalance and can have negative consequences. For instance, if all I think about is what COULD BE and do not get clarity on what IS, then I am likely to allow the things that need changing in the NOW to go unchanged and in the process the NOT YET becomes a more distant possibility. Likewise, if I accept that NOW is a picture of what is to come then I will cease increasing my level of aspiration for a better future, my NOT YET. What is needed is for us to hold both ends of the rope tightly. The tighter they are held the more tension is created, and the more tension there is, the more potential energy there is for the NOT YET to become a reality.

Without a Vision the Real You Dies

Vision, your desired future, produces a sense of hope and hope is like a tree. A tree produces oxygen for us to live; it takes the life-sapping carbon dioxide and converts it into life giving oxygen. It has become apparent to the medical world that when a person wakes in the morning with a sense of purpose they are likely to live longer than a person who wakes believing there life has no point to it. Purpose is hope; it is life giving, quite literally. The result of no vision is that we incubate a losing conversation.

View the Immediate through the Ultimate

Let me give you a suggestion in line with our theme of conversations. I want to take you to your front room where you are laid on the sofa. You are in the last days of your life and those close to you are making their visits to see you. You have plenty of time to think because your body is weak but your mind is still engaged. You have your final conversations with those you love. What do you want those conversations to be like? You have an opportunity to think about the key areas of your life, such as your finances, relationships, health and your development and how these were used to serve the people you loved the most. No one wants to have a conversation filled with regret and so thinking about these ultimate conversations throughout our lives will keep us on course to leave a legacy that will continue beyond us.

See my personal example overleaf*

Conversations that matter	This CONVERSATION WILL sound like this...
PERSON: LEANNE	*It was my honour to be your husband and I loved being faithful to you and keeping my promise to love and honour you. I served you in such a way that enabled you to become more than you thought you could have been because we were one flesh.*
PERSON: ERIN	*I loved your mother to show you how you should be loved should you choose to marry. I invested time and energy with you making you feel like you were the most important person in my life.* *I have done my best to build a foundation that will enable you as a woman to build something far greater for God and for others and do more than I ever could.*
PERSON: BETHAN	*I gave my all to create a place of safety and security that would also inspire you to take risks and to think big. My goal has always been that my relationship with you would give you permission to be the champion that you are. Do not settle for less than God's best for your life, from the relationships you keep to the goals you set. I hope and pray that my legacy for you is something that you are proud of and is a continual source of blessing to you.*
PERSON: REUBEN	*You were entrusted to me by God and I have given my everything to be the best example of a husband, Father and leader that I could be. The time we spent together was the most precious time and I thank you for allowing me to invest in you. I hope and pray that the foundation I have built through my example will be a springboard that will help you reach higher and go further to changing this world for good.*
PERSON: FRIENDS	*I led you with a desire to lead as Jesus led. I gave my best to see you become all you could be. I was willing to both challenge and encourage you because I loved you enough to want you to succeed. As I sowed into your lives my life was richer for it and I counted it a privilege.*

Let me encourage you: the script has not yet fully been written and even if you have regrets you have time to create more powerful memories that will dwarf the regrets. Past failures and regrets can be woven into the tapestry of an amazing story and fuel a fervent belief that you are going to end strong!

This kind of tension produces enough energy to power personal change. The goal is to allow the NOT YET conversations of your BELIEFS to lead your feelings, manage your thoughts and inform your choices. This will indeed activate the results you are looking for in your life.

I encourage you regularly to look at the pictures of the people who ultimately matter in your life and build every day around the WHO of your legacy. The more I choose to replay these conversations the more desire it creates in me to pursue the winning life.

THE WHY—*The Soul of my PURPOSE is WHY I am Alive*

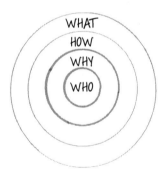

PLOT—The Ultimate Story Line

Your potential is a story line that will play a key role in the lives of other people

Imagine your life as a film in the making. The strength of a film is its storyline. While a producer can pay immense amounts of money for special effects the storyline is central to its success and the reason people remember it. How would you want people to sum up the storyline of your life? Would they be able to find a storyline? Is it memorable?

One day the film of your life will be passed on to loved ones and friends. Whilst every film has many characters and scenes they all have a central plot. The better the plot the greater the film and the more the characters come to life. You have an opportunity to shape the plot of your life.

I have helped many people to try and get clarity on their cause or plot over the years.

You can gain clarity on the PLOT of your life by asking yourself four questions. The more you ask them over time, the more clarity you will get.

PLOT questions

What is the PROBLEM you solve?

What do you LOVE to do with or without being paid?

What is OBVIOUS to you and not obvious to others?

What TALENTS do you have?

Let's look at these four dimensions of PLOT:

Problem you solve

What is the problem that you are drawn to? What is the challenge that gives you energy—the one you would spend time trying to solve without being paid for it? When this problem is absent from your schedule and focus you become frustrated and bored.

Love to do

What gives you energy and sparks your imagination? What connects and resonates with you on the inside? What do you use free time to do? What do you gravitate towards even while on holiday? Your plot is bigger than a career; it spills into every aspect of your life because it is your passion. You dream one day about this being a major focus in your life.

Obvious to you

What is obvious to you and is not so obvious to everyone else? What forums do you find yourself in? Do you sometimes find them frustrating because you keep seeing the same potential outcome but others just do not seem to get it?

Talents you possess

What natural abilities do you have? Whilst every strength and talent can be developed, what comes naturally to you? Is there something that you are unaware of how good you are at it because it seems so normal for you to be able to do it? Others compliment you in this area and often believe in you more than you do about your future potential.

PLOT questions	
PROBLEM SOLVE What is the problem you solve?	
LOVE TO DO What energises you?	
OBVIOUS TO YOU What is obvious to you that isn't obvious to others?	
TALENTS & ABILITIES What talents do you have?	

From what you have written in the boxes, can you now come up with a theme that suggests a PLOT? A good theme communicates a message or makes a point, whether it's good overcoming evil or the underdog overcoming the odds against success. What is your theme? Is it one that impacts others for good and leaves a positive legacy? As we will learn throughout the winning conversation our PLOT theme should be about others.

I like to think of your PLOT theme as the message you want to repeatedly communicate directly or indirectly through everything you do in life. What do you want to constantly reaffirm through every area of your life?

Over time I realised that the theme of my PLOT was that I wanted to communicate to every person 'there's more in you than you think!' This now helps me to create focus.

There are so many options of what I can do with my time but I want to make sure that my time is re-enforcing the theme of my life. When this happens you come alive and you are willing to go to extreme lengths to make sure that the message is communicated to the world around you. Without a message everything can become meaningless. Your message does not come from the outside in but is in you already.

Clarifying your message is not an overnight task and you may want to revise it many times. However, because you are in the process of seeking clarity you will start to experience the benefit of such soul-searching right away.

What do you want your message to be?

Sometimes our gut response is the most accurate. It is important to remember that this is not about what you are supposed to say but what you want to say. Sometimes when we have lived a certain way doing a certain job for any period of time we feel like we ought to say something that people expect. However, this may actually be suppressing the real WHY of your life.

Without much thinking, write the first message that you think of when it comes to your life.

_____

_____

Can you see why it is so important that this exercise is carried out before you get into the details of daily decisions? Reminding yourself of your message daily is important if you are to keep the winning order.

It helps if your message has an image that you can quickly recall. When you are engaged in your daily activity it is easier to measure what you are doing against what you see yourself doing. For instance, I picture myself like a fisherman throwing nets into the ocean and drawing what's under the surface into the boat. The net represents questions. I am a fisherman of potential. Therefore this image encourages me to live out my WHY in my daily interactions.

What image helps to represent your message?

_____

_____

The image may not directly reflect HOW you will outwork your WHY but like my image may simply be a helpful way of explaining it. I encourage it to be simple enough that you could explain it to a six-year old. Albert Einstein was reported to have said, 'If you can't explain it simply enough then you don't know it well enough!'

First thing in the morning and last thing at night refresh the WHO and WHY of your life and stir the right mood and drive into your being. This means that your DOING will serve your BEING.

You can download the tools from this chapter free of charge at www.thewinningconversation.com

Day 5: The Winning Goals

HOW—How am I going to ultimately outwork my core message? How do I view my future? How do I get to that 'not yet' goal that I feel is in me to achieve? How does that inform my daily focus?

WHAT—What am I doing with my daily choices to support my purpose? Does my practice match my potential? Unless I get clarity on what I am actually doing as opposed to what I feel I am doing then I will not be able to successfully PLOT my way forward.

Once we have clarity on the core circles we can start to work on the outer circles of HOW and WHAT, PRIORITY and PRACTICE.

If the inner circles represent the ultimate picture of our life, then the outer circles represent the immediate choices and decisions that we need to have in place. I call this the 'winning goals' that facilitate the 'winning purpose.'

THE HOW—The brains of my PURPOSE is HOW I am going to live

PRIORITY—The Ultimate Priority drives the Immediate Priorities

Not many people would argue with the fact that prioritising is important. However I believe we can prioritise incorrectly. The winning conversation is not about efficient prioritisation but effective prioritising. It is possible for me to prioritise a list of activities efficiently however it may not be effective because I have not allowed my CORE legacy to drive the process. Effectiveness is about prioritising the right things in the right way. I can simply become a manager of tasks if I prioritise from the immediate demands. However if I step back and allow the ultimate legacy to lead my priority process then I will be effective.

The ULTIMATE Priority—The NOT YET

I believe everyone should work towards having a NOT YET goal. This is something we want to have achieved that is not fanciful thinking but a deep desire we believe we can achieve. We build our lives around this goal and our mindset is 'when' not 'if' this is going to happen—hence the reason for calling it a 'not yet' goal. There is no question of it becoming a reality. If we question its possibility then we become indecisive about how we go about moulding our lives around that goal.

Go to the finished film of your life and ask what you want to have accomplished through your purpose. It is common practice when an author or script writer puts pen to paper that they start by thinking about where they will finish. A champion will have a 'one day I will…' dream. It may be vague to start with but it will be a picture of a certain accomplishment in life. While many people regard this as 'wishful thinking,' the champion believes with absolute certainty that this will happen and they have a strong idea as to how it will happen. It will happen through plotting a course that requires holding in tension that 'one day' dream with making 'one degree' improvements and changes every day, ones that have a significant bearing on a person's destination in life. These changes in and of themselves seem insignificant; however, over time they accumulate to bring about the result. Live each day believing that…

I WILL get there…ONE degree at a time!

It's the apparently insignificant choices and decisions in our daily lives that are shaping the ultimate story and legacy of our lives. A steering wheel in a car not only negotiates the obvious twists and turns on a long journey but actually produces thousands of tiny adjustments that alter the direction of the vehicle by the smallest of margins. However without these adjustments, these incremental decisions, the vehicle would end up far from the desired destination.

My NOT YET goal...	KEY MILESTONES
30 years from now I WILL...	
5 years from now I WILL...	
1 year from now I WILL...	
1 month from now I WILL...	
1 week from now I WILL...	
By the end of today I WILL...	
My NOW choice is that I WILL...	

It is important that we sketch out what we think we will need to do between the NOT YET and the NOW that will bring it into a reality. We can do this by completing the statements in the diagram.

A book I would encourage to you read to further develop this mindset is *The One Thing* by Gary Keller. Gary asks a question that helps me every day to focus: *What is the ONE thing I can do today which means that everything else becomes easier or unnecessary?*[2]

The IMMEDIATE Priority—The NOW

Your ultimate goal will come with a handful of disciplines that will be required in order for it to become a reality. The key for a winning purpose is to identify what these are and to make sure they are part of our daily focus.

Some of these activities can be expressed by asking and answering the following questions:

'In order to achieve my ultimate goal I can see that daily I need to be………'

Like me you would have experienced what life feels like when living in reactive mode. You would have heard yourself and others saying 'it feels like all I am doing it putting out fires!' This is a description of outside-in living. It is allowing what is around us to determine HOW we live and HOW we feel. The reality is that many of the things that become demands in our lives genuinely need dealing with so the answer is not to ignore them.

I am not a big believer in endless 'to do' lists. I encourage you to think of four or five activities that if you did these daily would keep you investing in the ULTIMATE goal of what you want to achieve.

As I mentioned earlier, the winning purpose is about effectiveness over efficiency. Therefore I believe in <u>time focus</u> rather than <u>time management</u>. How is my time serving the ultimate picture of what I want to achieve and the theme I want to convey in everything I am doing?

2. Keller, Gary. The One Thing. Great Britain. 2013. John Murray Press. Hodder & Stoughton

Firewall Focus

If you imagine your daily demands that you have to carry out and respond to as small fires, these will naturally vie for your attention. The demands of other people will always be presented as the things that MUST have your immediate attention.

When a building is in the planning stage, one of the fundamental principles influencing the designer is the necessity to create 'firewalls'. These are protected areas that prevent fires spreading throughout the entire building.

My aim is to create four or five firewall focus activities in my daily routine that keep me highly effective and that must be protected from the many other fires that need to be put out. They are the activities that take precedence over anything else that may come my way.

So for me my immediate priorities are as follows:

Firewall 1 - Study, write and think

Firewall 2 - Ask others questions that increase my understanding, enabling me to prepare and plan better

Firewall 3 - Coach key team members helping them find progress in what they are doing

Firewall 4 - Forward plan by staying a week ahead

I will make a list of all the activities (A = activity) I need to do on a blank sheet of paper or a flipchart in no particular order and then box my firewalls. This way I always know that by prioritising my firewalls I am protected from an ineffective use of my time. This is prioritising from the inside-out. Any fires (activities or requests to act) outside of these will either be delegated or dealt with in any remaining time I have.

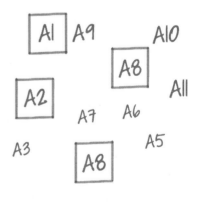

THE WHAT—The muscle of my PURPOSE is WHAT I am actually Doing

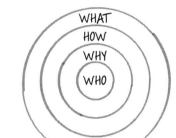

The final part of this process is to align the intentions I have to my actions. Without action my best made plans are powerless and remain wishful thinking.

The alignment of the tyres of a car to the wheel and vehicle is essential in order not to lose valuable energy and potentially lose control of the vehicle. The same is true when it comes to our journey toward our winning goal.

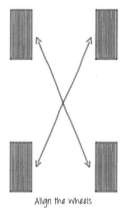

Align the wheels

The signs of a car's wheels being out of alignment have striking resemblance to our lives being out of alignment. The car starts to drift to one side because one of the tyres is not aligned correctly and creates wear and tear on the other wheels. Even when on a straight road—where typically less movement is needed on the steering wheel—tension is needed on the wheel in order to stop the vehicle drifting.

Our life is out of balance when certain priorities are not receiving the necessary investment. When we invest according to principles and create a healthy rhythm we experience the enjoyment of the journey.

Each tyre represents a key area of life that needs investment in order to get you to the destination of your goal and establish your legacy.

RELATIONSHIPS

MONEY

HEALTH

DEVELOPMENT

You steer these through the following pattern from the inside-out:

PRINCIPLE behind the Practice:

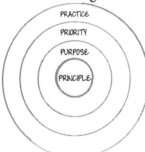

The Winning Conversation starts with what you believe so it is important that you constantly clarify what you believe about your key priorities. What timeless principle are you allowing to lead your feelings? If you imagine the principle as a command, it serves as a referee, pulling you into line when your thoughts and feelings start to drift. You need a set of rules if you are to achieve the results that your potential is capable of achieving.

PURPOSE driving the Practice:

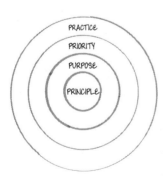

What is the WHY of the priority? This is your desire, what you really want. Circumstances can distort what we really want in life so it is important to ignite our desire regularly so that we stay on course to reach our desired goals. Your true desire is a 'soul statement' and it needs to move our emotions whenever we mediate on it.

PRIORITY positioning our Resources:

This is now the practical attribution of time, money, effort and everything else attributed to the priority. It is important to refine our priorities so we are not simply creating a checklist of activity, but a rhythm of activity that goes from being first nature (consciously having to think about what we are doing), to second nature (sub-consciously working according to a priority system).

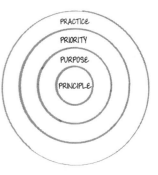

Below are example tables of how a person may choose to fill in their LIFE alignment plan:

RELATIONSHIPS	GOD	WIFE	CHILDREN	FRIENDS	COLLEAGUES
Principle	God is Spirit and I am a Spiritual being	As I treat my wife I treat myself because we are one	If I don't lead my children someone else will	Who I am is who I attract	I serve others and elevate them above myself
Purpose	I want to be a 'rock' to those in my world	I want my relationship to go from strength to strength	I want to be the trusted voice in my kids' lives. I have around 18 years	I want to leave my friends always feeling bigger after being with them	I want my work place to become a tight community of friends who cheer one another on to success
Priority	1.Morning reflection/ prayer 2. Listen to uplifting podcast each week 3. Share from a book I am reading every week with someone	1. Date time with wife 2. One evening a week together 3. Small gift every week that shows my appreciation for her	1. Three times a week share short story before bed 2. Spend one-on-one time with each child every week 3. One evening for family time and fun	1. Communicate my value and appreciation every Tuesday to three people 2. Connect over coffee once a week 3. Organise getting together twice a month	1. Communicate my thanks to three people every week in handwritten form or a phone call 2. Ask three people every week how I can help them do their job more effectively
Practice ✓ or ✗					

HEALTH	DIET	EXERCISE	REST
Principle	Not everything is beneficial and I will not be addicted or controlled by anything	My body is entrusted to me to look after	Set apart one day for rest and preparation in order to be highly effective the other six days
Purpose	The longer I live the more value I can add to those I love the most	Maintain High energy levels so I can keep up with my children	Stay fresh and sharp so I can engage with those I value most
Priority	Stay around 12 stone and maintain healthy BMI Low carbs Low saturated fats High Protein	3 x runs per week 2 x weight training 3 x abs training	Protect day off every week with my wife Six weekends off a year Only out two night of the week Average of 7-8 hours sleep
Practice ✓ or ✗			

MONEY	DEBT	GIVING	SPENDING	SAVING
Principle	I am not a slave to lenders	The world of the generous gets bigger and bigger but the world of the stingy get smaller and smaller	Always live well within my means	Compound effect. A lot of little makes a lot.
Purpose	I want to protect my freedom to respond to opportunity	I aim to increase my capacity to be generous	Make my spending follow my goals in order to fulfil my NOT YET goal	I want financial freedom for later life not having to reduce my standard of living
Priority	No debt except 25% of take home income for mortgage payments	10% charitable giving	Live off 60% take home	Set aside 15% of gross income into retirement fund Set aside 15% of gross income into savings for children's college and wedding fund
Practice ✓ or ✗				

DEVELOPMENT	COACHING	LEARNING	PLANNING	READING
Principle	'As iron sharpens iron, so one man sharpens another.'	My personal education is preparing me for promotion	Diligent planning is the key to success	Leaders are readers
Purpose	To win in life I need challenging and accountability	I become a better leader by becoming a better follower	Failing to plan is planning to fail and I am not willing to fall short of my NOT YET goal	There are riches in the experiences of other people that can add value to my journey.
Priority	Budget £x to participate in a monthly skype call with my coach and review notes weekly	Have a planned meeting with someone I can learn from every six weeks. Listen to a podcast/TED talk or YouTube clip twice a week	Find a quiet spot in the week when I can evaluate the week that has been and plan the week ahead	Read two books a month One self-development and the other a biography/autobiography of someone I want to learn from
Practice ✓ or ✗				

PRACTICE—The Immediate Results

Appraising and analysing our results reveals so much about what we truly believe. A plan is only as good as the evaluation that is carried out on it. Our results reveal our true beliefs and are difficult to ignore.

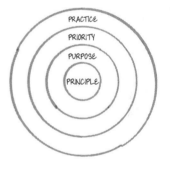

Give yourself a ✓ for every priority that was actioned or a ✗ for an activity that was not carried out unless there is a **genuine** reason.

Based on the overall % of results in the above 'practice' boxes tick the appropriate box below:

PRACTICE V POTENTIAL (tick)	0-25% 1 point	25%-50% 2 points	50%-75% 3 points	75%-100% 4 points
RELATIONSHIPS				
HEALTH				
FINANCES				
DEVELOPMENT				

Once you have ticked the appropriate boxes in the above table, add up the points of the columns your ticks are in. Based on a maximum points score of 16 points what was your score? _____

Which type of person have you been this week?

Consumer 0-4 points
Complacent 5-8 points
Competitor 9-12 points
Champion 13-16 points

My Overall **POTENTIAL**: I AM A **CHAMPION**

My Overall **PRACTICE**: I HAVE BEEN _____

The more I can demand an honest answer to the question 'why did I get that result…really?' the more I will be able to make the necessary adjustments with the steering wheel of my choices. If you have ever driven a car you will be aware that a journey consists of thousands of steering adjustments. While there are some obvious turns on the steering wheel needed to navigate the roads, there are many adjustments we make subconsciously. These adjustments are critical for the journey. There are many adjustments/choices we carry out without being fully aware of how they are steering us in our lives. When we stay UNAWARE of how negative choices are taking us off course by a matter of degrees every day we realise that this is the margin of error that costs us our potential.

"Success is nothing more than a few simple disciplines, practiced every day; while failure is simply a few errors in judgment, repeated every day. It is the accumulative weight of our disciplines and our judgments that leads us to either fortune or failure." Jim Rohn

Action is the best way to reinforce the belief that we have. It is actually the way we drive the conviction we have even deeper. Creating behaviour based on belief enables us to move from knowledge to understanding and over time that becomes wisdom. Wisdom then makes you a 'go to' person as you begin a journey of mastering those areas of your life.

The more clarity we can get on our **NOT YET** goal the more we can identify what we need to do in the **NOW** to unlock the results we are after.

If my ultimate conversation is that I invest heavily in the lives of my children and my purpose is to help unlock potential in people then I will want to make sure that I have set aside time and finance to facilitate this. Without planning I may sacrifice this for the sake of giving my time to others things, or, because I have overcommitted financially to something else, I do not have the finance required to invest in what I believe to be the most important people in my life.

Do you have goals in your finances? If not then how do you know if you are over committing in areas of lesser importance? Clarity is key in order to stay free to do what you value most. By keeping the ultimate conversation before us, we become people of principle making great choices with our time and finance. I know that I will never get the time with my children back again. I have approximately eighteen years to set a strong foundation for their lives but it will not happen by chance; it will happen by making great choices in the rhythm of my life.

The Power of a Number

The number we place next to our priority creates a positive pressure for action. The clearer the goal the clearer the expectation we are placing on ourselves. A number also helps us to evaluate when we have completed a commitment. Being aware of a completed activity is essential in developing a winning life.

Unleash the Power of Completion

When making your plans it is better to master a pattern that you can achieve than setting unrealistic goals that are currently beyond your capacity. There is a power in completing a task, activity or goal. The feeling of completion is a key factor in creating personal momentum. Therefore, increasing the size of the goal over time is far better than constantly not hitting goals. Incompleteness works against our progress; it demotivates us and causes us to give up on trying. While the road needs to show progress, it also needs to be steady.

The Lid that is Stuck

A friend of mine reminded me of that moment when a family member cannot get the lid off the jam jar despite trying everything. They pass it onto the confident family member desperate to show they can deliver the result only to find out that they cannot do it either. It goes round three more people until the youngest and unlikeliest member pulls it off. The truth is that it was the process of attempts that produced the result despite each person thinking their part made no difference and they failed.

It is the same when it comes to our winning patterns of behaviour. Do not decide whether a single activity was or was not successful based upon perceived results. While your time in the gym may not produce obvious results in that moment, it will be that moment when you catch yourself in the mirror after sticking to a regime that you suddenly see the difference. It has been the process and not just one single activity that pulled it off. Like the boxer who knows they cannot simply right hook all the time; they need the jabs to keep coming too. It may look like the hook won the fight but it was each jab that wore down the opponent.

The Significance of the Insignificant

We develop a losing pattern of behavior when we allow our perceived results to determine our actions. Let me give you an example. When I spend time with my children they are unlikely to communicate how my time with them has impacted their lives. In fact they are probably unaware themselves of the power of what is taking place. However, one key principle that we must realise is that it's the things in life that appear to make little difference that are making ALL the difference. I am amazed at the memories my children have of things I have said or done. At the time I was unaware of the influence I was having.

We are unable and unwise to try and work out the results of every decision we make. When we build our life plan around our core principles then we know we can have confidence that we will achieve the results we desire.

Over the next seven days I am going to unpack the pattern of the winning conversation you will need to adopt in order to win in every area of life.

You can download the tools from this chapter free of charge at www.thewinningconversation.com

Section 2: The Winning Conversation— I value My Self

Understanding how to unlock your winning self

Day 6: The Winning Conversation

If I asked you to name the most important conversation you will ever have what would that be? A proposal of marriage? A conversation with your child about the birds and the bees? How about the conversation with an 18-year old as they transition into adulthood? Or the final conversation with a loved one on their death bed? There is no denying the significance of these conversations. However, there is one even more significant conversation!

Let me give you a clue. The most significant conversation is not an event; it is the conversation you most frequently have. Whoever this person is will have an incredible influence on you because they are the greatest stakeholder of your attention. So who is it? A parent, best friend, spouse, child? They are all stakeholders and influencers but there is a conversation that holds a greater sway than all these people put together.

So let me put you out of your misery…

The most important conversation is taking place right now. No, it is not me with you; it is actually happening in you right now. Wait a minute, you may say. Talking to yourself has gone down in history as the first sign of madness. I beg to differ. In reality it's an indicator that you are alive! We talk to ourselves all the time but most of the time we are unaware of its significance and influence on our lives.

All the results of your life are tied into your ability to master your own conversation. My journey in writing this book started from a place of frustration. I became really unhappy with the fact that I kept making plans and decisions but not following through with them. I was discontent with the results of my life. I was aware of my ability to influence my results but I was not fully aware of how much control I had to do so.

Through my study of ancient Biblical wisdom I began to see a pattern that unlocks the potential inside a human being. It is my joy and privilege to share this with you.

Blissfully Unaware

If this is such a significant conversation then why are so many unaware of it? As human beings we develop a natural bias towards the things that can be seen and a cynicism for what is invisible. Most people base their beliefs on what can be evidenced with the human eye. The saying, 'seeing is believing,' has become a philosophy that most people adopt. And yet the most significant forces in our lives are those that we cannot see. The wind that blows cannot be seen and yet no one can deny its presence because they see its effects. The conversation that takes place within us is unseen and yet we know it's there. However, we greatly underestimate its impact on our lives.

Every Conversation you have is Defined by the Internal Conversation

As you read this book now I know that I am not the only voice in the conversation. In fact I know I am not the most influential voice. The most influential voice is the one inside you filtering and processing how you think and feel about what you are reading.

Can you hear it? This conversation is constant. There is a constant dialogue between our subconscious (what we are unaware of) and our conscious mind (what we are aware of). So when we think we are not thinking something, the truth is the conversation is taking place. We even learn as human beings to ignore the conversation. However, pressing the mute button on the conversation in our conscious mind does not stop the effects of the conversation anymore than closing our eyes and putting our fingers in our ears stops the effects of the wind from influencing us.

The quality of your conversations with others is set by the quality of your internal conversation.

Life is all about the conversation. Without conversation we cannot earn money to buy the basic necessities of life. Without conversation we cannot build relationships and enjoy life-giving community. Without conversation we cannot learn and be educated. Conversation is pivotal to life and how we develop. Many people are unaware of the influence the conversation we carry on the inside has on the conversation we have on the outside.

Let me give you an example. Have you ever held back from introducing yourself to someone you would really like to get to know? Yes, me too. I guess you did what I did and spoke to someone you already knew or someone who felt easier to approach. Why was that? I can guess what you said in your conversation. You told yourself 'they look too busy.' 'I wouldn't know what to say.' 'I'll introduce myself next time.' The reason I guessed is because I used to do the same. What is happening is that your sub-conscious belief leads to a feeling that makes you feel unauthorised to have the conversation. You are filled with inferiority but your conscious mind is great at making excuses that justify your beliefs. These then inform the choice that it's ok not to make the approach.

Who knows what could have happened had I believed I was authorised to approach this person? What opportunities, what other relationships? If you need convincing, look at the key milestones in your own life to date. I will guarantee that a conversation played a key role in bringing that situation about.

I am excited for what could happen in the days, weeks, months and years ahead if you determine to develop a winning conversation. In order to unlock the potential of your life you need to understand the conversation you are having and what you can do to develop a conversation on the inside that will unlock incredible opportunity on the outside.

Getting Past the Layers to the Core

When it comes to our biology we are made up of layers and the same is true for who we are as people. Just as each person has a skeleton that forms the core of the body and is wrapped in layers of tissue, muscle and skin, so the unseen part of you is layered. At the core, we are spiritual beings, wrapped with a soul that carries our emotional capacity, our mind that carries our mental capability and our physical body.

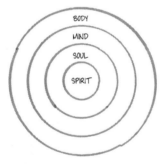

We know that there is a side to each of us that we can hide from the outside world. However, we are integrated beings and while we believe that the things we hide inside have no bearing on what happens to us, the reality is that it influences everything we do.

Opening the Lines of Communication

If improving the quality of our internal conversation opens up the conversations we have with others then our approach to improving those conversations can apply to our internal conversation. Conversations are improved when people learn to listen to one another and understand how they can add value to the other person in the conversation. This is how winning teams are built in business, sport and life. This is how we can build a winning conversation, by opening up the lines of communication between the four parts of us and getting them working in one direction. This is what makes a person fully integrated, or a person of integrity. The dictionary defines integrity as *the state of being whole and undivided.*[3] When each part is working together there is a synergy that unlocks the potential in us.

The Results are Wanted but the Process Ignored

Most people are dissatisfied with the results in their lives. However, many are unwilling to spend the necessary time to understand how they can get MORE out of themselves. Quick fix solutions are more attractive because they do not require 'major surgery' on ourselves and yet their results are limited and unsustainable. The winning conversation is for those people who have decided that it's better to take a longer journey to lasting results than stay in the land of 'fad' where we get excited in bursts but carry a continuous underlying knowledge that we are not really changing.

Life is full of distractions and there will be more attractive offerings on the table of HOW to use your time and WHAT you can do. However I am committed to helping you understand that if you invest in WHO you are and WHY you are alive it will result in you seeing MORE in every area of your life.

---

3. integrity. Oxford Dictionaries. Oxford University Press, n.d. Web. 23 September 2015.

Day 7: The Winning Voices in the Boardroom

Ever gone to bed feeling great only to wake up the next day feeling terrible? You were motivated one day to change the world only to step into the next day feeling unable to even face it?

What has changed? Our feelings certainly have but what has led to the change? Our feelings are unpredictable and do not make great leaders in the conversation we host. They can change direction easily and if they become the driver of the conversation we will end up in confusion.

When we adopt the winning flow to our conversation we correctly position our feelings under the authority of our beliefs. Our beliefs need to be principles. Principles are unchanging beliefs or values that have stood the test of time and are strong and positive leaders in the factory of our lives.

The results of your life are ultimately determined by your beliefs. Who you believe you are is the epicentre of what you will come to see in your life. While we cannot control every circumstance in life we can control what we believe about ourselves and how we process those experiences. As we saw with *Life Inc* in the parable, there is a boardroom at the core of your life and the voices that are allowed to speak set the rest of your life in motion.

The winning conversation takes place in the boardroom of your beliefs. There are six chairs around this table but two groups of six beliefs vying for a chair to be a voice that shapes your world. Whoever gets to sit in the seats has an opportunity to lead your feelings. You can trace who is at the table by analysing the feelings that you carry. Find the feeling and you'll find who is line-managing it.

The Right Leaders in your Boardroom

You may ask which beliefs should be adopted. The beliefs you adopt need to be those that are in line with the results you are trying to see. It is important that you have clarity on both the winning and the losing conversation so you stay aware who sits at the boardroom of your beliefs. Self-awareness is key to controlling your internal conversation.

The losing conversation has the following six voices in its boardroom:

LOSING CONVERSATION	DIMINISHING CONVERSATION	INFERIOR CONVERSATION	WORTHLESS CONVERSATION	FRAGILE CONVERSATION	FORGETTABLE CONVERSATION	UNNOTICED CONVERSATION
BELIEF	Predictable	Exclusive	Mediocre	Lethargic	Irrelevant	Apathetic

WINNING CONVERSATION	EXPANSIVE CONVERSATION	INFLUENTIAL CONVERSATION	VALUABLE CONVERSATION	RESILIENT CONVERSATION	MEMORABLE CONVERSATION	PROMINENT CONVERSATION
BELIEF	Creative	Inclusive	Excellence	Passionate	Relevant	Devoted

The Voice is a Principle

Principles are unseen laws that govern everything that is seen. In creation there are laws that govern the way we outwork life. The law of gravity has a defining influence on how we go about outworking our lives. You cannot defy a law; it is in place for as long as the world exists. You have to build your life around laws. Another law is the law of cause and effect. For every effect we see there is a driving cause. Therefore if we want to see something happen (an effect) we have to identify the relevant trigger to make it happen (the cause).

Stephen Covey in his book *Seven Habits of Highly Effective People* describes principles as the territory of a nation.[4] So for instance if

4. Covey, Stephen. The Seven Habits of highly effective people. New York City. Rosetta Books, 2009 Electronic edition

you were to journey into Alaska, the territory is already defined before you get there; its contours and characteristics preexist before your arrival. To make your way around Alaska you must first study the territory. The more you study the territory the easier and more enjoyable it will be to do what you want to do there. You start by studying what does not change and build your plans around that. You could take flip flops and a surf board with you but you are going to be disappointed because that activity is not supported by the territory.

Have you ever over-relied on a satellite navigation system (sat nav) to get you to where you want to go? I have. It can get caught out by traffic flow and incidents that happen beyond its knowledge. It feels a lot easier and quicker to simply jump into a car and let the sat nav do all the work. However, I have found the best way is to study a map before I set off so I get an understanding of the territory. Then, when I use the sat nav, I can spot mistakes or directions that are not going to help me on my journey. Knowledge of the territory helps me to overcome unexpected challenges that may occur on the journey.

The six voices behind the winning conversation are timeless; they are not bound by history, culture, people groups or eras. They are the six values that command your feelings, inform your mindsets and activate choices that produce corresponding results. They take the winning conversation from inside of you into the winning outcomes of life. We will look at these outcomes in the next chapter.

The Voice is a Revelation

The winning voices need to be more than a good idea for them to have an impact in your life. A revelation is something that you are certain is correct; it becomes a conviction -something you don't so much hold as holds you!

A revelation is not:
'I could be'
'I should be'
'I want to be'

A revelation is:

'I am'
'I have'
'I can'
'I will'

Revelation is the acceptance of a truth regardless of the evidence that you see around you. Just as planting a seed in the ground will eventually produce the plant that we see on the seed packet, regardless of how inconsequential the seed currently looks, so a truth that comes by revelation is a belief that I totally accept. The seed is activated when it is buried in the soil. The belief I accept as true activates the outcome I get. In short, 'I get what I accept.'

The Voice is your Identity

Your identity has nothing to do with what is around you and has everything to do with what is in you. The boardroom of belief is about identity, WHO you believe you are. Sub-consciously our daily choices are built around our understanding of WHO we are. Have you ever wondered why it is that some people can commit crimes against others as if they were worthless beings? We say 'how can anyone in their right mind do such a thing?' The answer is 'a person capable of such a crime views those people the way they do because of how they see themselves.' They may view themselves as nothing and the standard of worth they use for themselves becomes the standard they use for others. Hitler believed he was a superior being to the Jews and propagated a belief system around how he saw himself which was bought into by others who adopted the same belief.

On the other end of the scale we see the selfless sacrifice of other human beings laying their lives down for others—people who will go to extraordinary lengths to help or save others. Someone can sit and ask 'why would they do that? How did they go through with that?' In the process they may reflect, 'I'm not sure I could ever do that.' Again, peoples' actions start with WHO they believe they are. It is the epicentre of life. History is the sum total of the activities of people who have chosen to believe WHO they are.

Our belief systems and paradigms are largely created from the upbringing that has defined and developed us. There can be valuable components to our heritage that we would not want to lose. However, it is possible that we carry beliefs from our upbringing that prevent us from stepping into the greatness of our potential. Let me use a well known analogy to explain what I mean.

While walking through the forest one day, a man found a young eagle that had fallen out of his nest. He took it home and put it in his barnyard where it soon learned to eat and behave like the chickens. One day a naturalist passed by the farm and asked why it was that the king of all birds should be confined to live in the barnyard with the chickens. The farmer replied that since he had given it chicken feed and trained it to be a chicken, it had never learned to fly. Since it now behaved as the chickens, it was no longer an eagle.

"Still it has the heart of an eagle," replied the naturalist, "and can surely be taught to fly."

He lifted the eagle toward the sky. "You belong to the sky and not to the earth. Stretch forth your wings and fly."

The eagle, however, was confused. He did not know who he was, and seeing the chickens eating their food, he jumped down to be with them again.

The naturalist took the bird to the roof of the house and urged him again. "You are an eagle. Stretch forth your wings and fly."

But the eagle was afraid and jumped down once more for the chicken food.

Finally the naturalist took the eagle out of the barnyard to a high mountain. There he held the king of the birds high above him and encouraged him again. "You are an eagle. You belong to the sky. Stretch forth your wings and fly."

The eagle looked around, back towards the barnyard and up to the sky. Then the naturalist lifted him straight towards the sun and the eagle began to tremble. Slowly he stretched his wings, and with a triumphant cry, soared away into the heavens.

It may be that the eagle still remembers the chickens with nostalgia. It may even be that he occasionally revisits the barnyard. But as far as anyone knows, he has never returned to lead the life of a chicken.[5]

You see the point? The eagle allowed his experience and the sense of self-definition produced by those around him to shape WHO he was. He mimicked WHAT he should do and HOW he should live and his WHY for being alive became to survive as a chicken because he believed this was WHO he was.

The naturalist, however, introduced him to his design. He flipped the understanding of the eagle's belief system by convincing him of WHO he was based upon WHY he was designed.

The eagle in the analogy was not unhappy, was not crying out for change. However it took someone else who knew the bird's potential to bring it out of it.

In the process the eagle moved from surviving to thriving by living inside-out.

Day 8: The Conversation that Shapes my Identity

It all starts with WHO

Many people are unaware that every choice they make draws from the internal beliefs of WHO they believe they are. Therefore, any true and lasting change has to start at this level.

So WHO are you?

I do not mean what is your name? I mean what is your understanding as to WHO you really are?

Our lives are the sum total of the decisions we have made. We are who we are today because of the choices and responses to the events and opportunities in our lives so far. Have you ever questioned the origin of those choices?

Imagine the choices of our lives are like fruit that appears on a tree. The fruit is a result of a process. The process looks a little bit like this:

5. Theology News and Notes, October, 1976, quoted in Multnomah Message, Spring, 1993, p. 1

The feeding source + root of the tree + the branches = the fruit

Just as every piece of fruit that is produced is the result of a consistent process, so our decisions are the results of a process. The process works like this:

Who I am + Why I exist + How I choose to live = What decisions I make

Every one of us is operating from a concept of who we are whether we are aware of that or not. This self-concept is the critical starting point of our decisions that determine what we are becoming. If we want to see extraordinary results in our lives we need to daily operate with clarity concerning WHO we are.

Our self-concept, or idea of who we are, is **developed**, **defined** or **designed** just like the eagle in the story.

Developed by the Ideals of my World

The eagle was born into an environment that transmitted the message 'you are a barnyard chicken.' There was no role model or influence that gave him an alternative self-concept. His identity was shaped from the *outside-in*. As he grew he was treated like a fellow chicken by barnyard chickens around him. He adapted his behaviour until he was accepted by the culture he was in. Therefore his identity developed.

If pushed to answer the question 'who are you,' you might reply, 'I am simply a human being' and that level of identity satisfies you. Many people accept that who I am is simply the result of a natural process, a series of random events with no specific, overarching purpose. Whether you call that process natural selection or evolution they all are founded upon the belief that I AM the result of a process and therefore who I am is something that is developed between me and the process I am in.

Defined by the Ideas of Others

The eagle not only developed his identity but it was defined by the voice and activity of the farmer. His decision to put the eagle among the chickens had a critical part to play in how the eagle viewed himself. How others place us through their treatment of us is the other big life-shaping force. While they may not attribute the shaping to a specific supernatural being they do agree that there are unseen forces that help to bring an understanding about who we are and they are satisfied with that. They allow who they are to be defined by the people around them. What others say, think, how they have responded to life-shaping circumstances, have all played a role in their self-concept.

Designed by a mastermind

There are those who believe that their identity has been determined, that there is a mastermind, a supernatural being who has an overarching purpose in which every human being has a specific and unique part to play.

So I ask the question, whose concept are you? A concept is an idea. Those who believe their identity derives itself from a developing or evolving humanity would have to say that 'I am not an original idea, but simply part of a progressive series of random events.' Those whose identity is defined by life-shaping forces would have to say, 'I am what I am in response to life around me.' Those who believe they are the original idea of a divine being would have to say, 'I am who God says I am.'

I choose to believe I am designed.

However, regardless of your belief, you can take control of WHO you are today by owning the conversation inside of you. You can own a winning conversation by positioning the six winning voices that are in you at your boardroom table of belief.

The Voice is your Doorway to Tomorrow's Results

The size of the change is not equal to the size of the result

A seed is not equal to the size of the result it can produce. The critical factor is the process the seed is willing to go through to produce the result that is inside of it.

There will be words spoken over your life that you have always remembered and they have either had a positive or negative impact. To the person who spoke them they were simply words but you created an environment for them to grow and in the soil of your belief-system created a process for them to bear fruit. The result of those words has been totally disproportionate to the effort behind them. Those words were like seeds thrown onto soil; the conversation may have been over in a matter of seconds and yet they now influence the lens of your beliefs which in turn influences the thousands of choices you are making every week.

The winning conversation is not about WHAT you do it starts with WHO you believe you are.

From the inner room of your beliefs come the small choices you repeatedly make every day that produce significant results.

You may want to see significant doors of opportunity open up in your life but the size of the door is not equal to the size of the behaviour needed to open the door. You simply have to know what behaviour, carried out repeatedly, will unlock the door you want to see opened.

A key is insignificant in size compared to the door it opens and yet it is the very thing that produces the desired result. You need to carry the keys everyday and use them to unlock doors of destiny.

The six conversations I am going to encourage you to immerse yourself in every day look like six huge doors. These are the doors of potential that you have. It is important that you believe that they are doors that you can unlock. This cannot be wishful thinking; it has to be a definite belief that they are your doors with your name on and that you have the keys to unlock them.

The doors available to you through the winning conversation are on a street called 'CAUSE Avenue':

I am Prominent
I am Resilient
I am Influential
I am Memorable
I am Expansive

I am Valuable

Most people will look at these doors as if they are on an estate way out of their price range. They will look at them saying, 'they are someone else's front door. I do not belong or live here.' However, if you knew that these front doors had keys that you possess, and if you knew that what lies behind the doors belongs to you, then you would want to take possession of what rightfully belongs to you, right?

The doors available to you through the losing conversation are on a road called 'COMFORT Avenue':

I am Unknown
I am Fragile
I am Inferior
I am Forgettable
I am Diminishing
I am Worthless

Here is the rule to the winning conversation: you can only carry six keys on you at one time. You determine the house you live in and possess based upon the keys that you use.

The KEY of your BELIEF opens the DOOR of your RESULT.

Below are the six beliefs that open the six results of the winning conversation and the losing conversation:

LOSING CONVERSATION	DIMINISHING CONVERSATION	INFERIOR CONVERSATION	WORTHLESS CONVERSATION	FRAGILE CONVERSATION	FORGETTABLE CONVERSATION	UNNOTICED CONVERSATION
BELIEF	Predictable	Exclusive	Mediocre	Lethargic	Irrelevant	Apathetic
RESULT	Diminishing	Inferior	Worthless	Fragile	Forgettable	Unnoticed

WINNING CONVERSATION	EXPANSIVE CONVERSATION	INFLUENTIAL CONVERSATION	VALUABLE CONVERSATION	RESILIENT CONVERSATION	MEMORABLE CONVERSATION	PROMINENT CONVERSATION
BELIEF	Creative	Inclusive	Excellence	Passionate	Relevant	Devoted
RESULT	Expansive	Influential	Valuable	Resilient	Memorable	Prominent

It is really important you understand and picture these two very different places.

Our family once moved house to a bigger house on a

neighbouring estate. We had lived in this one house for almost ten years and became use to driving to it without giving it much thought. We would drive up a hill and then turn right onto this estate. When the time came for us to move we had to change that pattern. We had to drive up the hill and turn left onto a different estate. We had outgrown the house we were leaving and were entering into a much bigger house.

Even once we made the move there were many times when I would drive to the old house because it had become my default setting. I would do it without making a conscious effort to go to the new. It took quite a while of reprogramming to make the new house my new default. Even when I thought I had cracked it there were times, funny enough when things were not going well, that I would drive to the old. It was almost like my feelings were saying, 'Let's go back to the old.'

It is important you are fully aware of your default settings that take you back to the same choices time and time again. The winning conversation is about handing in the default keys every day in exchange for the keys to the designer house of your potential. This is a fundamental change in belief that will produce new patterns of behaviour.

The voices present in your boardroom of belief become the conversations you present to your world. The conversations you present to your world are the currency with which you operate.

The higher the quality of the conversation on the inside, the higher the quality of the conversation on the outside.

Day 9: The Winning Mood on the office floor

Every thought and action is influenced by our feelings. We are aware at times of the influence our feelings have but we are often oblivious to the undercurrent of emotion that is shaping the choices we make. The undercurrent of a river can look serene on the surface but in reality it is a powerful force determining where our choices will go. Like a boat that is not tied to the river bank, any choice that is not tied to a fixed belief will be taken wherever the river flows.

Feelings are a powerful resource and an essential part of unlocking our potential. Our emotions motivate us and move us toward action. We believe that our rational conscious minds are firmly in control of our choices when in fact our feelings hold the trump card in our decision-making. Our unconscious emotional state is firmly in control.

My dad used to allow me to sit on his lap and move the steering wheel when driving slowly in a car park. I loved it because I believed I was the driver. Whilst I had some influence, however, the reality was my dad was in control. He could put the brakes on, push the acceleration at will. Our rational and conscious minds are like the child steering, while the emotional unconscious mind is the daddy in control.

When it comes to influencing people to act a certain way we can try and convince someone intellectually but it's when we move them emotionally that we are most effective.

My Mood Moves Me

Have you noticed how your mood determines your movement? When you are in a great mood you may walk tall with confidence and a smile. If you are in a bad mood you may walk around looking at the floor, not engaging in eye-to-eye contact with people around you.

Have you ever had someone notice your mood? They may say, 'You've got a spring in your step,' or, 'Have you got out the wrong side of bed?' We are always in a mood of one kind or another. Moods are like the weather, sunny or stormy, dark even.

We can often allow someone to trigger a mood in us. Something they say either helps to lift the cloud or intensify the storm. That person has managed your behaviour by changing how you feel. The best sports coaches will be those who have the ability to influence the mood of the players. They will be great man-managers; they get alongside those lacking in confidence and influence their mood by instilling new belief, which in turn triggers a new mood. This new mood informs the new mindset and a new level of performance produces positive results. When a coach is failing, people will use the phrase, 'They have lost the dressing room.' What they mean is that the coach no longer has the ability to influence the mood of the players in a positive way.

The 'Brains' behind the Mood

Moods are powerful and are created from the part of our brain called the 'amygdala'. This part of the brain is responsible for our instinctive behavior. It produces powerful positive and negative emotions such as danger, anxiety, fear, excitement and pleasure. While we often believe our rational thinking is in full control (this takes place in the Neocortex), the amygdala is more powerful in its ability to shape behaviour. The winning conversation is about an individual taking control over this emotive engine through the power of choice and empowering a strong belief system to lead the way. This in turn can harness the potential of a persons emotive drive and rationale thought processes to create new and improved behavior patterns.

A mood is powerful and the mood of a person or group of people can positively impact the moods of other people. Our mood creates an atmosphere and the atmosphere and 'weather' of our moods determines what we can grow in the gardens of our lives.

Good 'Mood' makes Good 'Food'

The 'food' of our results—what we produce—is directly linked to the root of our mood. Imagine you are making a meal for some special guests one evening and you knew that the mood in which you undertake the cooking process had a direct influence on the taste. What would you do? Let me take a guess and suggest that before you start the process you would sit down and check your mood. You might ask someone to watch for any hint of a bad mood and point it out to you. You would have a strong word with yourself about any negative thought or feeling and get yourself into the right state of mind. You might put on some music, smile to yourself, or have a little dance in the kitchen, because you know positive movement has an impact on how you feel. Over time you would learn that what you focus on feeds your feelings and so you concentrate on the things you are thankful for in life. You think about your loved ones and precious memories. You might think compassionate thoughts about those who do not have the options of food that you have. You realise the more you focus on others the more you maintain the blue skies of your mood rather than allow low lying black clouds to fill the skies of your soul.

You serve up your food with confidence because you know you took control of the mood and therefore the food will be great.

It sounds simple and it is!

Great mood = great results

Negative mood = negative results

The longer you stay in a negative mood, the more damage you do to your potential results in life. When you realise that your mood is either working for you or against you, you start to increase your awareness of your mood.

My Mood is the Result of my <u>Soul Appetite</u>, <u>Soul Script</u> and <u>Soul Flow</u>*

<u>SOUL APPETITES</u>

How do I manage my mood? I need first of all to be aware of the two determining factors involved in the makeup of a mood. I am going to look at Soul appetites today and then soul scripts tomorrow.

Appetites Fed from the Inside-Out

Whilst other people can influence our mood, the purpose of

this book is to determine that our internal conversation will be a mood thermostat and not a mood thermometer. The thermostat controls the temperature whereas the thermometer reflects the temperature set by external factors.

Food and mood have a bigger connection than just my earlier illustration. Have you noticed the link between physical hunger and a negative mood? As a man I am all too aware that when I am hungry I am more prone to being short-tempered and abrupt because my physical hunger has created a new focus. My physical hunger is saying, 'Go look for food…now!' Anything that appears to get in the way of that, regardless of how important it may be, is prone to being pulled into the orbit of my mood. However, there are a number of appetites we as humans carry that we have to be aware of when managing and harnessing the power of our moods.

I remember being told time and time again by my parents that breakfast is the most important meal of the day. Even on the days when I did not feel like eating first thing, I would be reminded that it was still the most important time to eat, the belief being that this meal would set the rhythm and energy levels for the day. How I set my stomach up at the start of a day would influence the quality of my food choices throughout the rest of the day. In fact because what we eat influences our energy levels our choice to eat first thing or not can determine the quality of much of our day.

Every person has a physical appetite that needs satisfying but they also have appetites that are emotional and spiritual. These are part of our lives and just like the physical stomach they need satisfying. So what are these appetites?

Affection - to know that we matter to someone

Achievement - to know that we can add value and make progress

Authority - to know we have a voice that is heard

Acceptance - to know we have a place

Appreciation - to know that we are valued

Assurance - to know we are safe and secure

Throughout our lives we look for ways to satisfy these desires. How we go about that reveals something quite significant. We find our source for these appetites from the people and world that surround us. We carry a demand and we can often find a supply through relationships, health, finances and vocation. However what happens when the demand outweighs the supply is we facilitate an outside-in conversation! When our relationships are not providing enough appreciation, we then start to resent those people and either withdraw or resist, or we find alternative relationships. Why do so many marriages end in divorce? Why has the family unit eroded so much in recent decades? Why is teenage pregnancy continuing to rise? Why is debt at an all time high in most of the western world? Why is obesity such a problem for the health services? The quality of peoples' choices has deteriorated because they are desperately seeking to feed an appetite that needs to be satisfied.

The Problem with Shopping on an Empty Stomach

Have you ever been grocery shopping on an empty stomach? As you walk around, your hunger causes you to buy more, often things that take less time to prepare and that bring an immediate satisfaction to your hunger.

Making choices on an EMPTY stomach = Quantity of choices goes UP and the quality of choices goes DOWN.

However, if we eat a good nutritious meal and fill our appetite before we shop, there is less of a draw towards the bad food. In fact, we can easily walk past it and we can make better choices. Here is what happens:

Making choices on a FULL stomach = Quantity of choices goes DOWN and the quality of choices goes UP.

If we go into our day without satisfying our appetites then the same happens to our life choices.

Satisfy Appetites from Beliefs and not Results

The winning flow is about satisfying these appetites from belief and not from results. While results can create a feel-good factor our main driver for WHY we do what we do is based on the leader of the feelings we have. The winning conversation produces an internal satisfaction that feeds these appetites from the inside-out.

When we look in creation we can see this winning pattern. Whether you choose to attribute that to a deity or not, there appears to be a clear logic behind the systems that sustain the planet we live in as part of the wider universe.

The tree is a great symbol and example of this logic. A tree is visible from what we see above the ground. We can see the trunk, the branches and in the right season we see the leaves and/or fruit. However what is produced above is fed from what is below. The roots of the tree do not reach above the ground to try and find the source, they reach down. Why? Because the principle is that the source of life does not come from the outside-in but from the inside-out. The tree is a symbol of life and the principle that applies to it applies to us.

Find a Consistent Source of Supply

Let me be clear in communicating what I am not saying. I am not advocating living a monastic lifestyle where we become a community unto ourselves and we have no need for other people. The winning conversation requires community with others to have its full impact. It is good for people to have supply for the appetites from those around them; in fact, that is what produces a healthy community and facilitates healthy people. A tree benefits from the rain that falls and the sun that shines and these are external factors. However, first and foremost, it sends its roots down to find a consistent source so that when the supply from the external is not there, it can continue to grow and flourish.

The reason our default source becomes the external is because our intended source is incomplete. In the story on day 7 the eagle developed and was defined from the outside-in because he had no clarity about WHO he was. This reveals the starting point. Once we have in place the WHO it unlocks the next level of our lives which is WHY. The Eagle needed to know WHO he was in order to know

WHY he was alive. The eagle's purpose was to be a predator of the skies that could seek out its own food, not reliant upon chicken feed in a chicken pen. It needed the self-belief about its potential to be acted upon to create new results.

External frustration exists when I am trying to find a source to meet my internal needs from the outside-in. I can win in life if I seek deep clarity about WHO I am followed by clarity about WHY, and an intense desire to fulfil that purpose.

The Two Pilots

An airline pilot will fly his aircraft using a combination of conversing with air traffic control and liaising with his instruments. Ultimately this determines the destination and quality of the flight. If the conversations go well, you, the passenger, arrive at your destination; if they don't, then the consequences can ultimately be disastrous.

Most airplanes have two pilots. Let's use this as a picture. One takes the lead while the other is present to take over should he be asked. Pilot 1 is in place. His commands are based upon an identity we have developed and that has been defined by others. Pilot number 2 however, has clarity on the commands that steer us into WHO we are to be. Pilot 1 steers us to make choices that satisfy our appetites from the outside in and pilot 2 steers us to operate from who we are, a place of completion. Pilot 2 has the commands that help us live on a full stomach.

Every day we make a choice which pilot is taking the lead and that choice determines the flight path we take and ultimately our destination.

Feed to Feel to Focus to Function

Each of the 6 winning conversations starts with feeding a feeling with a belief. The more you feed your mood with belief the more intense the feeling which then creates focus. Your belief is that principle that is an unchanging law in your life. When you start living from a principle-centred life your life experience makes a quantum leap. The difference is like someone describing an event using Morse code and watching the same information transmitted through film in 3D high definition with surround sound. There is no comparison!

The winning conversation creates a winning mood. There will be times when our mood shifts but the aim of this conversation with you right here and now is to enable you to quickly change when it occurs. Having already introduced the voices of the winning and losing conversation we will look at the managers they lead.

The winning **BELIEF** feeds my **APPETITES** which creates the winning **MOOD**

WINNING CONVERSATION	EXPANSIVE CONVERSATION	INFLUENTIAL CONVERSATION	VALUABLE CONVERSATION	RESILIENT CONVERSATION	MEMORABLE CONVERSATION	PROMINENT CONVERSATION
BELIEF	Creative	Inclusive	Excellent	Passionate	Relevant	Devoted
APPETITE	Achievement	Acceptance	Appreciation	Assurance	Authority	Affection
MOOD	Enthusiastic	Curious	Grateful	Optimistic	Helpful	Expectant

LOSING CONVERSATION	DIMINISHING CONVERSATION	INFERIOR CONVERSATION	WORTHLESS CONVERSATION	FRAGILE CONVERSATION	FORGETTABLE CONVERSATION	UNNOTICED CONVERSATION
BELIEF	Predictable	Exclusive	Mediocre	Lethargic	Irrelevant	Apathetic
APPETITE	Underachieved	Unaccepted	Unappreciated	Unassured	Unauthorised	Undervalued
MOOD	Unenthusiastic	Uninterested	Ungrateful	Pessimistic	Unhelpful	Unexpectant

*Tomorrow we look at SOUL SCRIPT and SOUL FLOW

Day 10: Awareness of the script that forms the conversation

The Source of my conversation

My mood is the result of my <u>soul appetite</u>, my <u>soul script</u> and my <u>soul flow</u>

SOUL SCRIPT: The Manuscript of my Mood

Life can sometimes feel like a drama, something that's closer to the truth than maybe we realise. Every drama and play has a script that the actors are given in order to bring what started in the writer's mind to life.

Our internal conversation is the script for our lives. If we are determined to change the storyline of our lives then we need to take control of the script that is currently determining what is taking place on the stage of our lives. The soul is the central place for our script to be identified. Our feelings are interpretations of a script. So I call this our soul script.

Get your Hands on the Soul Script

When we look again at the story of the eagle (Day 7) we need to look at the conversation that would have taken place inside that bird and what needed to change in order for it to embrace its potential. The script might have looked like this:

'I am how I have been treated.'

The eagle was told he was a chicken and because this was backed by experience of how he was treated, this set his personal value. The flow of conversation was outside-in, and the conversation was a losing conversation.

We too can allow how we have been treated to become our soul script. We become slaves to our experience and the only way to change this is to experience something else. An idea is not strong enough. There is a power in an experience that cannot be rivalled. The eagle needed the naturalist to create a new experience for him.

'My Aspirations are set by my Surroundings'

The eagle had all the aspirations of an eagle drummed out of him because he believed his value was set by the surroundings of the barnyard. He feared what lay beyond the familiar and so stayed in the comfort of the familiar.

We naturally learn to reflect the environment in which we

are immersed. Only a revelation of another way can disrupt this mindset. Sometimes that disruption can feel like an offence. When what has been your familiarity is challenged it rocks your security. This can feel bad but it is important that we do not interpret all negative feelings as a negative thing. Having an operation can feel like a negative process and yet the surgeon's knife may lead to a positive outcome.

'The Unknown is not my Domain'

We know that the domain of an eagle is the skies but his internal script stated that it did not belong to him because he had not experienced it before. When we live from the inside-out then our experiences follow our beliefs and not the other way round. Therefore the winning conversation states 'the unknown IS my domain' because we have a goal that says the NOT YET rules the NOW and not the other way round.

It is not common for people to sit and really think about their *soul script* but when you realise that it is essential to unlock your potential then it has to become your business.

If the proverb ***as a man thinks in his heart so is he*** is correct, it shows us that the sub-conscious drives the conscious. We have to learn how to delve under the waters of our consciousness in order to reconfigure the script that drives everything.

For instance, the subconscious line, 'I am how I have been treated,' fed the eagle's conscious choice not to look beyond the confines of the pen. His choices all fell within the confines of what he was used to. Your dreams will remain fantasy unless you grapple with the reality of your soul script.

When you think of it, it's pretty scary to think how powerful our internal scripting is. However this book is good news; you do not have to stay where you are. You can change the script!

Failure to Change

Most people have tried at some point to change behaviour, through weight loss, career change or fitness habits. However, many fail to sustain new behaviour. Many never push through to a 'new norm.' Some briefly visit change but then return to the way things were. Why is that? Lasting change only takes place when it happens at a belief level. Our beliefs need to be immersed in the principle for it to move from a temporary visit to lasting change.

It took for the eagle to realise 'I am an eagle,' and ultimately to fly like an eagle, for the breakthrough to come. Too often we stick to the scripting that we carry and our scripting is based on our deep understanding of who we are.

Change the Script to Change the Storyline

What film do you want to leave others to watch when you have gone? What do you want your memory to be? You can influence that now. If we want to change the film of our lives, then the storyline has to change and the only way to change the storyline is to change the script. Our frustrating lack of results has to switch from a focus on HOW and WHAT and start with WHO. Who I believe I am will define all that I become.

If you want to be a winner in life then spend regular time understanding your soul script because it is the engine driving all that happens above the surface of your life.

A Different Script Requires a Different Voice

In the story of the eagle it was down to the naturalist to come along and be a different voice. The farmer was quite content to keep the eagle believing he was a chicken. Therefore his voice kept feeding the script that determined the belief system. It was only when a different voice came along with a different script that the breakthrough came.

A Champion Needs to Identify the Final Word

In any sport there is an adjudicator or referee, someone who makes the final decision on the course of the game. Their decision is the final word and when a debate or even fight breaks out over a difference of opinion about the direction of the game everyone has to abide by that call. The script of our life is the final word. Even when there is a battle of opinions in a person's mind and feelings (the soul), the contest will be decided by the spirit of the person. Have you ever felt like you are fighting a losing battle between what you want to do and what you end up doing? Well, you are fighting a battle and it will be a losing battle unless you change the referee.

In the story of the eagle, the naturalist became the new voice that had the final word. He changed the script, the belief, and the eagle was unleashed.

Throughout this book I am going to introduce you to six conversations that are taking place inside you 24 hours a day, seven days a week. This will start to reveal the inner conversations and start to outline the principles that need to be the new voice—the voice that has the final word in your life. I am going to walk you through how to change those conversations so that you shift from the ordinary to the extraordinary beliefs that will produce extraordinary results in your life.

The Root to the Fruit

When we hit a frustration we look to solve it through a method or a person. However, in order to change the fruit you have to change it at root level. Short term solutions are created through method changes but long term solutions happen when we seek to see the change in a person before a practice. The trouble is we often do not have the patience for this approach; we waste more time trying to solve things through methods.

If we are frustrated at our inability to be motivated, influential, effective, dedicated, confident or to add more value, then we might be able to make an incremental difference through behaviour change but it's only when we change the root beliefs that will we see a lasting difference. My root belief feeds me and this forms the substance of what I offer others to eat through the words I speak and the actions I carry out. What is the quality of fruit that I am giving my spouse, children, family, friends and colleagues? The script I rehearse internally becomes the quality of what I offer externally. It is time to get some quality control over the fruit of our lives and that starts with looking at what is feeding the root.

The Commands Control my Experience

The command centre of our lives is in the subconscious values of a person. This is like a satellite navigation system that has the co-ordinates for a certain destination. When you have it in mind to head to a different location you are going to be working against the machine. This will create constant frustration because you are battling against yourself. The only way to alter this is to alter the codes in the system.

If my commands in my spirit are set against the direction of my intentions then I will always be pulled back to my default position. I need to attach my intentions to the correct commands.

For instance, a default command that I have to watch is, 'You are worth what you achieve.' This means I can constantly make decisions to increase my personal sense of worth by overworking, getting too busy in too many things and putting incredible pressure on all areas of my life. This not only can affect me but my family, friends and those I work with. The commands of our sub-conscious not only affect us but everyone around us. It is possible that the commands we have in our hearts were exampled to us by our parents/leaders. We need to realise that we will reproduce the commands we carry in the lives of those who look to us also. This is a responsibility from which we cannot hide.

Learn to take time to think of the script that is shaping your choices, the root that is feeding the fruit and the commands that are creating my experience.

SOUL FLOW: Sow what I Want to Grow

If I want to take control of how I feel then I must understand that at any one time I am either in a state of CONSUMING or PRODUCING. A person's state is their condition, how they are positioned at any one moment. If I can understand at this stage that to unlock my potential I need to maintain a state of PRODUCING in order to host the winning conversation, then I will win in life.

A consumer is totally reliant on what happens around them to feed their soul appetites and to determine their soul script, how they feel about themselves. When you get clarity on your winning purpose you quickly realise that only a person in a state of PRODUCING will have any chance of fulfilling that purpose effectively. A person in a state of CONSUMING will be relying on external factors to get them in the mood to take on the challenge of their cause and to give them the emotional capacity to keep going.

The WHY of our lives is either set to CONSUMING—where my life is about ME, MYSELF and I—or PRODUCING—where my life is about me having a correct belief about MYSELF, MY FUTURE, so that I can serve OTHERS effectively.

Another way of putting it is that our lives are either set to PRIDE or HUMILITY. Pride is when the flow of my life is outside-in and when my ultimate underlying goal is to bring satisfaction to myself. Humility is an inside-out approach where my underlying drive and motivation is to serve others through helping them discover MORE for their lives.

You may say, 'Surely we all have to consume at points in life.' 'Surely there is a good pride. It isn't all bad, is it?' The answer is yes. Both have a place. However, it is when they become the 'driver' of our lives that we hit the big problems. In our rational minds very few of us would describe ourselves as CONSUMERS or PROUD people but remember our rational minds are the child on the father's lap. The question is, 'who is the Daddy?' If the underlying current is other people then we have a driver at the wheel that will take us to the destination of our legacy.

Day 11: The Winning Language

The Two Languages of my Soul Script

Our soul script is constantly informing our conversation. Even when we are not aware of thinking something, there is a conversation taking place. My wife will sometimes say to me 'what's wrong?' The truth is that I may not be thinking of anything at the time and I may not be aware that something is wrong, but she has learnt how to interpret my soul. Our presence is more than just physical proximity and external communication. Atmosphere is created from what we carry in our soul.

It is possible for us to deny our awareness of what we are carrying but others will sense what is inside us. What is present in our core we present to others, whether we realise it or not.

Our soul script comes in two languages. The language of the winning conversation is FAITH and the language of the LOSING conversation is FEAR.

The language of FAITH

Faith means to have complete trust and confidence. When our language is faith then it is full of hope, optimism, expectation and the result is CERTAINTY.

The language of FEAR

Fear is the opposite of faith. It is unstable because of a lack of confidence. Fear lacks hope, is pessimistic, expects negative outcomes, panics and the result is UNCERTAINTY.

The Winning Interpretation

Every day we are presented with many facts. Facts are pieces of information. Information is interpreted in different ways. The facts we are presented with get interpreted into our native soul language. If our language is fear than we translate everything into that language. FEAR or FAITH becomes the translator.

Two people can be exposed to the same circumstance and yet respond to it in two totally different ways. During periods of economic trial many will decide to hold tight to their money because no one is buying or investing. Why? They are fearful and

115

decide to grow small. Others see an opportunity for investing because the best time to invest is when most are not investing. The price goes down because the demand has diminished. However, when everything is going well and demand is high, so is the price.

Two people can be made unemployed. One can fear for the future because that is the only job they have done. The other may get excited because this is just what they needed to see them progress into something new, such as a job that has greater prospects and opportunity.

Two people standing on a beach can look at huge waves crashing down. One may stand back in fear of drowning. The other may don a wetsuit and fetch a board because it's a great day for surfing.

Your *soul language* filters the facts and gives them meaning. The facts are truth but the meaning is pure speculation. The language of fear will interpret events and feed it into a losing conversation. The language of faith will interpret events and feed it into a winning conversation.

How do we know which language we are interpreting facts Into?

The way we know is the process we use. Every person carries an internal interpreting process. These are made up of three activities intended to be used to create progress for the WINNING CONVERSATION. However, they can be misused and actually bring regression through the LOSING CONVERSATION.

The three activities are:

Counselling: This is the act of instruction. This activity involves the giving of opinions, advice and a judgment of a situation or person.

Consulting: This is the act of informing—giving information in order to make a decision or judgment.

Confiding. This is an act of trust and reliance. This is the recognition that the one in whom I confide will lead me to a decision. The one in whom we confide is the one whose track record we trust.

A person of FEAR will:

Consult FEELINGS: A consultant informs you. Feelings make awful masters but great servants. When my soul script is fear I make my feelings my master. Feelings should be like a dog owner who has their dog on a leash and under control, able to enjoy the animal and the companionship it brings. However when our soul script is fear, feelings become the dog with the human on the leash. The master actually becomes slave to the servant.

Confide in FEAR: You confide in what you trust. Therefore it is possible for people to trust their fears above anything else. There are many fears that seem extreme and almost unbelievable; however, what you trust you confide in. This belief then becomes extremely deep rooted and difficult to change. The only way to change it is through a new experience.

Counsel FACTS: The soul language of fear takes a feeling and makes it a belief. A seemingly good fact can be counselled into becoming a negative fact if fear is the language they speak.

A person of FAITH will:

Consult the FACTS: A person of faith is not someone who ignores facts or buries their head in the sand in order to remain ignorant. This kind of activity is actually fear disguised as faith. Facts are vital for a person of faith because they become useful navigation tools in getting from the NOW to the NOT YET. They become the co-ordinates that help line up the steps for progress.

Confide in FAITH: Faith requires a clarity concerning the NOT YET and allows it to lead the NOW. Faith is about the laws and principles in which we trust. We feel safer on the ground than in the air because we trust the law of gravity. We would not have that same faith in space because different laws apply. When we immerse ourselves in what we are certain of our soul script becomes one of faith. Fear becomes a foreign language to which we choose not to listen.

Counsel their FEELINGS: When faith becomes our language we instruct our feelings. A person of faith is not immune to negative or confusing feelings; however, they choose to process them differently from a person of fear. Uncertain feelings are reshaped and recycled and refuel the things about which we are certain. A person of faith acts like a tree in a community or team environment. They take the negative life-sapping feelings and convert them into life-giving positive feelings.

The Winning Disposition

There are three main subjects referred to in our soul script. The internal conversation will be about:

i) How we view OURSELVES

ii) How we view OTHERS

iii) What we seek to OBTAIN

The **losing conversation** will cause us to:

i) Be self-destructive in how we address/view OURSELVES

Our language of fear feeds a sense of inadequacy and worth. We demote our abilities for fear that an opportunity might reveal the 'truth' of what we believe about ourselves. Sometimes this self-destructive nature manifests itself in the hurting of other people. A coping mechanism for dealing with the hurt is to bring others into our internal experience. Self-destructive habits are evidence of a self-destructive script which is the language of fear.

ii) Elevate our needs before the needs of OTHERS

Fear of missing out based upon an internal lack of contentment results in a self-serving nature. 'Looking after number one' is based on a fear of missing out because others will not feed our internal appetites. The losing conversation believes that life is like a game of musical chairs. As time goes on chairs are being removed and we do not want to get caught without a chair when the music stops.

iii) Seek to OBTAIN a good feeling now rather than wait for a future moment

The losing conversation promotes the belief, 'If I can get a good feeling now then why wait? I may end up with nothing.' 'Why delay gratification when I may not have an opportunity to feel like this in the future?' 'Sure, it might be better to wait but my language of fear tells me it's better to get it while I can!'

The **winning conversation** will cause us to:

i) Build OURSELVES up

You can only give out of what you carry. Your winning goals involve resourcing other people and you can only give to others out of what you possess. A person who has not satisfied their internal appetites will struggle to resource others. To give courage to others you have to first be 'in courage.' How do you get 'in courage'? You simply learn to encourage yourself regularly. Therefore there is no room for a self-debasing script that subtract. The winning conversation is only interested in a script that multiplies the resource for the sake of the winning goals.

ii) Elevate the needs of OTHERS before ourselves

Helping others win is what the winning conversation is all about. Our NOT YET conversations with those we love require us to keep others before ourselves. Pride makes me push to the front out of a fear that I will not get recognition. However, the winning conversation understands that lasting recognition comes through humility and the promoting of others. This takes a secure person, a person whose soul script is in the language of faith.

iii) Be willing to put off a good feeling now to OBTAIN what we have NOT YET received

The winning conversation understands the principle of investment in order to produce a multiplication. The NOT YET goals require exponential and not merely incremental growth because the cause and need that you want to make a difference too will require this. Only a selfish person seeks to get just enough resource because their only concern is themselves.

Empower the Right Managers on the Office Floor of your Feelings

It is important that we manage the conversations taking place on the factory floor. We know the six managers of the winning conversation and the six managers of the losing conversation. We now know how to interpret the two different languages.

As we go through the six conversations we will look at examples of the soul script that we need to shut down and the soul script we need to incorporate in the conversation.

The conversation I want the most is the conversation I will host

Having spent thousands of hours with people who have shown signs of the losing conversation, it is actually quite amazing how many do not want to move from that place. The familiarity of the feelings it produces actually becomes a comfort to them. The proof of desire is in action.

Host the LOSING conversation and you will feel a LOSER

Why is it I can feel like a LOSER? It is because I lack a sense of completeness. Completeness is about wholeness.

The LOSING mood comes from the internal conversation that says:

i)   I do not value MYSELF

ii) I do not value OTHERS

iii) I do not value my FUTURE

Host the WINNING conversation and you will feel a WINNER

Why is it I can feel like a WINNER? It is because I have a sense of completeness. Completeness is about wholeness.

The WINNING mood comes from the internal conversation that says:

i)   I value MYSELF completely

ii) I value OTHERS completely

iii) I value my FUTURE completely

Day 12: The Winning Mindsets in the meeting room

Our mindset becomes the lens through which we view the world around us. I am short sighted and so rely upon glasses or contact lenses to give me the correct lens through which I can see the detail of objects that surround me. If I do not choose to wear them, then I struggle to make good choices because I cannot clearly see what is around me. I can make general decisions, but I cannot make focussed decisions which ultimately determine the effectiveness of my day. This means much of my day would be wasted trying to make the right decisions and correcting incorrect choices made because I did not have clarity of choice.

Your Mindset creates your Reality

Every day I adopt a mindset whether I realise it or not. Adopting the winning mindset is a conscious choice made at the beginning of a day that enables me to make quality choices. These choices then activate the results I experience.

The mindset I adopt is the tool I use to create my day. We are creative beings and must never underestimate our ability to create our reality.

Our mindset comes from our mind mix. When we choose to bake a cake we start with mixing different ingredients together. The ingredients we use determine the result of the cake once it has been cooked and then it has set. The cake set comes from the cake mix.

Our mind mix is the result of our beliefs and appetites that become established and set. Our mindset becomes the foundation upon which we can create the world around us. When we strengthen the foundations of WHO and WHY, HOW we live becomes stronger and our actions become increasingly confident.

The level to which we strengthen our mindset determines the strength of the reality we create. So how do we manage our mindsets? The best way to manage our mindsets is to view them as a map. When travelling you will often use a physical or electronic map. The choice to move in any one direction is based upon the map being consulted. Our daily choices are referenced against our mind map. If we want to produce winning results in life and yet use the wrong mindset it becomes like a person trying to make their way around London using a map of New York. Wrong turns will create frustration and little progress because the map being referenced cannot guide you to your desired destination.

If we knew the extent of influence that our mindset has on our daily lives then we would spend more time preparing this key area of our lives. When we spend time getting our mindset in place we are preparing for HOW we are going to outwork our beliefs and feelings.

Taking control of your life by adopting your chosen mindset and stepping into your day with confidence with a definite approach will cause the situations and circumstances you face to follow your mindset. When we fail to determine the mindset we use for the day we choose to negate our capacity to create our reality and expose ourselves to becoming created by our surroundings. This exposes us to the losing conversation because we are then at the mercy of other peoples' mindsets. Our thinking becomes a reflection of our surroundings rather than a creative force which shapes our environment.

Our mindset sets us up for success or failure before we even open our mouth.

Our Mindset is Created through the Thoughts we Agree on

The thoughts that I choose to agree with become part of my mindset. To choose not to deal with a thought is to agree that it can become part of the lens through which we view life. We allow the seed to settle into the soil of our minds.

A single thought is like a seed that is watered through focus. The thoughts we focus on are the ones we grow into actions and our actions activate our reality. Each seed contains the mix of our internal conversation.

New Thoughts start with new Beliefs

We change our thoughts by choosing a different belief. In doing so we create new feelings which in turn create new thoughts to feed through focus. The life we experience today is the result of the seeds we decide to focus on. No one else is responsible for our thoughts other than ourselves.

Your Mindset is your Life Filter

We live in the information age which means we are constantly bombarded with millions of pieces of information that fill our brains. This means that it is vital to set in place a filter system. We use filter systems on our email inbox to categorise, sort and order messages; this is vital because of the volume of emails that come our way. Without a system of filtering we can become distracted when accessing our inbox and valuable time is wasted sorting through the useful from useless emails.

Our mindset is that filtering process but the quality of the mindset determines the quality of the filter. The filter decides which thoughts we hold onto and which are discarded. If I have agreed with the thought that I am worthless, my mindset starts to hang on to any other thoughts that agree with it. By holding onto the thought I not only allow that seed to develop but other thoughts now gather with that thought and create a momentum in my thinking that will build over time and produce the wrong results in my life. Alternatively, to agree on the right thoughts creates a positive attraction to the right thoughts that will help build a mindset that in turn will build the reality that I seek to experience.

The following four mindsets are four sieves with which we filter the thousands of thoughts that enter into our minds and go on to create our reality.

The Four Mindsets

As we go through this book I will help identify the internal conversations of these four MINDSETS as a means of helping us identify which we have at any one time. The goal is to make the daily shift to the WINNING CONVERSATION, *the conversation of a champion.*

An ancient parable given by Jesus, founder of the Christian faith, describes how a farmer indiscriminately sows his seeds which land in four types environments with four different results. Some of the seed land on the path where the birds swoop down and consume it. There are no results. The second lands in shallow soil where rocks lie under the surface. While the seed starts to grow, the sun scorches the plant. The roots are insufficiently deep so the plants die and the results are short-lived. The third lands in soil and starts to grow but after a while the thorns and other weeds start to choke the seed's potential and once again the results are short and limited. The fourth group of seed lands in good soil and even though it takes longer the plant starts to grow. The plant is able to send its roots down deep and it has the ability to grow and ultimately bear fruit, producing significant results.

When I read this parable I see the four types of soil as four types of people who carry the four mindsets. It is only by approaching this book and its principles with a WINNING MINDSET that you will produce the WINNING RESULTS.

1. THE CONSUMED MINDSET

This person can be described as having:

Low self-belief, Low aspiration, Low focus, Low commitment

The CONSUMED MINDSET agrees with thoughts that...

- Doubt the possibilities life holds
- Undervalue a commitment to improvement
- Allow the bar of expectation to be set low
- Permit a high level of self-indulgence in the present
- Leave little room for the possibility of transformation

- Believe life cannot look vastly different from how it currently looks
- Place too much emphasis on past experiences creating an inflexibility to future possibilities
- Accept that their future has been predetermined by their past
- Believe life is a lottery and results happen by chance not by choice.

The content of this book will land on the SURFACE of their thinking and will not go any further.

2. THE COMPLACENT MINDSET

This person can be described as having:

Average self-belief, Average aspiration, Average focus, Low commitment

The COMPLACENT MINDSET feeds thoughts that...

- Promote quick fixes to lasting problems
- Avoid the path of resistance that brings lasting change
- Believe action is not urgent or even at times necessary to bring about results
- Pursue quick soul 'snacks' that bring an immediate sense of fulfilment not realising that they are simply hopping between short term fixes
- Create indecision
- When faced with opportunity to change their future will often lean toward what is known as opposed to what is unknown
- Believe talking is doing and so carry a false sense of accomplishment
- Avoid clarifying goals and evaluation for fear of revealing a picture that reflects badly on them.

The content of this book will land in SHALLOW thinking. There will be immediate results but an unwillingness to do the deep work will result in short term results.

3. THE COMPETITOR MINDSET

This person can be described as having:

High self-belief, High aspiration, Low focus, Average commitment

The COMPETITOR MINDSET feeds thoughts that...

- Desire and actively look for ways to change
- Seek success in every part of their life and carry a commitment to see it come to fruition
- Give space to anxiety which distracts and reduces focus
- Create a fear of getting it wrong, born of a desire for success, which rules their decision making process
- Believe 'the more I engage with the more results I will see'
- Believe that capacity is gifted and not created
- Accept a 'feeling' as a sign of progress as opposed to seeking facts that truly demonstrate progress.

The content of this book will get SWALLOWED by overwhelming feelings and distractions. A lack of results will create frustration and reduce quality decision-making.

4. THE CHAMPION MINDSET

This person can be described as having:

High self-belief, High aspiration, High focus, High commitment

The CHAMPION MINDSET feeds thoughts that...

- Believe every day is significant and the small and consistent choices made in each day have an ultimate bearing on where they end up
- Believe their problems carry potential answers that can fuel next level results and should not be avoided
- Believe they have a legacy to build which will impact the world around them
- Believe the bar for future results is set by their potential and not past results
- Believe every little choice or decision has an impact on results

- Believe the future will be greater than the past
- Believe lasting and sustainable results come from a commitment to a long haul process and not cutting corners
- Believe every common choice carried out in an uncommon way leads to uncommon results.

The content of this book will produce RESULTS because it becomes part of their daily conversation.

Determine the Mindset you Have and which you Want

Which mindset do you normally adopt and which do you want to have? It's important you are brutally honest with yourself at this point in order to make progress:

MINDSET	SELF-BELIEF	ASPIRATION	FOCUS	COMMITMENT
CONSUMED	LOW	LOW	LOW	LOW
COMPLACENT	AVERAGE	AVERAGE	AVERAGE	LOW
COMPETITOR	HIGH	HIGH	LOW	AVERAGE
CHAMPION	HIGH	HIGH	HIGH	HIGH

Get in the Right Lane

Imagine the four types of mindsets as four lanes on a motorway. We know that the first lane is for the slow moving traffic and those positioned in this lane are more likely to exit the road or break down on the hard shoulder. We know that the fourth lane is for those who are overtaking the vehicles in the other lanes. The default lane is the first lane and we want to keep challenging ourselves to move into the fast lane.

When we accept a mindset of the complacent or the competitor, those we influence or lead will get frustrated with us hogging those lanes and will either settle for a lesser lane or find someone who can help them overtake on the outer lane of the champion.

To key to developing a winning conversation is to be committed to tracing and trending. I will be encouraging you to stop regularly in order to analyse your tracks and see which type of mindset we have been using to filter our thoughts. This will then allow us to trend what will happen if we continue to travel in that lane.

This process will create self-awareness which allows us to understand at any one time which mindset we carry. This is a powerful position to be in because it means we can steer our thinking into another lane.

Alongside our focus on the winning conversation which includes developing a winning mindset, it is important continually to clarify our winning purpose. Our motivation to realise our potential as a champion is through a deep desire to achieve a goal that demands that level of commitment to our lives.

The size of my goal sets the level of demand for my personal commitment for change. More on this tomorrow!

Day 13: Winning Determination

Living Determined to make our decisions follow our goals

How does the winning mindset create a high level focus for our lives?

High level focus in life is the result of me adopting the right mindset. This involves a mindset mix (values + mood) and a clear future plan that demands high focus (the winning purpose).

The Mindset Mix

In following the flow of conversation from the boardroom of our beliefs and the office floor of feelings we now need to understand how these conversations feed into the meeting room of mindset creation.

A mindset is a mentality; it is the frame of mind a person adopts through which their choices will be informed. It filters the information going to the 'assembly room of actions' where the product of our lives is created.

My future is determined by my choices and my choices are informed by my mindset. These choices are shaping my future. A winning future requires a winning mindset. So what does that look like?

Each mindset carries the mix of self-belief (WHO I AM), aspiration (WHY I LIVE), Focus (HOW I LIVE) and commitment (WHAT I DO.) How these four elements come together defines the mindset that we carry.

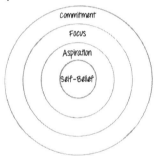

A winning mindset has high self-belief, high aspiration, high focus and high commitment and it will result in a person determining daily to have a:

PROGRESS Mindset

High level focus through prioritising ruthlessly

A progress mindset determines to focus daily on the journey before results. A champion understands that the winning, the result, is the bi-product of how I engage with the process. To focus on results first is an outside-in approach. It allows what we see to determine our next move. However we have already established that the pattern in life is that everything starts in an unseen form before manifesting in a seen result.

Progress is the result of focus. The way we practically focus is through prioritising.

We live unsustainable lives when we prioritise results over process. It will result in extreme moods and inconsistent motivations. It is our natural default to believe that life is good when results are good and life is bad when results are bad. However a progress mindset, whilst understanding the importance of results, will choose to have confidence in the process. A champion prizes the process and allows the process to take care of the prize!

When it comes to HOW we live our lives this mindset is developed through how we prioritise our lives around our winning purpose. A progress mindset is a mind mix of the belief that 'I am creative' and the mood that 'I am expectant'.

High focus creates proactive living as opposed to reactive living. Proactive living is where we are investing the right levels of energy and effort into the right areas to avoid living 'reactively' to life and to be ahead of the game at all times on the important issues. You will have experienced reactive living. It's when the 'to do' list always seems to have mastery over us rather than vice versa. It is the ability to work from a 'should do' mentality to a 'want to' mentality.

Proactive living is about keeping on top of the right things. People often say 'I am just trying to keep on top of everything.' When we look at that statement more closely we realise it is an impossible task. Only God can stay on top of **every**thing. We have to stay on top of **some**thing. This means we have to look ruthlessly at where we are investing our resource, our time, energy and finance. When we have clarity on a *winning purpose* then we realise that we have to lose many things in order to be on top of <u>something</u>.

We need everything to point toward something and when we can link it all to this something it becomes like a dot-to-dot picture in which the resulting picture is our winning purpose. We need clarity on what matters and what does not. Stephen Covey, in *Seven Habits of Highly Effective People,* talks about living from a place where our time is invested in the 'not-urgent but important.'[6] Many people live their lives acting on that which is 'urgent and important' and this means that we live reactively rather than pro-actively.

6. Covey, Stephen. The Seven Habits of highly effective people. New York City. Rosetta Books, 2009 Electronic edition

CONFIDENT Mindset

High level focus through presenting myself confidently

Confidence is about certainty, the ability to be assured of oneself regardless. Our confidence is tested most when it comes to our interaction with others. When our environment has the ability to make a judgment on us and form an opinion it causes us to become highly self-conscious. This is why some people prefer 'things' over 'people.' However when ultimately your winning purpose is centred on and around people, it is essential that we develop a confidence in front of people. This is not about the need for every person to develop a 'loud personality' because confidence can flow through a gentle and subtle approach. When we develop a confident mindset it feeds through into everything we do and opens doors in conversations with other people.

People are ultimately the cause that unlocks our potential. Therefore, growing our network of connections is vital. The confident mindset encourages this and informs our choice to engage well with others. The winning conversation has no limits in terms of what our potential can achieve and yet we often carry self-imposed limitations that prevent us from growing big lives. Our internal conversation makes a constant judgment about the people we meet. That judgment causes us to filter people into and out of our world. However, our judgment of people can often be wrong and so we can be unaware of the potential of the connection with that person. They may be the very person who needs what we have, or vice versa. They may have a connection, a piece of information or a problem that is directly relevant to us. Sight alone cannot determine this; it takes a conversation.

The competitor will strategically position themselves to be alone because they are determined to minimise 'wasting time'. There is nothing wrong with being strategic with our time and connections; as we have discussed, prioritising is vital. However, we must not be caught with tunnel vision when it comes to our connections because great opportunities lie in unlikely people. We have to manage the tension between staying smart with time and having an 'indiscriminate' approach to our daily connections.

A mindset that positions itself constantly for engagement beyond the normal boundaries of who we mix with is essential. It is only when we have a high self-belief in who we are and what we carry that positioning ourselves indiscriminately can be actioned.

DILIGENT Mindset

High level focus through practicing relentlessly

Diligence is about 'careful and persistent effort.' Diligence is a combination of our belief that 'I am excellent' and a mood of 'gratitude.' This mind mix creates a mindset of diligence. I demand high expectations of myself because I have a true appreciation of what I am dealing with. I seek to communicate high value through my approach.

Diligence is a high commitment to the outcomes we are targeting in life. It means that we need to embrace a commitment to practice relentlessly behaviours that will create the future for which we believe. We are the product we promote and this only comes through practice, practice and more practice. This means staying on something longer than most, investing more than others think sensible, eradicating anything that is reducing the impact of what we do. Like the athlete who practices day after day in an attempt to knock down the time it takes them to run the distance by seconds or milliseconds, we do whatever it takes to develop the one thing that we know is our gift to the world.

PERSEVERING Mindset

High level focus through persevering regardless

Perseverance is to persist in doing something regardless of difficulty or delay. It is a result of taking responsibility, to meet a self-imposed obligation. The more my winning purpose burns inside me the more I realise my life is obliged to see it come about. It is WHY I am alive! This obligation is necessary when it comes to the winning conversation. The responsible mindset comes from a belief that 'I am passionate' and an 'optimistic' mood that creates assurance and security in other people.

The deep desire and conviction of a NOT YET goal has a powerful way of pulling us out of how our NOW circumstances are making us feel and giving us the impetus to get back up and keep on going. The picture of the future and the size of our aspiration need to be such that, regardless of what is thrown at us, we are drawn to the future like metal to a magnet.

First thing in the morning we may not 'feel' like, living never mind pursuing, a goal. However the winning mindset makes the decision in the cold light of day to keep going because standing still, or worse still going backwards, is no option. Choose to view your winning purpose first thing in the morning and last thing at night every day.

SINCERE Mindset

High level focus through promoting others selflessly

Sincerity is the ability to operate in a way that is genuine and without manipulation. We all carry a natural connection to sincerity. So when it is presented to us in another human being, we connect to that, we sense it, we feel it. In fact sometimes it is only when we experience sincerity that we can distinguish between that and duplicity. You often need to experience the right and the wrong in order to make the distinction. The sincere mindset is the mix of a belief that 'I am relevant' and the mood of 'helpfulness' that creates the platform to contribute.

The winning purpose is ultimately not about me; it is about how my life interacts with others. The moment life becomes solely about me I start to develop the losing appetites which can never be satisfied. To determine daily to compliment those we interact with, to make our conversations about them and not us makes us a MEMORABLE influence. People remember those who make them feel good about themselves. To encourage people at every opportunity creates **self-belief**. When I make others feel important I feel important. The more we action encouragement the more we believe in what we can bring to the world around us. We often wait for permission to believe in ourselves. However the winning conversation is about self-permission to speak words of kindness and encouragement. Our words of encouragement are like fresh air and people love to be around fresh air rather than the stale odour of the losing conversation.

DETERMINED Mindset

High level focus through pursuing my cause unreasonably

To be determined is 'to make a firm decision and being resolved not to change it.' When I am determined I become consistent in my performance. My consistency in being determined means I become reliable, establishing and building 'credits in the bank' with others. Relationships are all about trust. Trust is built through a determined effort. A determined mindset is a mix of the belief that 'I am devoted' and cultivating the mood that 'I am expectant' which produces the mind mix for the determined mindset.

The higher the level of expectation we can commit ourselves, the greater the resolve we produce. This causes us to stand out as prominent in our world. We become 'go to' people when there are fewer people that can be entrusted with a 'high trust' activity or responsibility. This makes you more valuable in your world.

Unreasonable Thinking

It is our ability to straddle 'unreasonable' levels of commitment whilst maintaining a reliable consistency in HOW we live that will determine the winning reality we experience. This all starts with our internal conversation.

"The reasonable man adapts himself to the conditions that surround him... The unreasonable man adapts surrounding conditions to himself... All progress depends on the unreasonable man."

George Bernard Shaw

Unless challenged, we will always see the reasons to opt out of the pursuit of our cause. Therefore we have to determine daily to pursue our cause beyond reasons that would stop us or slow us down.

High commitment levels that produce deep resolve are HOW

we start to impact the world around us. These commitment levels are exhibited in all areas of our lives such as our relationships, health, finance and development.

A mindset requires a corresponding action for it to create an outcome which is what we will look at in the next chapter.

Clear future plan

Frame the winning future you want to see

Most people frame pictures of a past event but it is also true that you can frame your future. Pictures are powerful and can help create perspective in our lives. When we look at a picture taken of a loved one it helps put the rotten day we might be having in perspective. However, what if you could combine the power of perspective with a vision of a goal that inspires you to stay on course to seeing it become a reality?

Imagine you are looking at a wall in front of you and on the wall you have a number of pictures framed. These pictures are snapshots of your desired future. What would you like to see happen in your lifetime? What goals do you have?

The job of a picture frame is to help create a boundary through which you achieve focus. The boundary determines what sits inside and what sits outside of the picture. The greater the definition of what is acceptable and what is not, the clearer the reality you will create in its formation.

A conventional picture frame allows us in the NOW to focus on BACK THEN. When we spend time looking at a picture framed on a wall or sitting on the sideboard at home we remember the time the photo was taken through the lens of all we have experienced to that point. You can look at the same picture a year later and it will be an enhanced experience because more has happened between the NOW and BACK THEN.

When I talk about the winning frame I refer to the ability in the NOW to focus on the NOT YET. The more time I spend getting clarity on these two points the more I get a perspective on what my next steps needs to look like. The frame informs me so as not to overstretch in my next step but also to set the bar high enough to stay on course for the goal.

The winning frame is about a picture that produces a perspective and helps to inform our choices. It becomes a perspective that helps pull you forward when things are tough. It also becomes a challenge to keep our self-belief, aspiration, focus and commitment high if we really do want to

What we Frame, we Form

What we frame in our minds we form in our day and what we form in our day we become tomorrow. The more you understand this the more you realise that no one else can take responsibility for how we are formed other than ourselves. We even admit this when we say things like, 'I am not in the right frame of mind.' These sayings describe the lens that people are currently using through which to view everything. Our frame of mind is our choice. We can carry a losing or a winning frame of mind.

Developing this level of self-awareness is crucial to developing the winning conversation. Our activity is like a train that runs along the tracks of our mindset. If we do not like the direction of the train, then change the tracks—adopt a new mindset.

Moment to pause: What images do I see that I can use to create my 'winning frame?' Why not take some time to collate images that best represent the product of the process you are embarking on? Taking a long hard look at this framed picture will remind you of the mindsets you must adopt in order to see it come to fruition.

Day 14—The Winning Choices in the Assembly Room of Actions

Without the assembly room in a factory there is no visible product. Everything up to this point is talk and theory. All the work in the boardroom, the office floors and the meeting rooms are about leading, managing and informing the workers what to construct in order to create the reality of the product. It is only when the assembling of a product has taken place that it can then be tested and improved.

Working on a perfect idea is futile because a process involves failure and error in order to root out imperfections. The winning conversation requires action and while not every action will look or create an obvious winning result, the process plays a crucial role in producing the winning conversation in you. Remember the prize is the process and when we focus on the process the prize will take care of itself.

Action creates experience and experience drives our beliefs and values deeper. Someone can prepare you for an experience through sharing facts, figures and an account of their experience but nothing can match the power of your own experience when you commit to action your beliefs. Action puts flesh on our beliefs, feelings and thoughts.

Our actions are the product; they are the end of a process over which we have full control. Anything beyond this point is outside of our control. Many people complain at their lack of results as if they were the victims of circumstance when in fact it has been a lack of action that has left the results 'deactivated.' The winning conversation recognises that until an intention is actioned we must take responsibility for our lack of results. It is only when we have taken responsibility for the whole process over which we have control that we can then start to take wider circumstances into account.

Our actions are our Benchmark

Our actions are the visible outworking of an invisible process. Therefore they become our greatest benchmark as to the quality of conversation that is taking place inside of us.

There are six actions that our internal conversation produces that help us gauge which voices have control at the boardroom of belief. Each of these actions is carried out with the purpose of activating the intended result.

You can simplify the winning conversation into this formula:

A Certain Intention (Belief + Mood) + Determined Action (Mindset + Action) = Extraordinary Results

The winning choices of a winning conversation are as follows:

COMMIT wholeheartedly

High level commitment to the choices that accomplish the goals of my cause

When we host the prominent conversation the resulting action is wholehearted commitment to the WHO of our cause. Therefore a true test of our internal conversation is how we treat others. When we lack compassion and affection then we are unlikely to be hosting the winning conversation.

Our commitment to ourselves is demonstrated through our commitment beyond ourselves. It takes someone who is secure in who they are and why they are alive to commit wholeheartedly to seeing others succeed.

An outstanding team is one in which each constituent part of the team focuses on a wholehearted commitment to the whole unit. The more 'unreasonable' this level of commitment, the more the team achieves uncommon results. An unreasonable commitment results in the individuals and the collective whole increasing in prominence.

The more we commit ourselves wholeheartedly to others, the larger our world grows. There is a proverb that says *the world of the generous gets larger and larger, but the world of the stingy gets smaller and smaller.* When we make our lives all about ourselves we shrink wrap our lives and become unnoticed.

COMPLETE well

High level commitment to complete actions well that are contributing toward the goal of my cause

There is a power in completion. The greater the size of the task, the greater the sense of completion it creates. This deepens our resolve and becomes a springboard for our winning purpose. Completion creates an inner confidence and strength. When we leave tasks incomplete they become a drain on our conscious or unconscious minds because we carry an awareness of what has NOT been done. While an activity is left incomplete the battery power which starts at 100% everyday diminishes at a quicker rate. Like an application left open on a computer or smart phone device, it requires power to be left running and if shut down this power could be used for an alternate purpose.

Incompleteness produces weakness. The more we leave incomplete the more unassured we become of the task at hand. This lack of assurance often lingers in our subconscious mind. We lack resolve because an incomplete activity becomes part of our internal conversation that says, 'You are behind. You are unable to finish. You are going to fail.' On the other hand, a completed task says, 'You are getting there. You have finished this and now you can finish something bigger.'

When we comprehend the power of completeness it makes us conscious of not taking on more than we can complete. With every agreement we make to do something the more we potentially expose ourselves to incompleteness. This is a tension to manage because for every task we take on there is an opportunity to unleash a new level of completeness which builds our lives.

When we complete tasks we not only inspire confidence in ourselves but we produce confidence for those we influence. The reverse is also true. Incompleteness creates weakness in a team or organisation.

A determination to persevere and complete in a team of two or more is a powerful combination. When we collaborate with others over a shared goal and embrace the power to complete then extraordinary results will follow.

The action to complete well comes from a certain intention that 'I am passionate' and cultivating an optimistic mood. This, combined with the mindset of perseverance, enables a person to increase in resilience. The more resilient a person becomes the more capacity they have for bigger goals.

CONTRIBUTE to solve problems

High level commitment to contribute in order to solve problems that allow me to outwork my cause

When asking people questions about what they really enjoy in life and what energises them, I can often boil it down to this: people love to solve problems for people. People love it when something they do creates a 'light bulb' moment. Whatever the context, from healthcare to education, there is something about our makeup that is designed to solve problems.

The question is not 'do I have a problem I can solve?' It is 'can I get to know someone enough for them to share the problem that they need solving?' We become irrelevant when we do not connect our problem-solving ability to the world around us. We then get feelings of being 'unauthorised', like we have no voice—no legitimate reason for taking space up on this earth. This sounds extreme but when the belief of irrelevance is left to grow it will produce this kind of fruit.

Our ability to communicate with other people is essential if we are to discover the solution of which we could be a part. The more we seek to bring solutions to a situation the more we come to mind when problems arise in the lives of those we have helped. This increasingly makes us the 'go to' person because one thing is for sure, problems will always arise in life!

Millions of pounds are wasted each year on advertising that seeks to grab people's attention when companies would be better off asking 'how can we create a relevant connection with these people so that we gain trust and become the 'go to' brand when a person has the problem that we solve?' We need to create relevant conversations because conversations build a platform and give us a place from which our inner message can be heard more clearly.

CONNECT widely

High level commitment to connect widely and indiscriminately in order to outwork my cause

If conversations are the currency in life then it would make sense that if a person wants to increase their influence, they will need to engage in more conversations. The goal of connecting with new people is to explore and discover more about the other person. It is only when you get an understanding of the person you are talking to that you can prepare to move to the next stage of establishing relevance.

While connecting with people for the first time is uncomfortable for most, it does create momentum in how influential I feel and in my internal sense of acceptance. 'Word of mouth' has long been the number one driver of products reaching more people. Conversations through connections create growth.

A person can have the greatest story, idea or solution to a problem but without the gateway of connecting there is no opportunity for our answer to find its question. There are people out there waiting for you to connect with them. The challenge is they often do not know it and do not reveal their 'need' of you in an opening conversation. Therefore it takes a self-belief that 'I am inclusive' and a mood of curiosity for a person to present themselves in order to connect. The desire and belief in positive results through a connection has to be greater than the fear of rejection.

CONSTRUCT imaginatively

High level commitment to construct through imaginative collaboration incorporating the gifts and goals of others

If we want to see more of something then we have to understand what the mechanism is for growing it. The imagination is our planning centre powered by our potential. Reality is not determined by what is seen but what is imagined and desired with certainty. Potential is reality simply in an unseen format. The apple tree inside a seed is real but unseen. When we collaborate to construct imaginatively with others the law of synergy kicks in. This is the principle that the sum total of two separate entities working and collaborating together is greater than the sum total of them working as individual units.

The ability to collaborate with others will determine the growth level we will experience as individuals and the impact we will have on the world around us. The temptation in any task will be to do it ourselves or simply to give it to someone else. While there are times for individual focus and delegation, there is a synergy in collaboration that will yield the greatest results. Two things happen in collaboration. Firstly, the quality of the idea will increase; secondly, the distance the idea will travel will also increase.

What we own we champion. If I create buy-in to my cause from others then they will want to champion it. The more ownership I can create, the more relational circles I can expose my idea to. Let someone who is engaged in a winning conversation in on your cause and construct with them imaginatively and collaboratively.

COMPETE differently

High level commitment to compete in a way that others do not to further my cause

Competition is essential in order to unlock our potential. However, choosing the right competition is also critical. The most successful people in life choose to make their greatest competitor their own potential as opposed to other people. Why is this? If there is an absence of strong competition in your environment then you will tend to use the nearest competitor as the benchmark. This can mean you stay in a place of maintaining what you bring rather than raising your game to new levels of effectiveness. Competing against other people and products has merit if done correctly. However, too much focus on what others are doing can create poor focus management. It can also create unnecessary demands for you to be something you are not. After all how can you compete like-for-like when you are meant to be unique? The result of comparison is that you recreate what others are doing as opposed to tapping into your own creative potential.

Every day that I decide to compete against my potential I have the opportunity to increase the value that I bring to the people in my world.

Section 3: The Winning Team—
I Value People

Understanding how to unlock your winning relationships

Day 15: The Winning People in my life

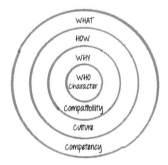

How do I know which relationships to select and which to relegate?

The challenge of life is often not a shortage of relationships but a shortage of the right relationships. While we will talk about the value of inclusiveness for gaining influence, a level of exclusivity is important when it comes to those we allow into our core relationships.

I have learnt that we will be attracted to certain relationships depending on our personality type. Regardless of our personality type, however, there is a pattern of principles that defines the process by which someone makes their way from the outer circle of our friendships into the inner circle.

When it comes to building any team—whether a team around my cause, a team at work or a sport's team—the principles are relevant to some degree in each context.

As with the winning circles it is not just about ticking these areas off; it's about order.

Who—The Character of a Person

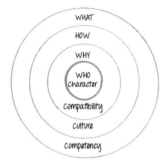

The company I choose to keep will play an integral part in the formation of my character. I can tell who my children have been with by their temperament and behaviour. This either serves them or subtracts from them.

Close friendship is spiritual; it can become the deepest connections that shape our values and beliefs. Their significance is unseen to us yet noticeable to others.

If you imagine your life as a brand, would your close friends add value to it or damage it? I am not trying to reduce friendships to a product but sometimes the only way of appraising our relationships is to ask questions that help us to make a principled rather than an emotional assessment.

When we make our way through winning conversations and we identify winning values we realize how important it is for those close to us to stand for the same values. The winning team we need is centred on the same values not just the same interests.

Relationship re-alignment is either decided by you or for you. In my experience while both routes are painful, to be proactive is the preferable route. There have been times when I have either not dealt with this myself or naively believed that it would sort itself out. This creates more damage to you, your family and the community you are a part of because those who align themselves to you also build relationships with others to whom you are connected. It's better to be proactive than reactive when it comes to realigning your relationships.

Conversation with myself: Which relationships are potentially out of alignment with my shared values?

Why—The Compatibility of a Person

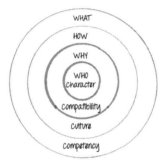

Relationships are about synergy, becoming more together than we could on our own. There has to be compatibility for synergy to occur. This is not about having compatible interests; it's deeper than that. You need someone whose soul is 'open for business.'

You may have had a friendship where the person is inconsistent; sometimes they are oozing with affection and admiration and at other times you feel like you are walking on egg shells. You cannot allow such people access to your soul; their instability produces instability for you.

The synergy of friendship is when both people feel like value is being added to them. It's mutual in its function and benefit. When someone has a low emotional capacity you will find it more draining than energising. Authentic relationships put the challenges of life on the table and do not seek to hide them. When only one of the friends puts their challenges on the table the other feels more of a project than a person and this is unhealthy.

You also have to know that revealing the challenge or the success is going to bring progress not problems. If close friends are threatened by your success or vice versa then you have a compatibility problem. Likewise, if the other person cannot handle the challenges you are processing then the same applies. This is not about the other person being able to help you; that is a matter of competency, something we will talk about shortly. Friendship is often about listening and presence, not problem-solving. If the person you open up to struggles to be present to you during times of need, you need to exercise realignment.

When I talk about realignment this is not code for 'getting rid of someone.' That is not the spirit of a champion. No, it means creating necessary distance. Be aware however that this can mean losing friends. Sometimes the emotional pain caused by a process of distancing means that others struggle to keep the relationship going. You just have to accept that sometimes relationships belong to seasons in life.

The stronger you develop your core convictions and values the greater the importance of compatible relationships. You need a team of people who are committed to the same journey as you. I do not mean people who are doing exactly what you are doing but people whose purpose in life is to be a producer and not a consumer in life. When this is the case you can be the catalyst to their growth and development.

It is important to listen to your instincts on the journey. Sometimes you get a hunch that your relationship is changing. You feel it in your soul before your head. While any alignment should be sensitive and gentle, it does need to happen if a person refuses to change from being a consumer to a producer.

As you read through the winning conversations in this book you will see clear ways of identifying where you are on the journey. This will also make you aware of where others are. Your journey will become an unnecessary struggle if you are not proactive with your relationships.

Conversation with myself: Do I open myself up to those in my close circle of friends? Do others open up?

How—The Culture of a Relationship

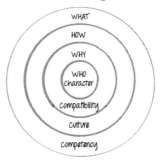

A culture can be simply defined as 'the way things are.' It is the expected norm of a group of people. A winning friendship is one where people are comfortable with the uncomfortable conversations. If I know that the other person is for my success and holds the same values as me then I must give that person permission to challenge me along the way. A good friend is not someone who just says what I always want to hear but is comfortable saying what I do not like to hear and what I actually need. This can create a feeling of adversity inside the recipient. However, a friendship that progresses through this discomfort goes to a deeper level. You want friends who leave you feeling built up not puffed up. A person who simply tickles my ears does not help unlock my potential.

In centuries past, oxen would be used to plough fields and a yoke would be placed on them. The key to cultivating the field was for the oxen to share the burden equally but also to pull in the same direction. When a relationship has a culture clash it can feel like you carry an unequal burden or that others are pulling in a direction at odds with where you are heading. Unless there is realignment there will be an increase in stress which at some point will break the friendship. This will also negatively affect the future harvest.

Conversation with myself: Who in my relationship circle is most closely aligned in HOW they outwork their lives? Does the time I spend with them reflect our close alignment or do I spend more time with people who are not as aligned?

What—The Competency within a Relationship

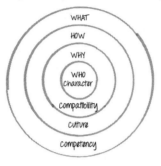

Competency is about looking at the quality of other peoples' relationships—the quality of their marriage, their relationships with other family members, their relationships with colleagues. You need people who are competent in these spheres.

Competency in relationships is to do with capability. If you are driven by a cause then you need people connected to you who will be able to add value to you and in whom you can invest. The aim is to create a synergy that so productive that you would be worse off without the relationship.

Conversation with myself: Do I have people who inspire me to raise the bar on my relationships?

The power of this book when studied with others is that it produces conversations where you can gain an understanding of where you and others truly are.

In the next two chapters we look at two principles that great relationships have—evaluation and accountability.

Whilst I encourage you to increase awareness of your current relationship team I would also advise you to increase your awareness of where you are at before making any major alignments in your relationships. We can often be quick to think others are at fault when actually it's our internal conversation that contributes to the poor alignment. This is where being coached by others is so important—the subject of the next chapter.

Day 16: — The Winning People around my Purpose

THE WINNING TEAM

Your team is made up of those who are specifically committed to being part of your journey toward your winning purpose.

Step 1: WHO - **The kind of people in my team**
Step 2: WHY - **The purpose for why they are in my team**
Step 3: HOW - **The prioritising of key environments in my involvement with others**
Step 4: WHAT - **The pattern of involving these roles and environments with others.**

The winning team requires four different roles. Every person needs these four roles in order to create a winning team that will help unlock their potential.

Step 1: WHO

The blend of people you need in your team

Counsel

*A person you go to for advice for specific **situations***

Who are the people that provide trusted advice in your world? Who are the 'go to' people that you know will understand you and help you think through the challenges you are facing? The more you become cause-driven, the more challenges you will inevitably face in the outworking of your potential. Having voices with permission to speak into your life is therefore essential. Do you have someone you trust enough to say 'no' to you, acting as a safety net should you ever be in danger of over-stretching yourself? These are experienced people who are open to sharing success and failure; they help you go further in life.

Such trust-filled relationships do not just appear and do take investment to build but they can become your most valuable insurance policy.

It is also important to recognise that as you pursue your cause you will become a point of 'counsel' for others. As you become for others what they need, you will discover the people that you need.

Coaching

*A person who trains and instructs in a specific **area***

Who challenges you about the goals that you set, holding you to agreements that have been made?

The American football coach Tom Landry says, 'Leadership is getting someone to do what they do not want to do in order to achieve what they want to achieve.' You do not go to a coach to feel better; you go to get better. We need voices that say what many people would not feel comfortable saying. We need those who understand our journey and our goals.

While we can achieve without a coach, I do not believe it is possible to fulfil our potential without one.

Part of the winning team involves us taking on the role of coach. It's important to have specific people we are helping to train and instruct.

Community

*A group of people you do life with around a specific **association***

A community is a people or group who hold something in common. The common ground could be biological, geographical, social or faith-based. A community provides opportunities for an individual to be themselves and contribute toward the benefit of the whole, and in so doing becoming a beneficiary of that community.

Healthy lives grow in community. The breakdown of community

in many western nations is the root cause of dysfunctionality. Therefore, the winning life needs to be centred on the foundation of community.

The more I invest in community, the richer my life experience becomes.

Collaboration

*A person you work alongside in order to achieve specific shared **aims***

When two or more people have a common goal they collaborate in achieving the goal. In order to outwork the winning life it is important we have people in our winning team who are on the same journey. Learning together is a key part of winning.

When a person is driven by a cause there will be times when the challenges can seem overwhelming. To have others that are with you to cheer you on is essential. We also need to be cheerleaders for others. Time involved in collaboration unlocks our potential as we become increasingly aware of our contribution in life.

To unlock the winning life, it is essential you have voices that are collaborating to achieve the same end goals.

Step 2: WHY

The purpose for why they are in my team

It is important to know WHY you have chosen that person and the purpose behind meeting with them. Always remember the purpose for choosing that person or group so that you can maximise your interaction with them.

Do not waste the time of the person you are meeting by not thinking through the issues or questions you want to discuss and the outcomes you are looking to achieve. Not to do this is to waste your time and theirs. When going to counsel, coach or collaborate, make sure that you have clear outcomes in mind.

You should be able to give a clear answer to this question:

I am going to see this person/s because they bring _____ to where I am at and the outcome I am looking for in meeting with them is _____.

Even in community it is vital you know 'why' you belong to it. When we lose the WHY we act out of duty and not desire. Duty kills our aspiration but desire brings it to life.

Step 3: HOW

The prioritising of key environments in my involvement with others

We can find our winning moments in three different types of environments:

Close Environment

The most obvious environment is one-on-one, face-to-face. This would have likely been the situation you envisaged when we identified the four types of roles that a person needs in terms of their winning team.

It is important to ask yourself 'is there someone else that could help me to a greater degree in the area I am seeking to develop?'

Once you identify this person then actively pursue how you can connect with them in this way.

Core Environment

In my experience this environment is the one that many shy away from. A small group of people can become a vulnerable place, one where we do not feel fully in control. However, this environment can actually be one of the most powerful. The reason is that people learn best through authentic interaction with others; the content is more memorable and the accumulation of life experiences more valuable.

While this is not a natural environment for many, it is an essential one for achieving the winning life.

Crowd Environment

This is any interactive environment involving a lot of people, either virtual or physical, which provides access to the roles we need. You might attend a seminar, course or presentation or you can be part of an online crowd. Either way, we can invest in such environments in order to find winning moments—moments in which I grow in a particular area of my life.

Step 4: WHAT

The pattern of involving these roles and environments with others

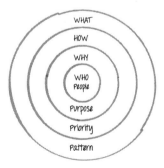

Create through Choice

Planning time with your winning team is essential. Creating

moments with them will not happen by chance but by choice. The winning life is an interdependent life. This is counter-cultural; western culture is based upon independent living. We will drift toward independent living unless we plan the involvement of the roles and environments that we need.

Good planning is essential here. We need regularly to assess if we have the right team at the right time and if we are investing the right quantity of time. In our weekly planning we need to identify the amount of time needed to invest with these people based upon the needs created by your goals.

Choose Consistency

Time set aside for coaching and collaboration needs to be a rhythm that you intentionally schedule. Whereas going for counsel can be more needs-based.

Community time needs to be planned; it is not just about existing in a community but actively investing. The old adage is true here: 'the more you put in the more you get out.'

Conversation with myself: 'What do I need consistently that only others can bring?' It is vital that the answer to that question gets planned in and if required a budget set against making that happen.

Day 17: The Winning Evaluation

THE WINNING TEAM

Evaluation is Innovation

You are not the finished article; as a winner, change has to become your best friend. Evaluation is the method by which we manage change. Change is a part of life and unless we are proactive change will happen to us rather than happen for us. Evaluation helps us to stay ahead of the change curve so that we can anticipate the change we need to create rather than wait for change.

Innovation is the process of changing old for new; it is the mechanism through which we facilitate our drive for positive formation. A drive for different results without a proper mechanism will create poor decision-making and ultimately frustration.

Evaluation creates Clarity

The winning conversation starts with creating self-awareness. Another term for self-awareness is personal clarity—an essential ingredient to producing health in any area of life. It is only when we can see clearly that we have the quality of judgment to make a great next step.

We evaluate what we are serious about making happen. Every day we make hundreds of evaluations. The areas we evaluate reveal what is most important to us. When I am walking with my children through a busy city I make many evaluations about where they are in relation to me. I do this because I value them and do not want to lose them. We make conscious and unconscious evaluations all the time because all progress in life depends upon it.

Progress without evaluation is called wandering and when we wander we cease to own the destination. The winning conversation is about getting to a definite place in life and not just taking a stroll.

Stay Informed not Ignorant

Why is it that we are sometimes happy to avoid evaluation? It is either because we are not really convinced of where we want to go or because of fear. We are afraid of the results. We choose to stay ignorant instead of informed. When we do this we choose to ignore the potential we carry. Our decision not to do something is actually a decision to do something. Choosing not to evaluate is to accept the life of the consumed or complacent person.

The Revolutionary Question

Every day we experience disruption. As I write this chapter I have experience several travel disruptions all before 10am! These have caused me to take several different routes. However these were essential for me to end up on the right train at the right time. The winning life is about welcoming planned disruption through the process of questions.

Before I set out this morning I had no questions relating to my travel arrangements because the route was familiar. However, as soon as a disruption occurred I had questions which led to me taken a different course—one essential for progress.

The reason we avoid evaluation is because it is more comfortable to believe we have all the answers rather than disrupt the status quo with questions. However, a winning conversation embraces the uncomfortable process of evaluation in order to create the necessary disruption that sets a person on the right tracks.

If we want to advance and grow the winning life then we need to embrace disruption.

A question creates the unrest required for progress. When we find ourselves wrestling with the right questions we will unlock the revelation that brings about a rebellion against old and familiar ways.

Find progress and behind the scenes you'll find pain. Progress follows in the footsteps of pain.

Here is the product of quality questions:

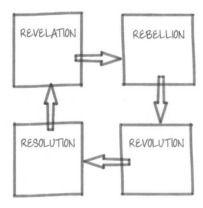

REVELATION—Find the Missing Piece

It is not what I know that is hindering me but what I do not know. Therefore to create the necessary progress I must get hold of the missing jigsaw piece of knowledge.

A question creates a vacuum for knowledge. By disturbing the status quo of a mindset, the mix can be altered.

Ask the revelation question:

What is it that I do not know that is stopping me progressing?

REBELLION—Stop the Subtracting Element

The deeper the question is, the greater the battle that can be created between the old ways (tradition) and the new path (innovation). At this 'T' junction a person can choose to progress into the new by adopting the new thought or rejecting it, strengthening the existing thought.

Ask the rebellion question:

What is it that I need to stop doing and why?

REVOLUTION—Establish the New Law

The adopting of a new idea based on the evaluation process requires a change of authority. The old idea loses its opportunity to influence our behaviour and now the new thought is given the ruling power.

Ask the revolutionary question:

What new discipline do I need to start doing?

RESOLUTION—A New Normal is Created

The power of new knowledge comes when it makes its way from revelation to resolution. Only when the new choice is repeatedly actioned will it become habitual and therefore part of our new mindset. Our mindset then becomes our pattern and others we influence are pattered in line with our example.

Ask the resolution question:

What can I put in place to make sure I keep doing this?

The winning conversation keeps evaluation as a core step. Throughout the six conversations I encourage a period of asking questions. I know what it is like reading a book that includes questions; the temptation is to run ahead and access the knowledge. Reading the book will undoubtedly create a <u>competitor</u> approach to life but my commitment to you is to take that up to the <u>champions</u> approach and that means not leaving out the uncomfortable bits. Going back to my analogy of putting a flat pack together, getting the 'jist' of what is needed ends up in me producing a weak product. Evaluation enriches the quality of conversation. The quality of your internal conversation determines the quality of your external conversation which in turn unlocks results.

Winners are Thinkers and Doers

You need space in your day to think and reflect. This will rarely feel like an urgent activity but it is a critical one. The quality of our action moments comes down to the quality of our thinking moments. Both are necessary if we are to win.

The problem is no one teaches us how to carry out the vital process of thinking. In my experience my thinking is planned and unplanned. My planned thinking time is always first thing in the morning and last thing at night. It is also part of my faith to spend time in prayer. During this time I walk through a process of evaluation.

My unplanned thinking time will be throughout my day. The more immersed in the winning conversation I become the more I use 'spare' or 'wasted' time as thinking time. Going for a walk or exercising has produced some quality 'unplanned' thinking time.

The pattern of my thinking time runs like this:

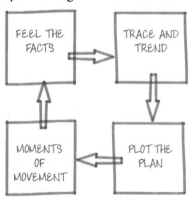

Feel the Facts

Taking time to look at how I have lived is an essential start. Replaying scenarios is often very uncomfortable. As a communicator the most uncomfortable process is watching a replay of your talk. However, it is only when we feel something that we are moved toward change.

Trace and Trend

Analysing past activities without a benchmark can be demoralising. A benchmark creates a sense of hope and expectation which motivates us to take the positive and negative parts of what has been and to fuel the next steps of what will be. The more clarity we can get on where we are the more we prepare ourselves for the next step.

It is good to ask ourselves where we would end up if we carried on doing what we have been doing. It is only when we understand the significance of the path we are on that we sometimes understand the importance of making a change now. Small choices never look significant unless we see where they are taking us.

Throughout the six conversations unpacked in the book we encourage you the reader to look at your most recent behaviour and to track the mindset out of which you are operating in order to know what needs to change to unlock the champion mindset.

Plot the Plan

Every day I reference the next 24 hours against my 'winning goal.' Holding the rope tightly between the ultimate goal (not yet) and the immediate reality (now) is essential for progress. Gary Keller encourages the reader in his book to ask 'what is the one thing I must do today such as by doing it everything becomes easier or unnecessary.' It can sometimes seem impossible boiling everything down to one thing. However it is not about achieving everything through one activity but taking out unproductive activities. This is based upon the theory that 80% of what is achieved comes through 20% of the activity.

Moments of Movement

The climax of our thinking time is about creating a moment that moves us to action. A few quality choices everyday will accumulate over time to produce the results we long to experience. The result of this moment is the winning conversation formula.

Moments of movement do not simply happen in isolation. We need moments when talking through our journey with a designated coaching partner. We also need moments in a community environment where other people who have been where we are and have successfully navigated their journey can encourage us with lessons learned.

I will go on to explain more about this in the next chapter.

Remember the formula:

A Certain Intention x Determined Action = Extraordinary Results

We are unable to become certain of something unless we have space to reflect. In this process of evaluation we are looking for an intense desire to develop which will push us over the line of intention to action. Unless we create a certainty and intensity we will be like the cartoon car races where the character runs out of fuel on the last lap only to stop right before the finish line. We must not end up empty handed because the moment never created the movement that brings the win.

Day 18:—The Winning Accountability

THE WINNING TEAM

Every step of the process of the winning conversation is essential. This final stage is often treated as less important in life and yet actually makes ALL the difference. We often <u>overestimate</u> what we can achieve on our own and underestimate what can be achieved in a collaborative community.

Nature reveals the secrets of success. For a plant to develop there must be a healthy environment. For the winning conversation to bear fruit in our lives we need the right environment in which to be planted. If the quality of our external conversation unlocks the winning results we want to see then we need an environment where that conversation can be developed and honed. We need to be among people on the same journey who can help us and provide us with an opportunity to help others. We need a healthy outflow and inflow in order to grow the conversation that is inside us.

If 'conversation' is the currency of life, then community is the marketplace for these transactions.

The three vital elements that a healthy community creates are:

i) Accountability

Without accountability we are saying that we can achieve the results we desire by ourselves. Independent living is not the highest form of effectiveness. Interdependence is the pinnacle. When I understand that the answers I need are in others, and that I am an answer to others, the more I build relationships that focus on winning together rather than winning at the expense of others.

Whether it is someone trying to lose weight, get back on course financially or become an elite performer in their field, accountability is the only route to sustainable and high-level results. We need accountability to people who have been there and done it, along with those who are at a similar point in the journey.

ii) Authenticity

One of our biggest hindrances is our natural tendency to project the person we want to be rather than who we really are. Self-awareness requires total honesty. This is unachievable while feeling the need or expectation to be someone that we are not.

A healthy community is an authentic one, a place where we can be real. It is exhausting trying to live as someone else. The intense pressure of being under the scrutiny of other people creates the feeling of being trapped. If everywhere I go I have to try and pretend to be someone I am not, I suffocate under the mask of my alter-ego.

The winning conversation requires us to be authentic and to journey with others who, like you, desire to live from the authentic place of who they are. This is not only liberating but exciting.

An authentic environment allows for a person's strengths and weaknesses to be addressed creatively because two key ingredients are present:

a) Trust

Trust is the oxygen of authentic relationships. Trust has to be cultivated in order for relationships to flourish. Trust cannot magically happen. The more trust I develop with someone, the more I let the real me out. The more I allow people to see the real me the more the community is enriched. The more a community is enriched the greater potential there is for growth.

b) Security

Security is about feeling safe enough to be yourself. When a person is insecure they feel unsafe being who they are in the company of others. They grasp after worth through titles, achievements and possessions. True security is about living life from an unchangeable centre. The only thing that cannot be taken from us is our identity; therefore this needs to be the foundation of our authenticity. Security about who we are is a constant investment. Without that investment we will lose strength over time because we exist in a world that propagates the lie that personal worth is the result of external gain and achievement.

iii) Agreement

Our financial wellbeing is determined by the financial agreements we make. Many people get into debt because they are unaware of the compound impact of many small agreements or contracts. In our internal conversation we are constantly making contracts and agreements with ourselves. We agree with thoughts that come into our minds or assumptions that are made as a result of how we interpret our circumstances. I have discovered that I have signed up to many internal agreements that would have better come under the scrutiny of a friend who helped me to read the small print of what I was believing about myself. Community provides perspective and perspective helps us to make quality agreements with ourselves about ourselves.

Agreement is also the basis of goal-setting. When we keep our goals to ourselves we limit our capacity to achieve it. However, when we 'let the goal out of the bag' in the presence of other people we increase our capacity to achieve it. It becomes a reference point in our external conversations. When we do not make an agreement in a community of people, one of two things will happen. It will become increasingly difficult for the person to connect into that community because the embarrassment of not completing a goal makes it more desirable to run away than to take responsibility and ask for help. Or the desire to continue in that community and play our part in its health will cause us to complete on the agreement that we have made.

This is How we Roll

The term 'this is how we roll' is a statement about the culture of a person or group. It is about the prevailing attitudes, behaviours and characteristics that become the expected norm.

Speaking of rolling, as part of developing *winning communities* I have developed the *winning dice*. This carries six statements designed to remind us of the six conversations contained within this book. Creating a trigger that keeps the conversation alive is essential for life-change.

These statements or sayings become part of the language of a group and help solidify the culture. You could develop your own sayings. You can create axioms that trigger the principles and values that produce winning results. These statements appear on the seventh day of each conversation that we are going to unpack. To find out how you can get a hold of your *winning dice* go to www. thewinningconversation.com

What does a winning community look like?

Your winning team needs to be people who are committed to the process. It can be as small as two people or as large as twenty people. In my experience the optimum number is ten to twelve. This gives enough diversity of experience to create a rich environment for growth. Each person needs to have a desire to contribute to the process and not just consume. Houses make great environments but so do coffee shops, conference or community facilities or even online environments. My experience tells me that a house is often the most conducive environment.

When you find the most profitable environment, follow these steps:

Step 1: RECALL Together

Recall Winning Moments

The winning conversation needs to be an immersive experience so starting a session with 'winning moments' will help create an atmosphere of belief and positivity. This also motivates people to have stories to share. Stories are powerful; they become useful tools when trying to coach other people.

Recall Teaching

Asking someone to go through the book and remind themselves what a conversation looks like can help in two ways. Firstly, it keeps the flow of teaching fresh in the group because new perspectives are given as the principles are brought to life through experience. Secondly, it creates an atmosphere for assessment because individuals will be evaluating their recent behaviour through what is being said.

Step 2: REVIEW with Others

Taking time to review the questions from the winning

accountability sections of this book is a great way of igniting conversation within a group. The questions give permission for people to be authentic in their assessment of their week and in their evaluation of how they are currently doing with their conversations.

Step 3: REFLECTION to be Shared

The way to increase learning is by putting the learner in the position of teacher. Everyone in the group should be encouraged from time to time to be the teacher as part of their journey. Ask someone to come prepared with a reflection that can be shared. Sharing this reflection will enrich relationships creating much needed moments of movement.

The following basic structure can be used:

i) What I realised for the first time/again this week is ………. (share the thought)

ii) The change I need to make is ……….. (share the action point)

iii) Can you help me make it …………… (invite help and create accountability)

The group can create online communities, blogs and resources that launch new communities and help more people.

Find a Coach

As well as learning communities the most intense form of coaching is one-to-one. Asking another person to coach you who is already successfully developing the winning conversation is an essential step to greater results. The level and quality of accountability a person puts in place determines the quality and quantity of results a person produces.

Become a Coach

The more you teach in a specific subject the greater the learner you become. Becoming a coach of the winning conversation will again raise the quality of your conversation in life. The more you work at unlocking potential in others the more you unlock your own potential.

Section 4: Be MORE prominent

Day 19: The Winning Conversation makes you MORE Prominent

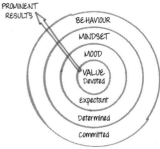

In a team there has to be a leader and in a meeting there has to be a chairman. Devotion is the chairperson of the winning conversation. He is the one with the agenda. Devotion keeps all the conversations on track.

The definition of devoted is to give all or a large part of one's time or resources to a person, activity or cause.[7]

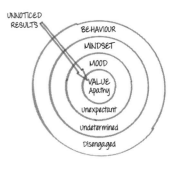

Being devoted is not about something; it is about someone. The potential of our lives is unlocked when we centre our cause on a person. The pursuit of possessions creates shallowness in our lives because there is no spirit in an inanimate object. Devotion is about unlocking our spiritual capacity, the core of a person. Have you ever struggled to describe how you feel about someone you love and value? This is because your connection is not simply physical, mental or emotional it is spiritual. It goes deeper than human intellect or even emotion.

There is a MORE prominent place for you to attain and the

7. Devote. Oxford Dictionaries. Oxford University Press, n.d. Web. 22 September 2015.

route is through your devotion to the cause of lifting the lives of other people. Your future is bigger than you could imagine and it's going to take you to places that you would not believe if you adopt the winning conversation.

When I host the **prominent** conversation I become…

1) MORE Others-Driven
Confidence comes from focussing on others more than myself

It is easy to get caught up in the detail of life that we lose sight of WHY we are doing what we are doing. Life is to be enjoyed but enjoyment is the bi-product of being driven by a cause. The moment we make enjoyment the goal we centre life on ourselves. It becomes about WHAT we want and not WHO we are meant to be devoted to.

Charles Dickens' *A Christmas Carol* tells the well-known story of Ebenezer Scrooge. Ebenezer was devoted to WHAT he could accumulate until he was taken to a vantage point by the ghosts of Christmas past, present and future where he could see how futile his life had become. It was only when he was able to see an ultimate picture of his life did he make a change. His philosophy from that moment became about WHO—improving the lives of people such as Bob Cratchet and Tiny Tim. When this became his driver the real Ebenezer came alive because his WHAT served a WHO, a person. He was now devoted to people and not the inanimate and lifeless world of money.

Whether it is looking into the eyes of a child starving in Africa, a sick parent, a newly born child, your spouse or a close friend, deep down you know that you are not just gazing into flesh you are gazing into another realm. You are connecting spiritually.

I believe we are spiritual beings. If you have ever been present when someone has died, you know that they are no longer present with you. The physical body is there but you know the person has gone. You are left starring at an empty shell. You sense this emptiness because human beings are spiritual beings.

If the spiritual dimension is the deepest part of a human being then it follows that when you devote yourself to another human being you will be raised to the highest place in their eyes. My wife is the person of greatest person of prominence in my life. Why? Because of her devotion to me. Devotion creates prominence.

A champion allows the voice of *devotion* to shut out the default voice of apathy. Apathy creates a loss of interest or concern in people. Interestingly it means to be without suffering. When people let us down and hurt us, as we do them, we can often feel that life would be better without people. But when we allow ourselves to feel the pain of other people, we position ourselves to find clarity in our purpose. Being exposed to the reality of other people's suffering is a necessary part of our personal development. It softens our hearts and causes us to realise that our lives must count for more than just objects. Suffering is of great significance when it comes to unlocking a person's potential. Suffering produces endurance, endurance produces strength and strength produces confidence.

2) MORE Aware of Your Journey
The big picture should drive the small decisions

We would never pack our suitcases, get on a plane or train and not have an idea of where we are going. We build everything around a destination. It determines what goes in the suitcase, the mode of transport, how much we take with us, who goes with us. Devotion asks the question 'who is this all about?' When you know WHO your life is about then it empowers you to get clarity on WHY you are alive, HOW you should live and WHAT you should do.

Devotion enables you to keep one eye on the end point while making decisions from your present position. There is nothing more frustrating than getting lost in the detail of options and possibilities. I remember entering a maze at a theme park with my children. There was not much time left before we had to vacate the park. We had long enough to go into the maze and make it out—or so we thought! We got lost. And we got frustrated. We had no idea of our starting or end point. What we really needed was a map.

We get lost in life when we forget our starting point which is also our end point...the WHO of what our lives are all about.

WHO your life is about is down to you to decide. However, once you get clarity on it then this becomes the starting point of every decision because it is also the end point of what is ultimately most important. Whenever you face ambiguity or periods of frustration you know that your sense of WHO will provide you with a point of clarity to work from every time—everything else falls into line behind it.

3) MORE Compassionate
Compassion creates clarity

When our lives are centred on a cause we become more sensitive and aware of people's pain.

You may wonder if that is a good thing. However, the realisation that there is something inside us that could meet the needs of another human being with a problem or with pain unlocks the deepest and most powerful motivation of all.

I guarantee that when you host the prominent conversation and allow devotion to sit in the chair of the boardroom of belief you will discover energy like no other. You will wake in the middle of the night with ideas; you will find yourself missing lunchtimes because you were so absorbed in thinking up ways of solving that problem. When the voice of devotion is at the table of conversation you become invigorated because you have tapped into the power of compassion. Your spirit has drawn alongside the person with the problem or pain and that shift in you draws the best out of you.

4) MORE Loyal
Loyalty to others builds a bigger world for you to live in

The more your life becomes others-centred the more people matter to you. This means that your choice of relationships becomes even more critical. When you become cause-driven you will inevitably align your relationships to people who have a compatible or identical cause. When you get a convergence of cause and you understand the power of multiplication, you invest in those relationships at a deeper level. Through this conversation you will come to realise that MORE comes out of you when you become MORE loyal to people who have the same cause. You may find someone who carries a vision that connects to your winning purpose and that the way to unlock what is in you is to serve their vision. Remember, we are in an interconnected world and we work best when we are interdependent not independent.

The synergy of this depth of relationship is unparalleled. In a world where people shop around for WHAT they can get, loyalty has become rare. This highlights the common belief that independence is the highest goal. If you can unlock the power of loyalty in your relationships, your group, your organisation, then you are on your way to prominence because you become one of the few to be harnessing this powerful human desire.

5) MORE Affectionate
Prominence in the eyes of others is powered by our emotional capacity

Devotion produces affection and affection shown to others attracts people. Affection is in fact the most powerful leverage of influence. You have heard people talk about 'heart ruling heads.' This is usually a negative statement about the power of affection. When you move someone emotionally you go under the radar of their rationality. When this influence comes from a manipulative source, it is dangerous. When it comes from an altruistic source, it is an unstoppable force for good.

You can only be affectionate when you allow people to get close to you. Sometimes this can be hard for those whose trust has been abused in the past. This shuts down their emotional capacity and significantly hinders their capacity to influence through emotion. They often overcompensate through their intellect, or through a dominating physical presence. The only way to break down those barriers is to become *devoted* to a cause, and specifically to someone.

The more you devote yourself, the more affectionate you become and the greater prominence you have in the eyes of those who connect to who you are.

6) MORE Noticeable
Our prominence should be determined by the size of the cause and not by the size of the personality

What does being prominent actually look like? Prominence is someone who projects an internal value that catches the attention of people. Such people become more noticeable. This has nothing to do with external appearance. Some of the world's most influential and prominent figures are not externally impressive. But they have presence; they host the winning conversation which in turn creates an alluring sense of intrigue. When they enter a room people become aware that something bigger is present. It is not them; it is what they are hosting.

When you are immersed in this conversation you will start to see how people respond to your presence and how it is missed when you are not there. Our motive is not to be prominent; our motive is to embrace and communicate the cause that demands more prominence.

When prominence becomes the prize we can end up in apathy because we try and win affection from the outside-in. We believe we can achieve this through investing huge amounts of time and money in accumulating the external things that will create the attention and affection we crave. Like feeding any internal appetite from the outside-in, no amount of feeding it will create the satisfaction desired. Prominence will be the product of us prizing the devotion to a cause.

7) MORE Discerning
When a person's true cause is themselves they will drain and not motivate you

The more devoted you become to a cause the more you can spot the difference between those who are motivated by what they can bring to it and what they can get from it. I use the analogy of the school play and the rescue mission. When the cause becomes a 'school play' it becomes about which part the individuals get to act. Their concern is how this play can fulfil a desire and a dream.

To the devoted person the cause is about a 'rescue mission.' When a disaster takes place, people offer whatever help is needed because they have a full awareness of the cause. It would be inappropriate and unthinkable to offer help with conditions because the rescue mission is a cause and the cause drives a person, not their preferences.

The more devoted you become the more aware you are of people who want a cause to serve them. At first people can look like they are pursuing the same goal until you notice subtle differences that unravel their true motives. These people are more damaging to your cause; either they change or you realign your relationships with them. This conversation will produce a sharper discernment in you because you are more focused on WHO and WHY than HOW and WHAT.

Day 20: The Winning Voice of Devotion

Devotion is not WHAT I do, it is WHO I am

To be a person of devotion I have to immerse myself in the commands that are going to lead me into the right feelings. The more I immerse myself in the belief that I am devoted, the more prominent I will become.

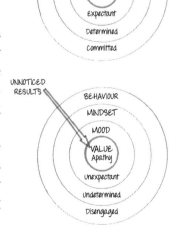

i) I AM Chosen

My cause has chosen me

The power in devotion consists of knowing that you are chosen by your cause. The reason I know a cause chooses us is because I have spoken to many people who have tried to walk away from their cause but could not. They thought they had hold of the cause but the cause had hold of them. At times this can feel frustrating, especially when you like the idea of escaping challenging moments. However, deep

175

down you know you could not do anything else. You just know you have to stay in pursuit of the path chosen for you.

Conversation with myself: What cause is choosing me?

ii) I AM a Change Agent
I am the change I want to see in the world

To be an agent of change you have to apply yourself to the change that you want to see. When the voice of devotion is released in our lives, unimaginable change can take place. We can see the power of devotion released through natural relationships, like the amazing story of John and Aileen Crowley, the true tale behind the film *Extraordinary Measures*.

John and Aileen Crowley were on top of the world. With a brand-new Harvard Business School degree, three beautiful children, a new house, and a great job, they thought that they had just entered the best years of life. Then doctors diagnosed their two youngest children with Pompe disease, and everything changed. Fifteen-month-old Megan and five-month-old Patrick were given only months to live. Pompe disease, the Crowleys were told, was so rare that no company had bothered spending the money needed to sponsor research. There was no cure, no treatment, only the gradual degeneration of muscle so that at the end the children would be unable to walk, eat, or even breathe on their own.

It was a nightmare but John Crowley refused to accept this death sentence. Determined to find scientists who could develop a replacement enzyme that would keep the disease at bay and his children alive, Crowley quit his job as a financial consultant and invested himself and his life savings in a biotechnology start-up company. In just over a year, Novazyme Pharmaceuticals Inc went from an endowment of $37,000 to $27 million and was sold to Genzyme Corp soon after for a news-breaking $137.5 million. But the struggle wasn't over yet; scientific setbacks, accusations of conflict of interest, business troubles, and the children's own worsening condition would test the limits of John and Aileen's minds and hearts as they fought towards a cure. These devoted parents, along with the help of those who joined the cause, eventually discovered the miracle that would keep their children alive.[8]

Many people would have accepted the predicted outcome that was given to John and Aileen but the power of the devotion of a father towards his children enabled them to keep on going.

You too can see the change that you want to see if you are willing to devote yourself to the cause. But it will not happen without a fight; it will not happen without the winning voice of devotion. Jean Nidetch says, "It's choice—not chance—that determines your destiny."

Every day I have to devote myself 100% to the cause, willing to sacrifice whatever it takes to unleash my potential.

Conversation with myself: What change do I want to see that I must first allow to take place in me? What does that look like?

iii) I AM the Size of my Foundation
The height of your promotion is determined by the depth of your devotion

When someone has a grand design for a house they have a vision of a totally new home, a picture of something totally different from what they currently have. The size and quality of what they can build is set by their self-belief.

The kind of house a person refuses to live in becomes part of the process of getting them to the house they can see. They create movement toward the goal by selling their previous property. This creates a feeling of 'no going back' as they purchase a property that is often uninhabitable and requires a definite plan of action. While this position seems undesirable it actually creates movement toward the desired goal. They embark on the process of building with a sense of desperation that failure is NOT an option. Then the revolution begins as they dig down deep to turn this from a 'potential disaster' to a dream home. It is a long process but they resolve to stay the course until the picture in their minds becomes the reality before their eyes.

8. http://pr.harpercollins.com/books/The-Cure-Geeta-Anand/?isbn=9780061800450

It is important to count the cost of being cause-driven. If you have ever witnessed someone who undertakes a grand design project, you will know that it usually demands far more than the owners ever realise. They prepare themselves as best as possible but the actual experience involves emotional, mental and physical demands that call on everything a person has. However they know that this is a home they are likely never to leave. It is the fulfilment of a vision; it is a dream. This is not a makeover; it is a grand design.

The most significant part of the build is the foundation. Get this wrong and the rest of the house will be flawed. The depths they plumb determine the heights they reach.

There are real parallels between building a grand design and the voice of devotion chairing the winning conversation. This will lead to you becoming more prominent but the height of your promotion is linked to the depth of your devotion.

Conversation with myself: What are the 'grand design' changes that I sense I may be required to make to follow my cause?

iv) I AM my Uniqueness
It's not about making life easier for us but making it better for others

We live under a constant pressure to conform. In a commercialised world we are encouraged to adopt the fashions, personas and patterns presented by the media, public figures, movie and sports stars. We are sold 'instant' success stories and our young people grow up believing that they can sit back waiting for 'it' to happen. The voice of apathy says, 'You can wait for the instant; it's much less work,' but the aim of life is not to make it easier but about making it better for others.

When the voice of devotion is contrary to the current of society, my internal conversation reminds me that 'I am my uniqueness.' The voice of devotion rejects <u>sameness</u> and digs deep to celebrate what is different about an individual.

My pursuit should not be where the 'herds' go but an exploration of where I am different. I believe that there is an assignment for your life and it lies in your difference, the very thing that sometimes you get embarrassed by but are passionate about. If I am going to build my life around a single focus, then it has to be my difference; that is my cause, my reason for being, my 'because.'

Conversation with myself: What is my uniqueness? How could it be linked to the things I am sometimes embarrassed about?

v) I AM being Trained by my Pain
The pain of the process makes you fit for your purpose

When you pursue a cause you are embarking on a painful journey. If devotion is becoming aware of me being an answer to someone's problem and suffering then I know I will have to journey into that pain in order to bring the answer. There is a deep shift that happens in you during this journey. Your cause requires you to be shaped internally in order to bring the change in someone else's world. The pain of the process makes you fit for your purpose.

As well as moments of great highs, there will be times of tears, hours in the night when you are unable to sleep, but that is okay because you are aware that the voice of devotion is orchestrating an internal change that is preparing you for external results. In this process, books that describe the lives of pioneers and those who contributed their life to a cause are a key part of your winning journey. A book gives you access to a person's pain and joy and the lessons they learnt along their journey can be priceless.

Mother Theresa spoke about the time when she visited the home of a poor family whose children were starving. They had not eaten for days and it had taken its toll on their bodies. She took the family a small bowl of rice and gave it to the mother, only to be amazed as she divided the rice and proceeded to leave the house. When Mother Theresa asked where the Mother was going the woman said 'I am going next door because they are hungry also.'

This level of devotion inspired devotion in Mother Theresa. That is the power of devotion; it is contagious. Once you have encountered someone who has devotion at the conversation table you realise you have met someone that can influence you to be bigger and better in this life.

Conversation with myself: What pain do I carry that is actually preparing me for my purpose?

Vi) I AM focused on one Person
A picture stirs desire in me which motivates me to keep going

They say pictures speak a thousand words. Your cause should be crystallised into a picture. When your mind recalls that picture, it should inspire you to keep going. I can see my children reading this book in the future. In moments when I have felt like exiting this writing process I have recalled that picture. This inspires me to stay devoted and keep going regardless.

To have a picture or scenario that you can quickly envisage at tough moments will prove invaluable. When someone tries to convince you to compromise on your cause, picture yourself explaining to them why you could not follow through with your cause. Do you think now that you are going to compromise? No. We think in pictures so create and determine your own picture today. It is this picture—this imagined future—that brings direction to your attention, assets and activity creating intense focus.

Conversation with myself: What picture creates a burning desire in me that will help prevent me slipping into an apathetic state?

vii) I AM shaping my Convictions
A conviction is like the rudder of a ship; it carries incomparable power to turn around the toughest situations over time.

A cause flows from my convictions and my convictions become the rudder of my choices. A small rudder can turn a big ship just as a seemingly small choice can turn a life around. No one else sets these convictions; they are the conclusions that I have drawn over many years. Therefore the voice of devotion seeks to keep us aware of the convictions directing us.

The state of being continuously convinced of your cause through tried and tested experience is evidence that the voice of devotion is at the table of conversation. Remember, it is the voice that keeps the other voices on track and moving in a uniform direction.

Create more time and space for the voice to speak and you will continue to become more convinced. The stronger the conviction the more desire you have to discover your convictions. Immerse yourself in your conviction and you heighten your awareness of the jigsaw pieces, the pieces of information, the contacts, the opportunities that you collect along the journey to take the vision from the unseen to the seen.

Conversation with myself: What are the things you are currently being convinced of? How will this belief potentially shape your future?

viii) I AM Steadfast
Not everyone will champion my convictions and when this brings natural disappointment I will use it to further solidify what I believe

You might think that everyone in your world will cheer you on the more convinced you become of your cause. However, you may be surprised at who does <u>not</u> cheer you on. At that point you need to allow the voice of devotion to remind you that challenges come in order to solidify your position. The more steadfast and resolute you become, the taller you stand, the more prominent you become. The more 'shoves' you get the more rungs up the ladder of prominence you will go.

Conversation with myself: What disappointments and discouragements have created instability in my convictions? How can I use this positively to reinforce what I believe?

ix) I AM Dying to Win
The feeling of dying precedes the greatest feeling of WHY you are alive

There is much that the voice of devotion will ask of you; at times you will say, 'It feels like I am dying.' Relationships will change; where you live may have to change; activities, jobs and habits will all be brought into question. All this can feel like a kind of death.

Picture the process a caterpillar goes through in order to become a butterfly. The caterpillar has an identity of its own which is why it is called a caterpillar and not a butterfly. However, it enters the chrysalis phase where the caterpillar dies in order for the butterfly to break out. For the caterpillar to win it has to go through a death process.

There is a process of death during the pursuit of the cause. As I wrote earlier, Michelangelo created one of the most famous sculptures in the world. It is the sculpture of the biblical figure Kind David. When asked how he created a piece of such beauty, he said that 'every block of stone has a statue waiting to come out.'

Your cause will take you from a block of stone to the true you. Just as the process of chipping away stone brings mess and discomfort, so will the process of developing your devotion. However, just like the statue of David, a new, true you will break out. This is the purpose for which you were born.

Conversation with myself: What am I avoiding that is actually going to set me up for success? What will happen if I follow through on this action?

x) I AM Discovered through my Weakness
My weakness is the gateway to my greatest strength

No one likes to talk about their weakness because we all like to project strength. Yet the voice of devotion will remind you that while most people try to cover up their weakness, our weakness is actually the gateway to our strength.

Some questions that may stir you in your thinking about the cause for your life might be:

What are you ashamed of?

What have you battled with that no one is aware of?

What is the weakness that, if you could trade it in for strength, you would do so in a heartbeat?

I would like to suggest that there could be a dormant strength behind your weakness. A world driven by the 'outside-in' philosophy creates an expectation that weakness should be hidden. I challenge you to work against this flow and be like the boy who shouted out from the crowd that the emperor had no clothes on. Be brave enough to state what is obvious to you and by doing so give permission for hordes of other people—who live with weakness that they do not know how to handle and will not speak for fear of how they will be perceived—to rise up with new strength.

I encourage you to explore your weakness and start to view it as a gift rather than a penalty. Remember the world's version of strength is actually a mirage; the real strength lies in someone who embraces their cause through their weakness. Your struggle to break out of the chrysalis of restriction is actually forming you. To interfere in the process of the struggle is actually to prevent the formation that strengthens the wings of the butterfly so it can fly.

Conversation with myself: Based on the answers to the questions in this section, what battles and weaknesses are actually forming strength in you?

Day 21: The Winning Mood of EXPECTANCY

Unlocking the power of WHY creates expectancy

My WHY is my PURPOSE. My purpose is the vision of my life. My vision is the future that I choose to have. The power of vision is that it ignites hope inside me. Hope has an unrivalled way of lifting negative mood clouds that drift into the horizons of my thinking. The winning mood is stimulated when I choose to keep clarifying and reminding myself of my vision, my winning purpose. I must follow the pattern of the winning purpose from the inside-out, from the WHO to the WHAT. The power of our WHY is the power of positivity that creates motion in our lives.

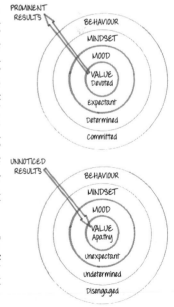

I am having the PROMINENT conversation led by the voice of devotion which means I choose to put myself in an EXPECTANT mood.

Every Day is a Piece of the Jigsaw

A mood impacts the way I feel, think and act. Among the average 'cloudy' moods that exist in my world, I will be a ray of sunshine that is prominent because today is another piece of the jigsaw of my vision.

The reason I act in an expectant mood is because expectancy is the state of knowing <u>something</u> is definitely going to happen that will build the unseen vision into the seen reality. While the details of exactly HOW and WHAT this looks like today may be less than clear, the certainty that 'it is on its way' shapes how I position myself. Expectancy is the state of fixing my attention and readying myself. It is the fertile ground in which possibility can grow.

'Expectant' is a word used of a woman to describe something unseen that is growing inside her that will eventually be brought into visibility in the world. Its reality is not defined by it being visible but by an internal process that is being worked through on a day-by-day basis. Expectancy makes me pregnant with the hope of something new taking place. It starts with an unseen mood but produces 'seen' results. This is the power of the winning purpose; when you carry vision, the unseen actually presides over the seen. You live with the reality of the un-birthed vision because like the unborn child, it moves in you and struggles inside, creating positive discomfort. Opportunity is all around us but it waits for us to perceive it because *believing is seeing.*

To be in an un-expectant mood means being consumed by lack of opportunity. My attention lies in a broken state, flitting from one thought and idea to the next with no coherent connection. Un-expectancy is an insular state in which our perspective is wrapped around our emotions. This mood tends to cause us to care little for others and our future, which is why we can make costly mistakes while in this mood. We have no clear plan or purpose that gives us a reason to protect our future.

Expectancy Eradicates Uncertainty

In the world of sales and retail, people understand the power of expectancy. Expecting every person who walks into a store to want what you sell has a profound impact on results. Those who apologetically approach customers in an almost embarrassed way create an atmosphere for a negative outcome. Even if the customer responds positively, the shock the salesperson now feels can create second thoughts in the mind of the customer. After all, confidence breeds confidence while diffidence breeds timidity.

When a person adopts an expectant mood it has an undeniable effect in their lives. We are attracted to certainty, to positivity and to belief. We are spiritual beings and belief is the currency of the spiritual dimension of reality. Therefore when someone operates at this level it has a deep and often mysterious influence over others.

Doubt, on the other hand, masks our potential. Your potential is as real as the things that you see. However, doubt about your potential creates a distorted reality that prevents you believing that you can become more.

When it comes to expectancy concerning our potential, this is not like hoping for good weather. We have no control over the weather; we only have true control over what is in us. Our potential and therefore our purpose is not 'out there' somewhere but resides inside us. Therefore we can live each day with a mood of expectancy that says we can create the reality of the vision that energises us and stirs our soul.

Expectancy Enables me to Ride the Waves

My expectant mood will enable me to ride the waves of difficulty. Storms are a part of life and while I am not in control of the turbulence I may face, I am in control of how I respond to create progress in my life. I can determine that my mood is led by my devotion to my cause.

I will keep my eyes on the horizon of where I am going and when waves try to catch my attention, while being aware of them I will keep them in my peripheral vision and not my line of sight.

My future will keep me in expectant mood.

Choose to be Aware of your Soul Script

How I feel has a direct impact on the choices I make. Our feelings form our moods and these exist for a positive purpose. They are an integral part of us outworking our beliefs and engaging with the world around us. Feelings need to be instructed and directed to fall in line behind our beliefs. They then become a powerful asset for you to win in life.

Our feelings revolve around three major focus points.

1) How I feel about myself
2) How I feel about others
3) How I feel about the future

Let's see what happens when our soul-script is dominated by a conversation of apathy and when it's dominated by a conversation of devotion.

The Losing Soul Script of Apathy:

When APATHY leads my conversation I am a CONSUMER and my lack of AFFECTION leaves me feeling an overwhelming sense of being UNDERVALUED and in an UNEXPECTANT mood

'To be undervalued is to feel unappreciated and underestimated.'

The script of the apathetic conversation will shape our perspectives in such a way that we will be _self_-destructive, _me_-obsessed and _now_-focussed.

Self-destructive statements from an *apathetic* belief sound like this:

i) I am just one of the crowd
ii) I am nothing special
iii) I have no purpose
iv) I am not significant
v) My pain proves my lack of value

Me-obsessed statements from an *apathetic* belief sound like this:

i) I have my own problems to think of
ii) Life is about survival

iii) I will help others when others help me

iv) When I have everything in place, I will think about helping other people

v) Giving to others means less for me

Now-focussed statements from an *apathetic* belief sound like this:

i) There is nothing to suggest that my future will be better through helping others

ii) You cannot be sure about tomorrow so live for now

ii) If I take on the problems of others then it will take away from my future

iv) I cannot risk my prospects for the sake of others who may not want even want help

I can often be unaware of the statements that are informing my decisions. These statements are often feelings and so I do not naturally quantify them in words. However, hosting the right conversation means describing the feelings we have in terms of statements.

Write them out and look at them in front of you.

If you are not happy with the descriptions you have then you can change them by changing the belief. Your feelings are subject to your beliefs, so if you are unhappy with your feelings, change your beliefs.

The Winning Soul Script of Devotion:

When DEVOTION leads my conversation I am a PRODUCER and feel AFFECTION because I give it and produce an EXPECTANT mood

'Affection is when someone has an affinity with something or someone. Affection and admiration produce a feeling of respect.'

The script of the devoted conversation will shape perspectives in such a way that I will *Value Myself, Value Others* and *Value the Future.*

i) Value Myself

ii) Value Others

iii) Value The Future

When I am filled with affection I am able to focus beyond myself. I do not hunger after affection from the 'outside in'. When I know the voice of devotion is at the table I have a centre that can help me bring order to my fragmented life. Life stops being a random series of events and becomes intentional and purposeful. Living beyond myself means that my relationships are enriched because they are not me-focussed. I use my assets, resources and energies to be generous. The more I give, the more enriched my life becomes. What I sow, I reap. The positive 'coincidences' that follow are the fruit of the diligent process of showing affection to others. The voice of devotion says, 'There is an endless supply of affection that is unlocked when you build your cause around serving others.'

Turning up the Voice of Devotion

When devotion is at the table of my internal conversation, my external conversation becomes 'others-focussed.' Others become more concerned for me because my focus is them not me. I will approach everything through the lens of my cause knowing that if I prioritise the main thing then everything else will fall into place around it. I do not have to focus on how I get promotion if I focus all my efforts on the promotion of others, especially if that is centred on my cause. Despite the strength of opposition from my selfishness, which is in turn driven by apathy, devotion has the final word.

So what does the new script sound like?

It flows *inside-out* and makes the following kinds of statements:

Statements that *Value others* from a *devoted* belief sound like this:

i)   I am needed by my cause and those it will help
ii) I am energised by purposeful living
iii) I matter in this world
iv) My weakness will produce strength
v)   I celebrate my difference

Statements that *Value others* from a *devoted* belief sound like this:

i)   I am concerned how others feel
ii) I am strengthened by those who seek to discourage me
iii) I will put others first based on my choice and not their reaction
iv) I will help others find their cause
v) I will be aware that the issues of people go deeper than what I see and I choose to see past any offence and see their need

Statements that *Value my future* from the valued belief of *devotion* sound like this:

i)   My future is bigger than I could imagine because it is bigger than me
ii) My future will count and will enable others to have a better future
iii) I do not have to worry about getting *affection* in the future because I have a consistent source
iv) My health must be ready for the demands my devotion will require
v) My finances are being ordered so that I will have freedom to focus more time on my cause in the future

Conversation with myself: It is important that I create a time of reflection to identify my current soul script and make the necessary decisions to change it. The examples on this page are not exhaustive. I must discover my specific narrative and make choices to change any outside-in statement as I seek to host the winning conversation.

Day 22: The Winning Mindset of being Determined

I have the DETERMINED mindset and this will influence HOW I live out my winning purpose today.

To be DETERMINED is to make a fixed decision and produce a consistency of behaviour in line with that decision.

My abilities are unlocked through new beliefs that form new attitudes. It is not that I could not do it before. It's that I did not have the belief and desire to sustain the activity. Now that the voice of devotion is at the conversation table of my life, I am in an expectant mood and I know I have a determined mindset.

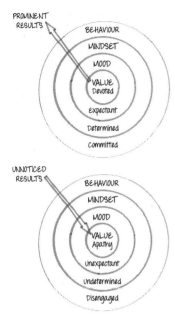

As a winner I believe that my results come through the steady pursuit of my goals and are solely my responsibility. If I fail to prepare, then—as the saying goes—I prepare to fail. Therefore as a winner I resolve to adopt a determined mindset showing care and consideration to my daily choices knowing that they steer the course of my life.

The DETERMINED mindset means that daily I am:

1) Determined in my Focus through Quiet Reflection
Quality choices require quality times of reflection

The voice of devotion gets louder the more I create space to think about the people to whom I am devoted. The clearer the picture of the person I am to help, and the more time I spend responding emotionally to that, the stronger the desire I have to make a difference.

Solitude solidifies our convictions. In a world of competing voices, devotion is given prominence and its voice echoes through the day whenever I allow it to speak. While many think the one who shouts the loudest gets noticed, the reality is that they are ignored as quickly as they shout. It is the voice of devotion that counts. We need to set ourselves apart to hear it.

2) Determined to Embrace Moments of Development
I can become better rather than bitter

I understand that the process of being devoted to my cause will involve hurt and pain. Therefore, when struggles come I will get stronger; when bitterness tries to set in, I will get better. Getting bitter is to lose control of my life; getting better is taking control. You can take control because you now host the winning conversation.

I realise that when struggles come, my mind and soul will be thrown off by the voice of apathy trying to get me to resent people. For me to resent and want revenge means giving a dirty cup of water not only to that person but to every person with whom I interact because it all comes from the same source. Every relational transaction is now tainted. I need to protect the source so every struggle will enrich what I carry and not poison it.

3) Determined to impact the Lives of Others
I grow self-importance when I make others feel important

Every person has to deal with insecurity. Insecurity is the belief that my position of value is under threat because someone else appears to be doing better than me. It is a lie that says there is a shortage of importance, therefore I must fight to have some and not give it freely away to other people. However, the devoted voice reminds me that my prominence is not dependent upon the level of prominence achieved by others; it is about me fulfilling my unique assignment. Therefore I can promote others because I am people-focussed and not position-focussed.

4) Determined to Adopt the Change I want to See in my World
I can initiate the change I want to see

Your life is the sum total of the decisions you have made up to this point. While you may not have been in control of all circumstances, you have been in control of your responses. Life is shaped by our responses. Any internal change can be initiated. While it may not produce immediate results, it will start a process of creating the right feeling, the right thoughts and then appropriate action. Action that is then repeated consistently will become a habit and habits shape you.

To initiate is the ability to begin or follow through a plan or task. So what do you want to change? What areas need to change to facilitate your cause? People live in the prison of 'I can't change.' We need to realise that we can change. Nine out of ten 'can'ts' are actually 'won'ts'. If we have courage and take initiative we have the power to start, stop or change anything.

191

Some people are happy to allow life to happen to them. But people who are initiators shape their own lives through their decisions. You can write your own history; it is not a foregone conclusion. Devoted initiators are contagious and create momentum. Be a part of the epidemic!

5) Determined in my Willingness to Embrace the "Unreasonable" Demands of the Cause
When my cause feels "unreasonable" I know it is growing me

To try and fulfil our cause within reason is simply to perpetuate the status quo. It is the person who is willing to embrace the unreasonable approach who will rise to prominence. Being immersed in the devoted conversation means more questions will be asked of what you are doing and why you are doing it then if you were to take a well trodden path.

Your cause will demand:

An unreasonable amount of time
An unreasonable amount of attention
An unreasonable amount of commitment
An unreasonable amount of finance
An unreasonable amount of focus
An unreasonable amount of tenacity

Live beyond reason is life devoted!

6) Determined even in the Midst of Crisis
Crisis creates the opportunity to refine my priorities

There will be plenty of commotion when hosting the prominence conversation because you will be a catalyst for change. This change does not just affect you; it affects everything and everyone with whom you do life. You will be misunderstood, misrepresented and misinterpreted. Change brings the best and the worst out of people because people always ask, 'How is this change going to affect me?' Their answer may or may not be right but in that moment facts are irrelevant; it is how they feel. This defines whether they view change as positive or worthy of resistance.

When people struggle with change it challenges relationships, especially when close family are involved. As a visionary leader I know that much of the change I produce will not be immediately understood because it takes time for people to understand the merits of what the change could bring. Waiting for the penny to drop is demanding.

When demands feel overwhelming you soon realise the power of devotion. For me my devotion has involved centering my life on the immoveable principles of my faith. When I devote myself through the conversation of prayer it does not matter what the intense levels of demands are, or the chaotic schedule these times create; there is wonderful order and reassurance. You may or may not pray but you can create a time for reflection. Devotion deepens your sense of security in the midst of apparent uncertainty.

It is important that you never pin your fight on a person. If you want to bring true and lasting change then focus on the conversations people host. While it may seem that attacks are aimed at you, they are not; they are the outward expression of a fight that is happening around their own table of conversation.

When you host the conversation with devotion at the table you will find that stress becomes a source of strategy. Do not press the self-destruct button by taking comments personally. You are bigger than the conversation that produces the toxic words you hear.

7) Determined in my Approach
If I cannot do it with everything I have, I cannot commit to it

The voice of devotion views every activity as a key component of the cause. Each activity requires a wholehearted approach to produce momentum. If an activity is carried out half-heartedly then this not only affects the activity but gives permission for an apathetic attitude. This attitude will creep into other key activities. Therefore if I cannot discipline myself to give it my all, I should not do it at all. Regardless of the activity, when we are wholehearted we become full-hearted.

A full heart is one that goes deeper than simply aligning

circumstances with expectations. A full heart enjoys a deep feeling of satisfaction that can often come at the oddest of times, even when everything is not 'situationally okay'. It is a myth that we arrive at happiness as if it's a holiday destination. Happiness is a choice that comes when we connect with something bigger than ourselves. My heart is full when I give myself wholeheartedly to that cause.

In light of this the way to deal with moments of being disheartened is to commit ourselves wholeheartedly again to our cause. To be disheartened is a feeling and feelings can be created and the creator of feelings is choices. Devotion requires a wholehearted commitment that does not leave you feeling empty but full.

8) Determined to Equip my Successors
My success depends on me preparing others for success

No one can run your race and you cannot run another person's race. However, a champion has a responsibility for leaving a legacy. The size of who you are is not determined by what you achieve but by what you unlock in the lives of others.

Life is not a competition against others; it is a competition against your own potential. Your race requires you to set others in motion, to compel them to greatness. I have witnessed the sad scenario of people who are nearing the end of their race becoming more of a hindrance than a help to those running after them. Even men who have stood and promoted the notion that *success lies in our successors*, could not let go when others did things differently and potentially more successfully.

You are a champion and champions raise champions. Apathy promotes insecurity, so keep it away from the conversation table and enjoy watching others succeed. Practice celebrating the success of others. Make it a habit now. The best time to try this is when you sit in apparent defeat or failure. This is an unreasonable request I know, but that's the life to which you are called.

9) Determined in my 'Followship'
I apprentice myself to those further on than me because my progress demands it

The voice of devotion requires us to devote ourselves to leadership—to being led as well as leading. As you pursue your cause you will invariably lead others. We succeed at everything we track and trend. Who are you tracking and trending when it comes to leadership? Leadership is influence and you have influence. But others have influence over you. To produce great followers you have to become a great follower.

It makes sense that those who follow learn actively to honour the leader. This creates an empowering environment for that leader to flourish. In doing so, the followers benefit from a stronger leader. However, this is often neglected because as the leader is often the one in public view he/she will be the first target if they challenge the status quo or if anything goes wrong.

While every person has an equally important part to play in achieving the completion of a cause there is an additional weight that rests on the shoulders of those in leadership positions.

Honouring leaders in a special way produces a lift that benefits everyone. Honour is a product of devotion that creates a **LIFT** that brings benefit to you not only in the season you are in but in the future too.

Let's look at that word LIFT.

It forms a neat acrostic.

L is for LISTEN

Listening is especially easy when we understand what is being said and we agree with what is being said. However, there are times when we have to listen and learn with a confidence and trust that because of their unique position leaders can see things we cannot see. While we must test what leaders do and say we must not fail to listen to our leaders. Have confidence in the leader to whom you devote yourself. Give them encouragement. There is nothing more fulfilling for a leader than a follower who listens and applies what is being taught. The best followers are those who ask good questions and listen to the answers with open minds in order to gain understanding. Good followers also refuse to listen to the wrong voices that encourage them to take part in dissention. Devotion commands that any change comes through an honourable approach.

I is for INITIATE

Be a solution-bringer and not a problem-bringer. Lighten the load of the leader and you create an environment where they can perform better. Who benefits from a leader performing better? You do—the follower.

F is for FLEX

A leader operates best when they know they have a group of followers willing to change and adapt. When a follower remains flexible, they honour the leader. When we become inflexible in our approach we are in fact elevating our own agenda above the leader and devaluing the leaders gifting to lead us.

T is for TRUST

There is nothing more valuable to a leader than trust from those who follow. As a leader they will see and understand things before the follower. This creates a tension for the follower because our human nature likes to understand before buying into something or someone. If the leader has built credibility with you then you must allow them to access that credit in times of uncertainty or obscurity.

Always to assume the best is to demonstrate honour to a leader and creates a trusting environment. In an environment where trust is cultivated, healthy relationships are produced.

Honouring creates a LIFT that will bring about a benefit for everyone, producing greater results for the cause to which truly devoted people are in submission.

10) Determined to Create moments of Movement
I am addicted to making others feel bigger

I have played games with my children many times in which I

have purposely lost so that they can win. To see them enjoy the moment of winning does not anger me or make me feel small; in fact, quite the opposite. This is something we should seek for everyone. A truly devoted heart overcomes insecurity and enjoys seeing others win. This makes you prominent in their eyes because it communicates an authentic desire for them to succeed. Who would not want to be around or be influenced by that kind of attitude?

Conversation with myself: Which one or two statements do I struggle to believe? Which specific belief must I stay aware of and practice in everything I do today? I must remember that in order to achieve what I want most I must be willing to tackle what I want to do least.

Day 23: The Winning Behaviour of committing wholeheartedly

"WHAT I do today will be driven by WHO I am. My choices will reflect my character."

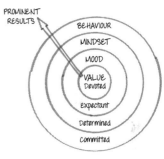

Today we look at some practical ways to look at how you can develop the winning conversation that will make you MORE prominent in life. The more you inform the right choices, the more you activate the results.

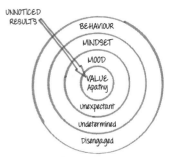

Devotion is the lead voice of the six sat around the meeting table of our beliefs. Devotion leads the discussion because everything forms around our cause. Our cause is the reason for our lives; it is our 'be-cause.'

Devotion needs to lead the boardroom of my beliefs and be the reminder that it is my picture of my preferred future that will lead the conversation. Therefore I must practice HIGH commitment in the choices that I make today.

Experience the Reality of your BE-CAUSE

We have already talked about the power of our imagination and the ability we all carry to use images to stir us emotionally to action. Today I want to achieve two things. The first is this: I want to help you experience your goal in your imagination.

Results are produced by certain intention multiplied by intense action. Therefore the clearer the picture we have, the more we can see, feel and experience the result before we reach it. Our imagination produces the image that eventually becomes what we incarnate in our choices.

Certain Intention = WHO + WHY

Certainty is about combining clarity and desire

WHO

If we are agreed that a cause starts and ends with a person, then WHO is the person or group that you want to serve through your purpose?

Can you see the face of the person and the context of the person/people your cause is trying to effect? If it is a group of people then imagine what they might be doing now. The clearer the profile of the recipient/beneficiary, the more clarity you acquire about what you have to do to serve them.

It is important that you keep clear about WHO your cause is about. Life is full of opportunities and choices and the challenge is to stay on a determined and defined path once you know your cause. People and organisations move off course when they lose sight of the objective.

Moment to pause: Look at an image(s) of the WHO behind your cause

WHY

Why do you want to bring a lift to that person or group? What is it that motivates you about them? What is it you seek to change in their life that will raise their life experience? What would you say to that person now about your plan and what would be their reaction? It is a great idea to talk through your cause with those people or those who represent that group. Their reaction to your goals will help inform you when you build and clarify your LIFE Map.

Use your imagination to see the end goal. What does is look like, smell, taste, feel or sound like? The greater the detail the more certainty you create. This intensifies your belief and expectancy in the end goal.

Moment to pause: Imagine the outcome of the change you are going to bring

Determined Action = HOW + WHAT

Determined action is about a clear plan backed by high levels of desire that produce consistent choices which get you to the end goal.

HOW

Imagine yourself living in the reality of your end goal. What would life look like? How would you behave? How would you approach your time? How would you apportion your time? What finance would you have? What relationships would you anticipate carrying forward? What demands would there be on your body and so what health regime would be required? What approach would be needed to sustain and increase the results you would be seeing?

When our minds spend time thinking about this the reality produces clarity on the difference between now and then. This may appear like two worlds. If your goal is big enough then going to a place in your mind when you are thinking about this will feel like you are visiting another planet. This may feel like fantasy to others but if it is built on a foundation of certainty that this is how things will be then it becomes fuel to make the necessary changes in HOW you currently live your life.

Moment to pause: Write down a short journal entry of a future day as if you were already living in the fulfillment of what you are trying to achieve. Now you have created a benchmark in your mind that will help steer you in your choices today.

WHAT

The way to pursue the cause is to act like the person you are becoming. The changes to how you live your life will not happen by chance; you need to adopt the winning mindset which informs the winning behaviour and activates the winning results. One way to help you challenge your current behaviour in the light of your goal is to find people who are already successfully serving the people you also want to serve, or people who have successfully served another group but have demonstrated they have navigated the path to achieving their goals. By default we like to swim in a pond that makes us look big. However, while this will stroke our ego it does nothing for us unlocking our potential. We need to be a small fish in a big pond so we can see how bigger fish swim!

Moment to pause: What can I do today that will create an action to drive deeper my conviction of the future I will obtain?

Plan a Rhythm of Resistance that Creates Positive Experience

The second thing I want to help you establish today is a pattern of daily challenges.

One thing I have found extremely useful is to have a challenge each day that keeps me a producer and not a consumer—that keeps me focussed on others and not myself. These challenges create moments of movement not only in others but also in you as you give. Those who are generous with their words and actions build a bigger life but those who withhold encouragement and acts of kindness shrink wrap their lives!

Daily Challenges that Keep Giving

I find that having a small daily routine that challenges me to act in line with the winning conversation is really powerful.

I have found that daily challenges:

Keep me Stirred

It is amazing how small acts of kindness can keep us stirred and in touch with people. It ignites a childlike excitement about life whilst all the time building a platform with people. It keeps my eyes off myself and on the cause, which is people.

Keep me Stretched

Our selfish and self-serving defaults are so strong that a selfless action everyday keeps me producing and not consuming. It creates a moment where I have to decide to point my value outwards rather than pulling value from the outside-in. It reminds me of my commitment to the winning conversation.

Keep me Sensitive

It is amazing how we can quickly become desensitised to the needs of others. Our daily pursuits will centre round our needs without us being aware of it, to the extent that we can become numb to the needs of those around us. Daily challenges keep us sensitised to the needs of people because they break our focus from 'our own small worlds' and encourage us to step into someone else's world.

Over the years I have refined and changed my daily challenges. Here are my daily challenges. You can create your own that help you stay stirred, stretched and sensitive.

Monday—Motivate on Monday

Share a motivational thought with someone at the start of a new week

There are quick and easy ways of sharing these thoughts with many people with the media outlets we have available. In order to increase the difficulty level, decide on a person who you feel needs encouragement because of the season of life they are in and share it face-to-face. Alternatively, share it over the phone. The more personal the thought becomes, the more powerful the impact is.

Tuesday—Talk up Tuesday

Share with someone how they are getting it right in something they do

The winning conversation is about seeing other people win. When we make clear to someone that what we have seen them do is praiseworthy, it produces a very clear encouragement to raise the bar in that area. When someone encourages me in my public communication it encourages me in that area to do more in the future. Talking others up with them present is powerful.

Wednesday—Wow on Wednesday
Give a gift to someone that takes them by surprise

Generosity is a powerful tool and you can really have fun with it. Whether it is buying someone a coffee in the cue at the coffee shop or having a gift delivered to a person's home or workplace, this raises the value placed on that person. Gifts given for no obvious reason—e.g. a birthday—reinforces the value you seek to bring to that person.

Thursday—Thank you Thursday
Communicate your thanks to someone for WHO they are

The words, 'thank you,' are greatly underestimated. Demonstrating appreciation unlocks powerful emotion that creates motion in others, whether you do it through a handwritten note or a phone call. To take the time to communicate your gratitude adds a value to the person that far outweighs the cost of the giver.

Friday—Fresh connection Friday
Kick-Start a conversation and show interest in someone you do not know

When a challenge involves an unknown person it can feel more difficult. Fear of how a person may react often prevents people pushing beyond the familiar. However, the more difficult a challenge may feel the greater potential there is for a positive result. New connections can lead to new relationships and new opportunities to serve the needs of other people. I have been surprised by the ways I have been able to help and support fresh connections that I have made over the years.

Saturday—Step up Saturday
Read, watch or listen to content that will challenge you to raise your game.

The weekend provides the perfect opportunity to invest in yourself. Saturdays are great for getting hold of content that will inspire or instruct you to think and act in new ways. The earlier in the day you get to access the content the longer you have to chew it over. When meeting up with friends or spending time with family you have opportunities to talk it over, creating deeper levels of understanding.

Sunday—Stand back Sunday
Reflect on the week that has gone and the week ahead

Reflection is powerful and Sunday still provides a great opportunity for me not to feel the pressure and demands of a world 'at work' and to take time to think. Thinking time is never an activity that feels 'urgent' but it is vitally important. Viewing the week ahead and building our approach and strategy can release a level of effectiveness that produces significant results.

Take time to revisit your 'Life MAP' and prepare to 'move through the gears,' increasing the momentum of the winning conversation in your life.

Increased Difficulty leads to Increased Results

In order to bring new depths to the winning conversation I encourage you to increase the difficulty level on your daily challenges. Imagine the daily challenges as weights on a dumbbell. The more you increase the weight and repetitions the greater the resistance you will feel, but the greater the potential results you will also experience.

The more the daily challenges become a habit the more enjoyment we get out of life.

Day 24: The Winning Evaluation

Benchmark which mindset you have when it comes to the PROMINENT conversation.

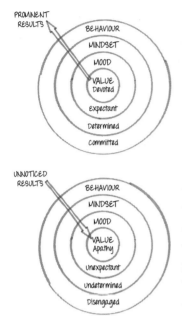

The fruit of my actions will reveal the root of the conversations I host. Today we are looking at 10 questions or statements we make based on situations we find ourselves in. I encourage you to be brutally honest as to which response most fits you. Tally up how many you answered according to which voice and make a decision to go back under the bonnet of your inner conversations to strengthen your foundation as a champion. If you feel frustrated then that is not a bad thing as long as you focus that frustration on making certain that you commit to hosting the winning conversation.

1) Success of others—What do you do when others are successful?

Consumed - I avoid the success of others because it makes me feel small. I will find fault in those who are succeeding to feed my sense of self-worth

Complacent - It is easier to deal with the success of others when you do not push too hard to pursue goals. There is nothing to compare against.

Competitor - I will learn from those who are successful.

Champion - I will help others learn from those who are successful and significant and celebrate what they have achieved.

2) Generosity—How do you view generosity?

Consumed - I give when there is an obvious benefit for doing so, even if that is just to give the appearance of generosity.

Complacent - I give sporadically, depending on how finances are at the time and the need that presents itself to me.

Competitor - I give regularly to worthy causes because I believe in contributing to society.

Champion - I create a rhythm of giving in order to intensify my level of devotion. Therefore my basis for giving is out of a need to give rather than the just nature of a cause.

3) Friends—How do you view friendship?

Consumed - Friends are about what they can do for me.

Complacent - Friends are about fun and enjoyment, sharing and caring.

Competitor - Friends fill my emotional tank. They are important relationships that provide a resource for the cause.

Champion - Friends are a community from which anything healthy in my life will grow. Therefore I must invest in community.

4) Partner—How do you view your partner?

Consumed - They are there to add to my life.

Complacent - They are someone I have got used to having around whom I must appreciate from time to time.

Competitor - I give my best when they give their best.

Champion - What I give is a choice I make and not based on what I receive in return.

5) Difference—How do you view those who are different from you?

Consumed - I view the differences of others as a disadvantage and seek to gather around me those who are similar. I have no time for people who don't think like me.

Complacent - I appreciate everyone is different but prefer those in my own tribe.

Competitor - I need different kinds of people to achieve the goal. I encourage discussion and openness between people in order to enrich life and achieve better decisions.

Champion - I seek to unlock the difference in others in order to help them succeed, regardless of whether it helps me towards my goal or not. I work hard at bringing people together—even those who repel each other—to get a blend of the differences. The bigger the repel, the greater potential for synergy. This requires skill and clarity of vision.

6) Up line leaders—How do you respond to those you report to?

Consumed - I give them what they require when I am treated well. I have no problem being involved in conversations that discuss how those leading should be performing better.

Complacent - I stay clear of dissenting conversations but do not actively discourage them. I just keep my head down and my aim is to go unnoticed.

Competitor - I exceed expectations in my performance. I avoid conversations that seek to demote those who lead me.

Champion - I seek to understand the challenges they face and actively do my best to create solutions regardless of reward. I try to focus everyone on solutions not problems.

7) Opposition—How do you respond to opposition?

Consumed - I will give as good as I get when others oppose me. I cannot be seen to be a doormat.

Complacent - I keep my head down and because of this I do not receive much opposition.

Competitor - I will not respond and give my energy to opposition. I will keep on track with the goals I know to be right.

Champion - I will use any opposition as an opportunity to demonstrate my pursuit for their best regardless of my internal feelings toward them.

8) Competition—How do you see competition?

Consumed - I seek to demote any competition in order to gain a competitive advantage.

Complacent - I accept my place in the pecking order and get on with life.

Competitor - I stay focused on what I have set out to achieve and don't allow competition to detract me.

Champion - I seek to learn and understand from competition and even seek opportunity for collaboration without deviating from the course.

9) Resentment—How do you view resentment?

Consumed - I put distance between me and them because otherwise I will react badly.

Complacent - I bury it and am good at compartmentalising.

Competitor - I can rise above any action that creates a feeling of resentment by focusing more on the goals ahead than the present negative circumstances.

Champion - I keep the conversation going and overcome feelings of resentment by promoting what I see others can become through acts of kindness and words of encouragement.

10) Coaching—What are you doing about getting a coach?

Consumed - I am waiting for someone to offer.

Complacent - I have met up with a coach and I try to make it happen regularly but struggle for time.

Competitor - I meet up with a coach and download from them.

Champion - I seek to add value to the coach and to coach others with what is being learnt, becoming a channel not just a reservoir.

PRACTICE V POTENTIAL of the PROMINENT conversation

Based on the answers to the above questions, how many times could you honestly say that your answer was that of a 'champion'?

Consumer:	1-2 times
Complacent:	3-5 times
Competitor:	6-8 times
Champion:	9-10 times

My Overall POTENTIAL: I AM A CHAMPION

MY Overall PRACTICE: I HAVE BEEN A _____

In order for my practice to match my potential I have identified the following three things I can do to unlock the champion in me:

1_____

2_____

3_____

Day 25: The Winning Accountability

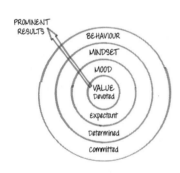

Pulling this whole week under the title of 'play the ace and not the joker' enables us to be able to review this conversation quickly. Using the dice in spare moments throughout the day, or in a small group, helps me to focus on the inner conversation of devotion.

The Winning Dice—***Play the Ace and not the Joker***

My prominence is directly linked to the value I place on the lives of other people.

A devoted person seeks to extract the highest value from life and does so by placing the greatest value they can on people. To play the ace in a game of cards is, in most games, to play the most powerful card. It carries the highest value and helps you win. Contributing in a positive way to people is involves an action that adds the highest value to another life. A person who hosts the *devoted* conversation becomes convinced that in every situation it is right to add value even when there are often reasons not to do so.

When a group of people agrees that this is the expected norm they collaborate to create an enriching environment that is healthy and therefore produces growth and results. This makes the group stand out because it is not the social norm to act this way. This unlocks more prominence for them and the cause they represent.

To play the joker is to use the card that carries the lowest value, the losing card. When we demote rather than promote people we usually do so in the belief that making the other person look bad and feel bad will in some way raise our prominence. While it may gain attention it will not produce lasting prominence.

There is MORE prominence in you when you play the ace and not the joker!

Step 1: RECALL Together

Here is a quick review of what it means to play the ace and not the joker so we can stay on course for allowing DEVOTION to have the loudest voice, thereby drowning out APATHY. Here is a description based on what we have looked at this week:

What does it look like to play the ace?

- We celebrate others even when we feel uncelebrated
- We're quick to respond positively to those in authority
- We go out of our way to make someone else look good
- We are sensitive to those in need
- We own the job of protecting the group/organisation/leaders/managers for the sake of the cause because reputation and credibility affects everyone
- We actively put others first
- We willingly make sacrifices to help others
- We go further than expected, beyond the call of duty
- We place a higher value on our finances, time and health because of the demands that will be required from the cause

- We find a coach/mentor from whom to receive but also to promote and encourage for their contribution

What does it look like to play the joker?

- We allow familiarity of life, relationships and resource to breed contempt
- We make ourselves look good at someone else's expense
- We demand to be honoured and promoted
- We put our wants before the needs of others
- We assume privilege
- We often talk without thinking
- We create relational alignment in order to 'climb the ladder.'

Step 2: REVIEW with others

Get together weekly with people who are committed to developing the winning conversations on the journey of this book. This week discuss the following:

i) What cause have you clarified so far?
ii) Who could you be coached by in order to support their cause but also receive advice and instruction on your journey?
iii) How could we support one another through the demands of pursuing the cause?
iv) Has there been a time when we have allowed ourselves to play the joker and not the ace?
v) How would our relationships be enriched by 'playing the ace'?'

Step 3: REFLECTION to be shared

Now create a reflection that you can share with someone in your group or someone else that you are coaching to be a champion in life. Why not take the time with your children, loved one, or friend and share what you have learnt? Simply sharing this reflection will accomplish much in your life and deepen relationships, enriching them with vulnerability and moments of movement.

Follow our basic structure:

i) What I realised for the first time/again this week is .....
(Share a thought that is authentically you)

ii) The change I need to make is ..... (Share the action point
you are in agreement over)

iii) Can you help me make it ...... ? (Invite help and create
accountability)

Once you have developed the habit of doing this why not
decide to turn your thoughts into a blog or even take your coaching
to another level. There is so much in you connected to your
commitment to stretch yourself.

Section 5: Be MORE Resilient

Day 26: The Winning Conversation makes you MORE Resilient

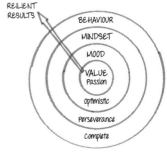

Let me introduce the voice of passion to your conversation table. A champion allows the voice of passion to speak over the voice of lethargy.

Passion is an intense desire or enthusiasm for something or someone.[9]

You are stronger than you realise; there is a tenacity and zeal inside of you that has not yet been fully seen. You have a capacity to go through harder situations and circumstances than you know. You have the ability to walk through the fire of challenge and the storm of problems and allow it to produce something in you that will last forever. You might be in a problem or challenge right now, or about to enter into that period. There is **MORE** RESILIENCE in you than you think!

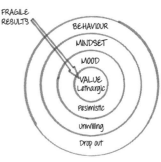

Resilience refers to a substance that has the ability to spring back into shape. It is the ability to recover quickly as a result of an innate toughness. This resilience is remarkable and is a key part of unlocking the message that is in you. The message needs to be birthed, refined and made ready to be told. There is no other path

9. passion. Oxford Dictionaries. Oxford University Press, n.d. Web. 22 September 2015.

for this than problems and pain. That may sound like bad news but that will only be true if you do not have a vision and goal to pull you through. The key to developing resilience is to have a razor-sharp vision that gets clearer, stronger and more intense the more it comes under pressure. Without vision the potential inside and the person you were designed to be can die. You will survive but something of your soul dies. This is why someone can become a 'shadow of their former selves' because the real person died in the fire of failure or drowned in the storm of setbacks. They did not have someone with them to help them keep their eyes on the goal and the joy of what the challenge was producing. However, you are different because you are a champion. To equip you to win, I am going to introduce the conversation that you can host inside of you that will enable your life to speak to your problems and challenges and produce MORE than you ever imagine!

When I host the RESILIENT conversation I become...

1) MORE aware of the calm in the storm
Determine to respond rather than react to the storm

When you realise that you host the voice of passion in the boardroom of belief you realise that regardless of what is happening around you, what is in you is stronger. This means that you could be in the midst of life's storms, with the boat of your life battered on every side, but you have the resilience to be calm, to choose to respond rather than react.

Our default reaction to outside challenge is to find an outside answer that will create the internal feeling we desire. What we desire when we face life's challenge is assurance. We have a human need to feel safe and secure. We are wired to find this in the things that can be seen and so believe that the answer is to have MORE of something that is visible than to believe that we have what it takes inside of us to be assured.

The starting place for the winning conversation is 'inside-out.' Every response to external problems starts with an internal step. This conversation will help you be the one boat that does not send out flares and S.O.S signals because the name of your boat is resilience.

2) MORE aware of a problem's potential
My problems can create more capacity in me

Have you ever asked yourself "Why are things in my life starting to feel tight and uncomfortable?" If this were someone's description of the place where they lived you would probably suggest a larger house or that they reduce the clutter in their existing property.

Our lives can hit points when it feels as if we are being torn apart at the seams. When this happens our response needs to be one of action. Sometimes simply prioritising what we do with our time, money and resource is the key, removing the things that are not a part of our future and giving more space to what is. Someone once said, 'Above all, be true to yourself and if you cannot put your heart into it, take yourself out of it.' But what if you have done that and it still feels a tight squeeze? Maybe it is time to identify and possess a more spacious place. This is the cry of the voice of passion.

The problem you face is like a squatter taking residence in a property that belongs to you but you have yet to possess. The voice of passion enables you to take control of the situation and get clarity on what you have to do to claim that space as your own. That space is your potential. Life is as big as you want to build it, but problems are your materials!

3) MORE self-confident
Confidence is built from suffering upward

There is an untapped confidence in you. Confidence gives a person an internal permission to act. Therefore the limits of our actions are usually a confidence issue rather than a competence issue. Competence can be learnt but confidence is a decision that what is in you is stronger than what is in front of you.

Your problems, anxieties and worries are like traffic signal lights. On the journey of life you stop and start because it feels like you are always sat at the lights and they are on red. This is monotonous and makes you want to get out of the car of your life and simply walk away. However, those traffic lights are simply a reflection of what is inside you. They will respond to your choices, particularly the choice to push past fear. When you do this they will switch to amber and eventually green. The more problems you face head on the more those lights turn to green and the further on the journey you can go.

It is time to leave the red traffic lights and face your challenges. They are not there to stop you; they are there to grow you. The lethargy you feel in the face of these challenges can and will be dispelled when you allow passion to rise. Passion is motion that is ignited by a choice. With passion you can rise in confidence and walk tall down streets that would formerly intimidate you. There's MORE resilience in you than you think!

4) MORE accepting of challenge
Let the storm produce the wind for your sails

The trouble with the word passion is that it is too often associated with romance. But the word passion is also a technical term referring to Jesus Christ, the founder of the Christian faith. This is why the Christian calendar has a Passion Week, celebrating the period between the Last Supper and the death of Christ.

In other words, passion is used of suffering not just sex.

Christ's vision and goal of salvation for the human race required an internal passion—an inner confidence and calm that on the far side of suffering he would ultimately win. So he was resilient; he turned the worst challenges and problems into his pathway to victory.

When you host passion at the table of conversation it creates a new dynamic, a new lens through which you view suffering. Rather than simply asking 'Why is this happening?' (the most natural response) the person of resilience is able to sit in a different chair and ask, 'What am I learning?'

Remember: potential is unlocked through passion and passion increases whenever suffering goes to new levels.

5) MORE persistent with passion
Passion balanced with patience produces deep resilience

While passion is described as a barely controllable emotion, resilience is really a refined form of passion. It is the ability to endure and persist toward a goal over a prolonged period of time. Many people use passion in small bursts but I would call that 'outside-in' passion—a positive experience that draws a positive response. Have you ever got excited about a new fitness programme? Have you ever made a decision to learn a new skill? In both cases, did you appear 'passionate' in the moment? People talk about the 'passion in the moment' but this is not the voice of passion that a champion hosts. If we are going to bring about a revolution in our world through our cause and contribution then we have to develop the discipline of passion.

In life naturally passionate moments are few and far between. If we lived off passionate moments we would be like a car stopping and starting. However, if we can develop passionate patience then while everything around us starts and stops our consistent passion will exceed everything around us.

As someone who will work with others to achieve your objectives and goals, you will need to know how to harness passionate patience. There is nothing worse for a leader than inconsistent followers whose enthusiasm is based on how they are 'feeling.' First you need to model the kind of passion you want to see through the discipline of passion.

Consistency is awesome but consistency on its own is not good enough. Consistency with passion is what gets you somewhere. I realised in my marriage that there was nothing more frustrating to Leanne than inconsistency in my demonstration of love and passion for her. I did not realise that it didn't just affect her; it affected me. I know that as a father, husband, leader, employer and friend, the greatest gift someone can give you is passionate persistence.

6) MORE resourceful toward others
People feed from passion

If you host the resilience conversation then you will start to notice the kind of people who want to engage in conversation with you. You will find that people will walk away from you energised. Why? Because passion is magnetic and contagious; it draws aspirational people to you who then leave with a greater belief that they can turn dreams into reality.

Some people may stop talking to you because your increased belief intimidates them. Some of those may eventually catch the fire of passion through you. Others may choose to believe the voice of lethargy. You will be able to talk to this person but not work with them. This is a conversation and a culture clash.

7) MORE listened to
The passionate pursuit of my cause gives permission to others to pursue their cause

One reason people will be attracted to you is because your passionate pursuit of a goal gives them a permission to believe too. When someone witnesses the ordinary side of your extraordinary belief they realise that they can add that extra to their ordinary. The quality of people you attract will depend on the depth of your passion and the size of the problem you are seeking to solve.

Day 27: The Winning Voice of Passion

Passion is not WHAT I do, it is WHO I am

To be a person of PASSION I have to immerse myself in the commands that are going to lead me into the right feelings. The more I immerse myself in the belief that I am passionate, the more resilient I will become.

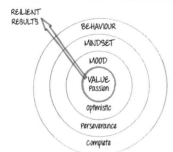

To be a person of PASSION I have to believe that...

i) I AM stimulated from the inside out
Initiate what you want to experience

To jump is to create external motion as the result of an inner decision. It is

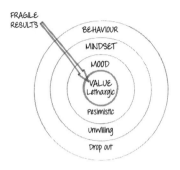

the ability to push yourself in a new direction at will. When I believe that I am passionate I believe that I can jump-start any area of my life through a passionate decision.

Enthusiasm is the product of either internal or external stimulation. A champion does not and cannot survive on externally stimulated enthusiasm otherwise known as hype. We live in a world that knows how to create hype! One definition of the word hype is *deception carried out for publicity.*[10] Huge amounts of money are used by advertisers to project images of people and products in order to persuade us that what we are seeing has a direct connection to what is being sold.

Advertising has learnt what images and sensory impressions will move us to action. Experts in advertising and marketing know that if they can convince us through images that purchasing their product will increase the value of our lives then we are more likely to buy and become loyal to the brand.

Branding is about identity. A Mercedes car will carry out the same function as a Ford but many people will purchase the Mercedes to build their personal brand identity. While the Mercedes may be better in terms of quality and engineering, what influences the buyer is the perception that the car confers a value that they want others to attribute to them.

Pictures of male and female models are therefore often airbrushed in order to create hype. But the reality is that such external activity cannot increase the value of who we are. When I talk about being passionate and full of enthusiasm, I am not talking about the result of external stimulation.

The enthusiasm a champion carries is a result of a choice that my inner passion is the only stimulus I need to get up and go for my goals. External stimuli can add extra impetus, as the wind does behind the car, but when the wind drops the internal engine

10. hype. Oxford Dictionaries. Oxford University Press, n.d. Web. 22 September 2015.

remains the primary driver.

It is interesting to note that the word enthusiasm actually comes from the Greek words *en* and *theos* which literally mean 'in God.' The enthusiastic person in the ancient world was in whom God was present. This highlights the spiritual roots of the word and further suggests that we must not be driven by man-made hype.

Conversation with myself: What do I need to jump-start today?

ii) I AM grown through tension
When I am in-tension I can create movement

Passion is quite simply my fuel to keep going on the journey of fulfilling my potential. Fuel is vital in creating movement towards a goal or destination and so we must always make sure the fuel tank is always topped up.

Where do we go to refill with the fuel of passion? What does a passion 'refilling station' look like?

Inside a car is a combustion engine. The combustion engine creates an explosion and out of that explosion energy is created that feeds motion. Combustion takes place internally. We never think of an explosion as a positive process. And yet this pressured environment produces the intense heat needed for positive motion. The greater the compression and pressure, the greater the explosion and the more energy is given to the motion. All of this takes place inside the car, hence 'internal' combustion.

You can have external combustion. Steam trains are driven by it. However, internal is far more efficient and more motion is created using less energy this way.

If I were to ask you what you think gives you passion, you would more often than not suggest positive experiences, such as encouragement, affirmation and empowerment from people around you. While these do give us a turbo boost, they are like

11. American Psychological Association (APA):
tension. (n.d.). Dictionary.com Unabridged. Retrieved September 04, 2015, from Dictionary.com website: http://dictionary.reference.com/browse/tension

the external combustion engine. They are not highly efficient over time because they are not consistent. They are not always there for us. We cannot therefore rely on external factors to produce the consistent fuel we are going to need.

The greatest asset we have is actually <u>tension</u>.

What is tension?

The dictionary defines it as 'The act of stretching or straining.'[11]

Tension is part of the created order. We live in a world where there are invisible pulls and forces that create tension. Out of that tension comes a balance that produces an environment for growth.

Tension produces fitness in the human body. Exercise is a mix of tension and release. The process of tension and release produces physical fitness.

Music is created because of tension and release. Every instrument in an orchestra creates its individual sound based upon the tension of a string, skin or the compression of air. That tension is then released and the sound is created. Something of resounding beauty is created through tension and release. However, our natural bent is to want the release of the sound without the tension. We want the release of fitness without tension in our bodies.

The winning conversation carries the belief that tension is good because it produces motion.

Conversation with myself: What tension can I start to view positively and why?

iii) I AM born to stretch
Stretch brought me into this life and it keeps me alive!

It was a stretch that got you into this world and it is a stretch that will get the potential out of you. Muscles are created to be stretched in order to give you increased strength and a capacity to do more. The same is true of any strength. A community is drawn closer together through hardship. The stretch causes people to reach out, to stretch further relationally. They lose their independence because the situation demands that they stretch in order to survive.

My marriage is strengthened through relational stretch which is the result of challenges.

My health is improved and strengthened when I stretch my muscles.

There is nothing like a recession to create financial health. The stretch causes people to call for help, to make realignments that can actually be the making of them.

When it comes to my goals, if they do not create a stretch then they are not the right goals. Own the goals and possess through them through stretch. It is what you were born for!

Conversation with myself: How has stretch positively impacted my life so far? Which area of my life needs to be stretched?

iv) I AM optimistic in the squeeze
My squeeze allows the world to see what I am made of

A squeeze is the result of external pressure. Sometimes squeezing produces something that you don't want others to see. *The Incredible Hulk* is about a man called David Banner. After being the subject of experimentation, anger becomes a trigger on the inside that makes him green, monstrous and violent on the outside. This causes him to spend all his time trying to avoid situations that trigger his rage.

While David Banner did not have control of what was in him, you do. What you immerse yourself in determines what comes out of you when the squeeze happens, and it will. When you immerse yourself in a principle that creates assurance, that feeling of safety and security will manifest on the outside when the squeeze comes.

Conversation with myself: What is my 'hulk' moment? How can I respond differently in that squeeze so that others get to see the new me?

v) I AM disciplined in my response
I can increase in responsibility when I improve in my ability to respond

Pressure is not all bad. Constant pressure with no let up will eventually produce negative results. However, pressure periods can be useful because they cause a change in behaviour and therefore a change in results.

Two people can experience the same pressure and yet respond in two ways. One allows it to hone their convictions and take command of their life; the other allows it to make them a casualty of their circumstances. The key word here is ALLOW because every person has a choice.

Passion, our fuel for the future, is created when we positively embrace whatever comes our way. So when we have a force that places resistance on us, or we face opposition that could be seen as negative, everything depends on our discipline. No one other than you and me can be responsible for this. We have a responsibility to apply discipline and in doing so produce passion for our purpose.

Resisting force/opposition + Disciplined Response = Passion for Purpose

Resisting force/opposition + Undisciplined reaction = Low aspiration + presence of excuses/blame

An undisciplined reaction is when we believe that the resisting force/opposition removes our ability to choose our response. Our reactions highlight our belief that we are not in control.

Does any of this sound familiar?

My kids are driving me crazy
You made me feel this way
My husband/wife is making my life miserable
My work is getting me down
I don't have the opportunity to do what I want to do
I can't get past my feeling of…
I fell out of love with them/it
I can't grow in that environment
I had to react because of the way they made me feel

An undisciplined reaction to an opposing force never creates a positive outcome, even though it is the way we are naturally wired. The voice of passion is the belief that I can choose my response and every response can build resilience.

Conversation with myself: Replay the last time you reacted negatively. How are you going to choose your response when something similar happens next time?

vi) I AM able to pause a trigger
Giving in to a reaction is to give up on an opportunity to build strength

When an opposing force triggers a reaction it is likely to be based upon what we have discerned physically and felt emotionally. Have you ever said, 'I did it without thinking'? That's a reaction. We fail to engage beyond how we physically and emotionally feel. When people challenge our reaction we excuse ourselves by saying, 'I reacted out of my feelings,' or, 'It was a natural reaction.' That is actually a correct interpretation of what happens, even if it is an inappropriate action. Maturity is when a person allows it to go to the next level which is for us to stop and think about a reaction or a response. The voice of passion creates a resilient ability to press pause in a situation, to stop and become aware of more than just feelings and physical realities.

To press pause at a time when it would be more natural to react is to take a higher approach that creates a better opening for a positive outcome. The winning conversation is more about valuing positive outcomes over a long term than satisfying feelings in the moment.

Conversation with myself: What triggers a reaction in me? In what way would a disciplined response build strength in me and those around me?

vii) I AM future
My future goal will produce my present experience

There is nothing like a clear picture of a preferred future to ignite fire in the heart of a person. If passion is grown and heightened in suffering then our ability to focus our feelings on a future picture rather than the challenge of now is critical. As a champion you do not have to live the life of the consumed and be led by your feelings.

I once had a dog who would decide halfway through its walk that she would stop and not walk anymore. Despite my attempts to coerce her forward I had to pick her up. I walked home in humiliation as I passed other dog owners who were taking their dogs for a walk in the conventional way!

The reason why this happened is simple: the dog had not been trained in her early years.

A champion takes control and leads their feelings through training them to reattach themselves to a picture of a different, brighter future.

Conversation with myself: In what way is my current challenge training me for the future?

viii) I AM able
Relegate the feeling of being UNABLE below the belief that 'I am ABLE'

When you feel like you have hit the wall and do not feel like you can go on, sometimes the only thing you can do is make a declaration: 'I AM ABLE to carry on.' While a simple set of words seems insufficient, actually the power of choice is all you need in that moment to kick start the feelings that will cause creativity to arise.

Conversation with myself: What do I currently believe I unable to do that needs to be challenged with my new belief?

ix) I AM able to pull my future into my now
My obstacle is simply the scenery along the route to winning

When you row in a boat race, the tension between where you are and where you want to go can become disheartening. This often happens in other contexts when we are tired and in a negative rhythm of life. Our attention gets fixed on the obstacle rather than the process of overcoming the obstacle. Simply trying not to look at the obstacle is not the answer. The answer is to intensify your focus on the finish and pull the finish line towards you, pulling your future into your now. Every pull becomes positive because your attention is a proactive decision to focus on the not yet rather than the now. This will result in a positive energy which inspires you and increases performance.

Conversation with myself: What do I believe about the obstacles I face? How do I need to view them in order to progress?

x) I AM comfortable with change
I grow more through the discomfort of change

We can be certain of one thing that will not change, that everything will change! Change is part of life. And yet many people openly admit and even comfortably declare that they do not like change! While this may seem insignificant, the words we profess reveal the beliefs we have. If change is part of life, why fight it? Why not embrace change? Change in itself it neither good nor bad. It is a principle.

While we are not in control of every changing element in our lives, we are in control of more than we think. Realising our potential is connected to our willingness to embrace change positively.

Memories are powerful and they can be used for good and bad. Memories can be the basis for gratitude. They can also create an unhealthy nostalgia where our fear of the future is masked by our hankering after the past. While you can shape your future you cannot escape back into the past. The Winning Conversation empowers you to embrace change and use the passion locked up in its challenges to build a resilience that unlocks the potential of your dreams and goals.

Conversation with myself: What discomfort am I resisting that I need to embrace?

Day 28: The Winning Mood of Optimism

Unlocking the power of WHY creates optimism

My WHY is my PURPOSE. My purpose is the vision of my life. My vision is the future that I choose to have and it is powerful because it ignites hope inside me. Hope has an unrivalled way of lifting negative mood clouds that drift into the horizons of my thinking. The winning mood is stimulated when I choose to keep reminding myself of my vision, my winning purpose. I must follow the pattern of the winning purpose from the inside-out, from the WHO to the WHAT. The power of our WHY is the power of positivity that creates motion in our lives.

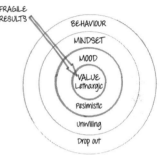

I am having the RESILIENT conversation led by the voice of passion which means I choose to put myself in an OPTIMISTIC mood.

Good will always prevail

The natural pessimist validates their stance by believing that they have chosen not to ignore facts and to embrace a greater level of reality than the optimist. The natural optimist on the other hand views the pessimist as a problem finder—someone who struggles to cultivate a 'can-do' mindset.

True optimists however do not ignore the facts. Rather, they have the ability to embrace facts. Whilst it may look like evil is winning the battle, the optimist believes that goodness will ultimately prevail. Every situation, however bad, can in the eyes of the optimist add value and play a part in an ultimately good outcome.

When I choose to put myself in an optimistic mood I am deciding to enjoy and not simply endure the process. While many things in life do not 'feel' enjoyable, I can choose to enjoy what the process will produce. Optimism is remaining cheerful and full of hope and allowing that powerful mood to navigate the choices of the day.

WHY this is happening is replaced by WHAT this is happening for

When negative things happen our natural response is, 'Why me? Why is this happening now?' This is not an empowering question because most of the time our answer is purely subjective. When my appetite needs feelings of assurance and my circumstances are negative, the hunger pains can become unbearable. If there is no change in mood then the belief a person embraces will be 'lethargy.'

However, when I am in an optimistic mood I respond to negativity with a proactive response: 'What can I learn right now that will get me to the place I am seeking to go?' This removes feelings of powerlessness and empowers a person so that they can determine the result of any situation. It moves them to ask, 'How am I going to allow this process to make and not break me?'

Optimism is confident presence

Optimism creates a hopeful confidence. Confidence is a powerful mood and mindset. It is contagious and can be hugely attractive in team or family environments. Confidence is not so much about rhetoric, although positive and affirming words will flow from an inner confidence; it is about presence. Optimism is created when I have an internal supply of assurance. I then produce feelings of security in the lives of others. This is profoundly attractive.

A leader is someone in whom people feel they can have confidence. They feel safe following them. The leader may not be the loudest voice but their inner confidence creates a positive awareness in others that it is safe to be under their influence.

Optimism is living to the optimum

The word optimistic comes from the Latin word *optimum* which means 'the best thing.'[12] Optimism is a state of being hope-full, believing the best thing will prevail. The medical and scientific world now accepts the link between a person's daily disposition of hope and their ability to fend off sickness. There appears to be an intrinsic link between hope and our immune system.

12. optimism. Oxford Dictionaries. Oxford University Press, n.d. Web. 04 September 2015.

We can all look back at negative events that actually produced a good outcome, one that we would not trade in for anything. The optimist is determined that they are never going to miss the opportunity within a difficulty because every event can be used for ultimate good if they are in the right state to process it correctly.

If I am in a pessimistic mood then the outcome is self-destructive. My mood is managed from the outside-in and my feelings rob me of the opportunity that obstacles present. Pessimism is the belief that life is working against me and ultimately my future is outside of my control.

Choose to be aware of your Soul Script

How I feel has a direct impact on the choices I make. While feelings do not and should not rule our actions, they exist for a purpose; they are an integral part of us outworking our beliefs and engaging with the world around us. Feelings need to be instructed and directed to fall in line behind our beliefs. They then become an indispensible asset to you winning in life.

Our feelings revolve around three major focus points.

1) How I feel about myself

2) How I feel about others

3) How I feel about the future

Let's see what happens when our soul-script is dominated by a conversation of lethargy and when it's dominated by a conversation of passion.

The Losing Soul Script of Lethargy:

OUTSIDE-IN

My mood is PESSIMISTIC which tells me:

Conversation lead: Lethargy
Conversation flow: Consumer
Soul appetite: Need Assurance

When LETHARGY leads my conversation I am a CONSUMER

and my lack of ASSURANCE leaves me feeling an overwhelming sense of being UNASSURED and in a PESSIMISTIC mood

'To be unassured is to feel fearful, apprehensive and undisciplined'

The script of the *lethargic* conversation will shape our perspectives in such a way that we will be *Self-destructive, Me-obsessed* and *Now-focussed*.

Self destructive statements from a *lethargic* belief sound like this:

i) I am not up to the change I want to see
ii) My past failures are evidence that I am not up to this
iii) I am what I feel
iv) If I try, I am setting myself up for failure
v) I am content with what currently satisfies me

Me-obsessed statements from a *lethargic* belief sound like this:

i) I cannot help my reaction; it's who I am. I can't be that person
ii) They make me feel this way and so how I feel is their responsibility
iii) I will reach out to others when someone shows belief in me
iv) I can always see someone more suitable for what is needed
v) Someone else will do something about it

Now-focussed statements from a *lethargic* belief sound like this:

i) My future will be a repeat of what I have seen in my home environment
ii) I am powerless to change my future
iii) I am never going to feel any different about what I am experiencing right now
iv) Maybe it has already been decided that I can't and won't...
v) I am a realist and so will not deceive myself with dreams or goals

We are often unaware of the statements that inform our decisions. These statements are often feelings and so we do not quantify them in words. However, hosting the right conversation means describing the feelings we have in statements. Write them out and look at them. If you are not happy with the descriptions, you can change them by changing the belief, the command. Your feelings are subject to your beliefs, so if you are unhappy with your feelings, change your beliefs.

The Winning Soul Script of Passion:

INSIDE-OUT

My mood is OPTIMISTIC which tells me:

Conversation lead: Passion
Conversation flow: Producer
Soul appetite: Full of Assurance

When PASSION leads my conversation I am a PRODUCER and feel ASSURANCE and I produce an OPTIMISTIC mood

'Assurance leaves us feeling confident, motivated and disciplined'

The script of the passionate conversation will shape my perspectives in such a way that I will *Value Myself, Value Others* and *Value the Future:*

i) Value Myself

ii) Value Others

iii) Value the Future

Optimism is a positive and assured declaration intended to give confidence. It is a state of certainty often required in periods of uncertainty. When you are immersed in a conversation of assurance it could be described as 'believing and feeling that you are more powerful than the challenge that confronts you.' Unexpected circumstances in life can create extreme uncertainty. We naturally try to shore up the foundation for our need to feel safe and secure by using external materials. Our jobs, relationships, finances and health can all provide temporary levies. However these all have limits; they are subject to change and are fragile materials.

A champion understands that this kind of optimism comes from belief. What lasts is what is unseen. Assurance comes from believing in a life-giving principle that is timeless and unchanging in every dire situation or circumstance.

Passion produces resilience and this becomes a source of safety and assurance for others. It makes you a leader worth following and a parent worth emulating. Everything you do carries the hallmarks of a safe feeling. Human beings are profoundly attracted to this feeling; more and more people will want what you have.

Turning up the Voice of Passion

The following statements are examples of the kind of script that flow from a conversation where passion is at the table. Remember, these statements produce feelings. Champions do not wait for the feelings to exist in order to act upon them.

So what does the new script sound like?

It flows from the inside-out and makes the following kinds of statements:

VALUING MYSELF

i) I am able to keep going
ii) My feelings are not an indication of my limits
iii) I will get through this and be thankful along the way
iv) This test will produce character in me
v) The size of the test reveals the depth of my potential

VALUING OTHERS

i) I can respond as I would want to be spoken to
ii) I will persevere to inspire others to go further than me
iii) Drawing on the strength of others is not weakness
iv) I will have the conversation when to avoid it would be easier
v) I am not running alone, others are counting on me

VALUING THE FUTURE

i) My future does not reflect my past
ii) My beliefs are the only limits I impose on my future
iii) I can persevere through this situation and it will enrich my future
iv) My mess can be my message

v)   I am the architect of my future

Conversation with myself: It is important that I create a time of reflection to identify my current soul script and make the necessary decisions to change it. The examples on this page are not exhaustive. I must discover my specific narrative and make choices to change any outside-in statement as I seek to host the winning conversation.

Day 29: The Winning Mindset of Perseverance

High level focus through persevering regardless

When I host the voice of *passion* in the *boardroom of my beliefs* I feel a deep sense of assurance and I know I can *persevere regardless* of what is happening to me. Adopting this mindset is the next stage in unlocking MORE resilience in my life which will enable me to achieve my *winning goal* in life.

When I adopt the winning mindset of perseverance, I realise that 'I can' master my approach to everyday life in the following way.

1) Persevere regardless of the fights that choose me
I can pick the size of my fights

We have all had fights. From the lighthearted play fights to those that create relational distance. What is it that causes us to fight? It could be a sense of injustice, a deep resentment, a sense of isolation or revenge for being wronged. We allow something that happens to us to get on the inside of us. What is external provokes an internal reaction.

Two people can react very differently to the same set of circumstances. So it cannot be the external circumstance that is the determining factor in the response. It has to be what is inside a person. An internal decision is made by one person to fight while the other chooses to reject the fight.

The size of the fight reflects the size of the person inside of you.

If I choose to allow a look, a comment or an offence to become my fight, then that circumstance actually reveals more about me than the other person. If I choose to fight someone based on the fact their behaviour annoys me, then I am deciding that the energy that it takes in engaging in the fight is worthy of such a cause.

Do you really want that to be your cause?

There are fights that are positive—the fight against injustice, poverty and corruption. When a person chooses to make a stand to combat such great evils, it reveals the size of what is inside them—a fighting spirit that enables them to overcome tremendous difficulties in their lives.

What we fight we become…so pick your fights carefully

I have seen people make a small offence their fight and this has shaped their attitude not only towards the offender but to everything else they see. They remain oblivious to it but the fight they have chosen has intrinsically shaped who they are.

A fight causes a person to engage every aspect of who they are with another person, circumstance or situation. No one ever walks away the same after full engagement in a fight. Why is that? It is because a fight enlists our core being (soul and spirit) and whatever we engage with at that level shapes the lens through which we view the world around us. Be aware that the fight you choose shapes the filter through which all your decisions are made.

There is a good fight and there is a bad fight. It is my belief that we all need a fight, a cause. It is time to lay down the negative fights and pick a good fight. You were born to fight and born to win!

2) Persevere regardless by correctly labelling my feelings
I can reassign meaning to my feelings

My feelings do not have to rule my life? We all have feelings but sometimes it can seem that feelings have a hold on us.

It may be a job, a season of life, a relationship or a period of intense ambiguity that appears to cause your life to be at the mercy of how you feel. However, I want to encourage you to see how you can use your feelings for the benefit of your future.

Sometimes you can just push through feelings and it's appropriate to do that. However, there are times when all we are doing is putting off having to deal with the cause. It's like shaking a can of cola: it's either going to explode or go flat. This is what happens to life when we fail to harness the potential of feelings and challenges.

Correctly labelling our feelings requires us to understand three questions.

i)   What is a feeling?

ii) What is a challenge?

iii) What do I want in my future?

Understanding the answers to these questions unlocks tremendous potential.

i) What is a feeling?

A feeling is an interpretation of an experience. People can interpret almost identical experiences differently. Two people can be made redundant from the same company, one says, 'This is exciting because it's a new opportunity to do something different, something I am more passionate about.' The other says, 'That job is all I am good at.' Who has the correct interpretation? Neither one is right or wrong because an experience can mean what you want it to mean. One sees it as an opportunity to bring about a better future. The other allows the circumstance to place a cap on their self worth.

Feelings are the result of the lens through which we view experiences. Feelings are not facts. A feeling is not the highest authority in your life; there is a greater authority and that is choice. You can choose to live under the authority of your feelings or you can make your feelings subordinate to choice.

The winning mindset will use feelings to fuel positive choices.

The more intense and regular the feelings, the more energy this mindset will put behind the choice that shapes the future.

ii) What is a challenge?

Challenges, problems or obstacles are merely facts that have yet to be interpreted. Many of us allow the challenges we face to become a mirror revealing 'truths' about who we are. Their only meaning is the labels we attach to them. Challenges can become what we want them to become. When used correctly they are an opportunity to hone a conviction. Challenges provide an opportunity to clarify our convictions. Convictions are choices that have intense desires attached to them. The sharper our convictions the quicker we make our choices and the greater quality they carry. Challenges, like feelings, have immense potential behind them if we learn to utilise them correctly.

The winning mindset recognises that a challenge is essential for progress.

iii) What do I want in my future?

Without a clear picture of a preferred future, our feelings and challenges can cause us to look back to a period when we felt better and things were easier. It can create an unhealthy nostalgia for the past. It can even distort the past, making it seem better than it really was.

The only valid direction is forwards. If we have clarity on what we long to see happen, our feelings and challenges can push us and compel us to reach and stretch into the future. When we do this our hearts are filled with a renewed sense of belief and certainty. My feelings and challenges are working for my good to unlock dormant potential inside of me when led by a clear picture or goal. Every feeling and challenge, regardless of how negative we perceive it to be, can propel us into a greater future.

3) Persevere regardless by relegating practice below principle
I can make my practices follow my principles

The antithesis of passion is lethargy. If I were to ask you to conjure up a mental picture of what lethargy looks like, what would you say? I am guessing we would all have similar images. Someone who cannot get out of bed or someone slouched back in an armchair maybe wearing their night wear in the middle of the day. The picture is one of inactivity, where any attempt to get motivated fails and the path of least resistance is the more appealing.

We need to be aware that at the root of this feeling is a belief. You can get out of that lethargic state but you need a new belief. When passion sits at the table of conversation I am reminded that to change a practice (the WHAT) I have to start from the inside-out with a principle. A definite decision to follow the command of a principle will kick start a chain reaction. It will inform my purpose which will determine my priorities and alter my practice.

When you do not feel like doing what you know you need to be doing imagine that principle as a person who reaches out their hand and pulls you up from your lethargic state into your passionate purpose.

4) Persevere regardless by drawing new conclusions
I do not have to settle for the conclusions I have; I can draw new ones

Our conclusions are the final judgment on something or someone. They are deep beliefs and scripts inside each of us. Some of these can be useful when it comes to fulfilling the plot of our lives. However, many may in fact be working against us—especially those that have already established how the chapters are going to end.

A lot of activity in life is futile if our conclusions go unchallenged. Challenging them is in itself a challenge because they are often deep rooted and shifting them is not a small overnight task. Our conclusions become fixed points to which our lives become firmly anchored.

What do these look like?

Let's take a conclusion about money: 'The accumulation of money is reflective of how good I am as a person.'

Finance Author and TV personality Dave Ramsey says, 'We buy things we don't need with money we don't have to impress people we don't like.'

The conclusion is based on a belief that 'my worth is determined by how I believe others see me.'

Here's a conclusion about faith: 'I must earn God's love and acceptance.'

Many people struggle to receive anything for free. Something inside has concluded that the only route to receiving is through earning. This is a self-destructive belief.

Here are other conclusions which form a losing conversation:

AFFECTION: I am worth only the affection I receive

ACHIEVEMENT: I am what I do; I will become what I have always produced

AUTHORITY: I am invisible to the world around me and have no voice

ACCEPTANCE: I am willing to do whatever it takes in order to feel accepted

APPRECIATION: The way I am made to feel is my worth

ASSURANCE: I am secure in what I possess

So what has this got to do with a mindset that perseveres regardless?

More often than not I watch football highlights as opposed to the full length games. When my favourite team plays and I know the result it determines whether I want to watch it or not. My motivation is determined by the conclusion I know. I will not want to miss the highlights of a great victory!

While it may not be in the forefront of our minds, the conclusions in our heart are determining the motivation for what we choose to do in our lives.

I have played in football games where I have simply looked at the opposition and said, 'There is no way we are going to win this.' I made a conclusion before kicking the ball. I see it in my children. They say, 'Daddy, what's the point? I will never be able to do it.' They draw a conclusion and the conclusions create their future.

The only way to combat this is to change the conclusions.

How can I identify the conclusions in my subconscious mind? They are exposed through the words we use—repeated phrases we speak and/or think that usually contain the words: 'I can't... I will never... That is not me...'

I am going to go a step further and say that phrases such as, 'I may... might... think... could... would... seem... possibly... probably,' are rooted in negative beliefs. Why? Because a conclusion carries no sense of question; it is a definitive statement. The winning mindset establishes positive conclusions that power us to keep pressing on regardless.

5) Persevere regardless through hiding in my belief
I can take cover in the shelter of my impenetrable belief

Our beliefs are tested when our world is shaken. Like shelter in bad weather, the effectiveness of the building's materials and construction are tested during the storms not the still days. In life it can move from a beautiful sunny day to a stormy day very quickly. What do we do when the weather turns bad while out for a walk? We run for cover and if possible get into a familiar place outside of the storm's impact.

I appreciate my home the most when I am inside and the storm is on the outside. When storms break out our beliefs are the shelter into which we can find safety and assurance. The storm will test the effectiveness of our beliefs.

When I look at key moments when I have stepped out and taken decisions that carried high elements of risk, the only way I coped was to have total clarity on my beliefs and convictions. The more certain my conclusions are, the more I feel safe when external challenges or storms seek to undermine that belief. To run and take cover in conclusions when everything seems uncertain enables us to use the storm for our benefit. Storms strengthen resolve and certainty. The more certainty we have in our hearts the more passion we ignite and passion is what changes the world around us.

This is how you unlock motivation. The storm can stir your appreciation for your beliefs and awaken the impenetrable, unstoppable and relentless conviction that you can, you will, you must keep persevering. It transforms your feelings, your thoughts and pushes you over the line into continued action.

6) Persevere regardless through turning annoyance into an assignment

I can turn my negative annoyance into a positive assignment

What do you regularly get annoyed about? Is there a recurring complaint? There is a seed in your annoyance that reveals something about your assignment. Everyone solves a problem and the problem you solve unlocks the story and the potential in you.

Your annoyance will be linked to questions you ask such as, 'Why does someone not fix this problem?' 'Why do people tolerate this?' 'Why are people remaining silent on this issue?' 'Why has someone not thought of a solution for this? Surely it's obvious.'

Persevering regardless is about proactively using what otherwise would cause you to quit to empower you to grow.

Step 1: Take your annoyance into a secret place

Annoyances are like manure; unless you do something useful with it then you become the annoyance because you begin to stink. Write down what you think someone could and/or should do about the problem. Start to ask, 'Could it be that it is obvious to me because I am part of the solution?' At this point it is important to do it alone so that you can distil your thoughts. When the annoyance has been directly impacting your daily life this act can be truly liberating because it creates an internal sense of hope and hope produces the quantity of assurance that we need if we are to be a winner in life.

Step 2: Don't get an opinion, get options

Spend time coming up with as many options as possible. Again keep this to yourself at this stage as opinions from others could interfere with what your annoyance is really showing you.

Step 3: Be ready to be part of a solution

Once you have distilled which annoyances are 'pointless' and those that are 'pointing' you in a certain direction, it is time to start telling yourself aloud, 'The solution to your annoyance is facing you in the mirror!'

Step 4: Write it down and as simply as possible

It needs to be simple enough that the clarity it gives you keeps your awareness heightened and makes you ready to further your solution finding process. When you daily repeat the assignment based on the annoyance, it keeps it bubbling away in your subconscious which means the moment you meet someone or see something you can start to piece the puzzle of your assignment together.

If the annoyance affects you regularly then writing it down every time it hits you will help you remove yourself from a reaction. Remember this little saying, 'What gets penned, gets perspective.' There is something powerful about penning down our thoughts and feelings. For many years now I have typed out or written thoughts, frustrations, feelings and prayers; it has been powerful to help me get perspective. It is also a great source of encouragement when you take time to be grateful.

Step 5: Wait for the right time to share it

There are people who are ready to run for you. They are 'make it happen' people who have a part to play in your story. This is where the interconnectedness of life gets really exciting. Believe it or not, there are people waiting for your annoyance to surface; it will form a positive step to making a difference.

Step 6: Prepare yourself for the cost

Your annoyance will not let go of you. This is what makes it an assignment. Sometimes you will feel like giving up and want to walk away because it will demand everything you have but then you realise it has hold of you, you do not have hold of it. What you cannot shake off shapes you.

Most stories worth reading have low points where the main character hits 'rock bottom.' You will hit this at some point. Sometimes things get worse before better but this is because the story you will make will first make you. Whatever you do, keep going.

A stagnant annoyance with no investment of movement will embitter you. While there may not be an obvious outward change to your annoyance, the most important factor can keep on changing and that is you! Water the seed of your belief and protect the soil of your mind and the growth will take care of itself. Invest in your winning conversation and the results will follow.

Step 7: Get ready for it to grow you as you grow others

Your passion will point to a place that seems beyond you. You know it's your assignment when it looks like it must belong to someone else and yet a little part of you dares to believe it's yours! There is one principle that needs to be remembered if it is truly to be your assignment. If it does not involve helping others connect to their assignment it is not your assignment. A champion knows that the winning conversation always involves helping someone else to host the winning conversation in their life.

Seize this moment and get on with your assignment!

7) Persevere regardless and you will produce what you are looking for

I can be a super-cow and not a selfish-cow

When I lack a sense of assurance I become insecure. Insecurity is when something or someone makes me feel unsafe. When this happens I start to centre my attitude and activity around how I feel. This state of mind makes me a consumer and I stop giving out for fear of me appearing to have less. When I am insecure I lock myself in my own world and shut the door on the needs of others.

I call this the 'selfish cow' syndrome. If you are near a window, look out and imagine a cow stood there. Now go with me and use your imagination to hear the cow whining and wailing out loud,

'Will someone please give me a drink of milk?' 'Why are you selfish people not helping me?' 'I deserve a drink of milk. Can you not see all that I do, all that I contribute?'

What is wrong with that picture? You may ask 'Why does a producer of milk need a drink of milk?' A selfish cow is someone who has the ability to be a super producing cow but expects others to make the first move. The way for the selfish cow to get a drink of milk is to produce it.

A person who is passionate does not wait for a feeling of security to come in order to give assurance to others. They produce assurance for others and in doing so create a personal sense of assurance. Stop being a selfish cow and be a super cow!!!

8) Persevere regardless by creating constant change
I can incrementally control my rate of change through daily changes that build resilience

We have established that change happens. A sign that something is healthy is that it is changing. Your body is constantly changing, replenishing nails and skin amongst other things. There is a continual renewal process taking place in your body which determines your health. The winning mindset embraces change because it daily chooses change. By creating daily incremental changes you will be more ready for any change that is determined outside of your control. Creating momentum in personal change will get you ahead of the game.

Continually refining and reviewing your Life MAP and immersing yourself in the *winning conversation* you will be challenged to keep making small adjustments. Small adjustments over time help you prepare for or even prevent the trauma that can happen when major changes come in your life circumstances.

9) Persevere regardless by learning to feel a choice before I make it
If it feels good tomorrow, I will do it today

Have you ever picked up a large packet of biscuits, opened a cake or large bag of sweets and known that you have the potential to keep eating them until you run out? Despite knowing there is a high possibility of you doing this, you still go on and do it? Later you regret opening the packet because now you feel bloated and lethargic.

What if you could harness the feeling of regret in the moment before you picked the packet up or even when you are in the supermarket walking past the shelf? Our default setting is, 'If it feels good, do it.' However we know operating from that premise will get us into all kinds of situations that we would not want. A champion can pull a future feeling into the now moment and then decide to feel the benefit.

You can take this practice to any area of your life. How do I want my children to feel about me when I am drawing my last breath? I want them to be thankful for a father who was faithful to their mother. I need to visit that place and feel it. Then should temptation come to be unfaithful, I can draw the future feeling into the immediate moment.

10) Persevere regardless by recycling the past into fuel for the future
I can make use of any experience to create momentum toward my goal

Passion recycles everything into fuel for my future through disciplined choice.

"Where there is muck there's brass!" This was a phrase that originated from Yorkshire, England, in the 20th century. The expression suggested that even the things that people throw away have the potential to create money (brass). Whether it is waste from animals or scrap metal from old appliances, this saying communicates the opportunity that lies behind seemingly unwanted things.

Millions of pounds are being spent today to see how waste can be used to produce valuable energy for homes and businesses. Again, 'unwanted' things are being seen as opportunities to extract something of value.

There are many unwanted things in life and not just mere household items or waste. Life is full of unwanted situations and scenarios—unemployment, relationship breakdown, financial troubles, missed opportunities, health problems, to name but a few. While no 'sane' person would choose to go through these situations, these circumstances have value that needs to be extracted.

The mindset of perseverance identifies a problem as potential. Where there is an obstacle they observe an opportunity. Rather than being filled with hopelessness and despair this mindset produces greater levels of hope because there is 'brass where there is muck'—there is something I want inside something I do not want.

'The more muck the more brass' means 'the more problems the more passion' and the greater the promise must be!

Choose your response today to fan the fire of passion with the oxygen of hope.

Conversation with myself: Which one or two statements do I struggle to believe? Which specific belief must I stay aware of and practice in everything I do today? I must remember that in order to achieve what I want most I must be willing to tackle what I want to do least.

Day 30: The Winning Choices of Completing aggressively

Today we look at some practical ways you can develop the winning conversation that will make you MORE resilient in life. The more you inform the right choices, the more you activate the results.

To be a winner you have to learn to fight. It is in the fight that the voice of passion will be required to produce the perseverance necessary to complete what you have started. By doing this the new you will shine through. Your resilience will then become part of your reputation as a finisher and not a quitter.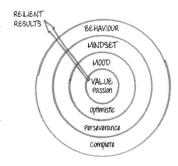

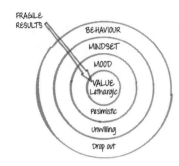

So what can you do practically to help unlock the potential of passion in the conversation of your life? How do you cultivate the resilience that allows you to cross the finish line of your goals aggressively?

FIGHT TO THE FINISH

Daily you will need some time to prepare yourself for the day. While this could be at any time I believe first thing in the morning is the optimum time because it means that you are then in a state of readiness throughout the day.

FIGHT

Find a place
Immerse
GRAB the new
Hold down belief
Test through practice

Find *a place*

When living the winning conversation, which requires an inside-out paradigm, it is vital that you find a place of stillness because how you set yourself on the inside will determine what makes itself to the outside world.

Immerse *yourself*

Create an opportunity at the beginning of the day to read this book and/or other books that produce life-giving principles. Allowing these to soak into your thinking is vital as it feeds your belief system.

As well as this you can listen to material in the car or on the commute, read a book during break, discuss with others. Create the immersive experience you need.

GRAB *the new*

Embodying the new conversation does not happen by chance; it happens by choice. It will be more of a wrestle than a soft encouragement to oneself—such is the strength of our defaults.

Two moves are critical in a wrestling fight: the grab and the hold:

THE GRAB:

Galvanise Gratitude
Review and realign
Affirm I AM
Believe I CAN

Galvanise *Gratitude*

Decide on at least three things to be grateful for every day. Think about these and allow the emotion of gratitude to oil your passion motor. Never underestimate the power of gratitude.

Review *and realign*

When reviewing the previous day or the day so far, are there any actions I need to take? Do I need to ask forgiveness from someone? What did I do right? What needs more investment? Where have I left the course and need to steer back onto the right path? Doing this daily means smaller changes. The longer the gap between reviews the more severe and difficult the changes. Doing this daily increases assurance and confidence and builds resilience.

Affirm *I AM*

Every investment and correction starts at WHO I AM. So what do I need to affirm today? This book is designed to be a continuous conversation and so read some of it every day and stay on course.

Believe *I CAN*

Make a definite decision that you can and remind yourself what you CAN now do. Remember it will require FIGHTING talk with yourself and brutal honesty.

THE HOLD:

Hold down belief

When we hold down a belief long enough over time it will create the change of mood, mindset and behaviour we long to see. In wrestling, the hold is the final move that leads to victory. The one performing the move holds the opponent until there submission is communicated by either the opponent or referee. Hold a belief long enough and the internal components of your soul, mind and body have to submit to it.

Test through practice

Only an experience will solidify the belief so FIGHT to decide what challenge you will embrace today to set another brick in the building that represents the grand design of WHO you are. Imagine yourself operating the winning conversation in a situation you choose to encounter today.

If we repeat this process daily then the beliefs we hold down and practice become our habits. If our habits are the shaping force behind the person we become then we need to give them daily health checks. What are the habits with which have I made a personal agreement to develop? Which habits am I keeping and which am I breaking? What habits do I need to start?

Sometimes we need to stir up our positive aggression that will create forward progression through creating a controlled crisis:

COMPLETE A CONTROLLED CRISIS

With business and commerce so reliant on the internet and new technologies, many companies will enlist the help of security experts to help look for the flaws in their systems so that they can identify the holes and fill them in. Many former computer hackers who illegally gained access into top companies have been put to good use and been offered legitimate work. The old adage 'it takes one to know one' comes to mind here. What better person to help prevent hacking than a hacker?

What the company is doing is very smart. It is in fact creating its own controlled crisis. Why do this? The board realises that not all crises are bad. Look at the diagram on the right:

These companies are creating a 'controlled' crisis in order to prevent the destruction that comes from an 'uncontrolled crisis.' Have you ever witnessed a bomb scare where a suspicious package is identified and the bomb squad use a radio controlled robot to go in and create a controlled explosion? They do this to prevent an uncontrolled explosion which could result in mass damage to buildings and more importantly human life.

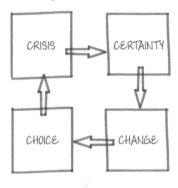

The more controlled crises created by a company in the area of their security, the more likely they are to reduce the chances of uncontrolled crisis.

So what are the benefits of a crisis?

A CRISIS LEADS TO CLARITY

The most recent financial crisis that started in 2007-2008 resulted in the closing of many businesses. It was not the crisis that caused the companies to become sic; rather, the crisis revealed severe underlying and preexisting health issues. It created conditions that exposed many false assumptions made by business owners and leaders. It highlighted the weaknesses and even corruption of principles that had become integral to the culture of many businesses.

The financial crisis forced every business and most of the world's governing bodies to get clarity on the reality of their finances, systems and legislation. While profits declined as confidence in the markets shrunk, all eyes were on the expenditure lines that had not previously been scrutinised. In the UK it revealed many areas of wastage in our government departments. Every practice in every company was questioned in a bid to reduce costs—the one area that could be controlled.

When a person suffers a heart attack, it is not the heart attack that produces the crisis. If the heart attack is the result of blocked arteries then it could have been years of bad eating habits and lack of exercise. In this situation, the crisis simply highlights and makes clear the already existing problem. While a medical opinion may not have voluntarily been sought before this moment, it will now because of the urgency precipitated by the 'uncontrolled crisis.'

If clarity is essential for preventing the destruction from an <u>uncontrolled</u> crisis, then it makes sense to create a <u>controlled</u> crisis where clarity can be revealed now rather than later, when it might be too late.

CLARITY LEADS TO CERTAINTY

Once clarity has been gained, people usually ask, 'How can we prevent this from happening again?' This question is frequently asked in an 'uncontrolled crisis.' Disaster proves to be the emotive catalyst for a positive response. It is often the case that victims of crimes where loved ones are lost will use the crisis as a means of positive response. It will often be said, 'If this loss can prevent the loss of others then this death is not in vain.' As human beings we need to feel that there is purpose even in the darkest hour because purpose is the result of hope and we are wired for hope.

When we find ourselves in a situation that is out of our control we long to find something we feel we can control. While a crisis which has happened in the past it out of a person's control, a future which has yet to be determined is still potentially in our control.

The more CERTAIN a person becomes of the CHANGE they want to see, the more likely they will move from an intention to an action. Certainty is about what we believe and what we truly believe in our hearts is what will become a reality in our lives. The more secure the belief, the more secure the chances of it becoming a reality.

CERTAINTY LEADS TO CHANGE

There will be things in your life as there are in mine that have taken place because at a point in time we were certain of it. This could be a positive or a negative outcome but either way our level of certainty would have played a key role. The greater the certainty, the higher the commitment we have to the outcome becoming a reality. Our certainty becomes our purpose, like the rudder on a boat. Our priorities are shaped and these produce the outcomes we see.

If we prioritise good health, based on a certainty that we will be in good health, then the chances of us being in good health are heightened. If we prioritise good finances, based on a certainty that our finances will be healthy, the chances are we will be financially fit.

CHANGE CREATES MOMENTUM

There is nothing like a goal being achieved to inspire a drive in us to identify another goal to go for. The more you create controlled crisis the more clarity you produce, the greater the certainty and the more change you see. The more goals reached, the more crisis you want to create.

Ask yourself how you can create a crisis in the four key areas that are your CAUSE, RELATIONSHIPS, FAMILY, WELLNESS, FINANCES and HEALTH. The areas where you want to see change will determine the kind of crisis you need to create. Which areas of your life scored low when you took the test at the start of the chapter? Was it your relationships which may include your marriage? If you do nothing about that your current behaviour is feeding an uncontrolled crisis down the line. It is time to get ahead and to create a crisis now.

Based on your current assessment of the results in these areas of your life, what kind of uncontrolled crisis could take place? When is the likely chance that will happen if you did nothing about it? Allow this process to create an emotion in you that inspires you to get a picture of a preferred future. Stir yourself by creating a crisis.

WHAT IS MY NEXT STEP?

Once you have created crisis in the four key areas of your life then make sure you action the following four things.

STEP

Share it. With a person or people you trust, share the crisis you have created and the goals this has now produced. When our goals are not shared they have a lower chance of being achieved. Sharing produces much needed accountability, a personal pressure that keeps us motivated in making the necessary choices.

Teach it. After learning the principles in this chapter, why not teach them to others? The best way of learning is by teaching. The more I can repeatedly teach something, the more I will own and embody the teaching.

Exercise it. A muscle that is not exercised cannot grow. The more you exercise your muscles the more you feel like exercising them. Identify ways in which you can exercise these principles and keep on with them.

Picture it. Picture yourself having achieved the result of your goal already. The more you can capture that picture the more emotional energy you create for achieving that goal. Believe you have already won. Now it's about getting what is in you out of you!

Day 31: The Winning Evaluation

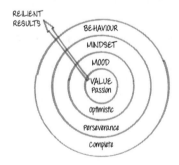

Benchmark which mindset you have when it comes to the RESILIENT conversation.

The fruit of my actions will reveal the root of the conversations I host. Today we are looking at 10 questions or statements we make based on situations in which we find ourselves. I encourage you to be brutally honest as to which response most fits your nature. Tally up how many you answered according to which voice and make a decision to go back to your inner conversations to strengthen your foundation as a champion. If you feel frustrated then that is not a bad thing as long as you focus that frustration on making certain your commitment to hosting the winning conversation.

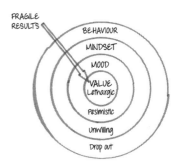

1) Capacity—Can your capacity be increased and how?

Consumed - My capacity is something I don't give much thought to, I fill my time and when it's full it's full.

Complacent - My capacity can possibly be increased when the opportunity comes to offload responsibilities. I'll just wait and see.

Competitor - I actively seek to get more into my life in order to grow my capacity and yet this can produce an adverse effect I struggle to complete things. I guess that's just the price of busyness.

Champion - I actively seek to grow my capacity through tackling and completing the right tasks. I understand that my capacity is not grown through busyness but effective use of my time.

2) Wholeness—Do you treat your emotional, mental, spiritual and physical components equally?

Consumed - I do not think that they are equally important.

Complacent - I try to think about all four as I see their benefit but I am not actively looking to grow each area.

Competitor - I know they are all vital to my wellbeing but I tend to favour one over the rest.

Champion - It is vital that I learn to invest in each area as this gives lift to my whole being. Balancing my accounts helps me unlock my potential.

3) Confidence - Is confidence something you actively seek to develop?

Consumed - Confidence is connected to the type of personality you are. A person can become more confident but this is limited by their personality type.

Complacent - I feel more confident when others encourage me based on what I have done. Therefore the more I get around people who encourage me the more confident I will become.

Competitor - I will not shy away from opportunities to grow my confidence. When they present themselves to me I will evaluate them.

Champion - Confidence is grown through my willingness to embrace challenge. I will daily challenge myself to step beyond what is comfortable which will deepen my convictions and build confidence in me. My level of confidence is in my hands.

4) Completion—How important is it to complete what has been started?

Consumed - Completing tasks is admirable but not essential.

Complacent - Completing tasks that have the highest importance is important and trying best to do the same with other tasks is advisable.

Competitor - I attempt to complete everything but with my desire to grow I always have more to do than I can possibly complete.

Champion - Completion is vital. Therefore I will take time to assess my ability to complete a challenge. Self doubt decreases the more I take on bigger challenges and commit to complete them.

5) Enthusiasm - How do you view enthusiasm?

Consumed - It is good to be enthusiastic but this can only be expected in those areas people like.

Complacent - Enthusiasm is important to achieving a good result. Enthusiasm, however, is unpredictable and not always within a person's control.

Competitor - Enthusiasm is very important because how I feel while doing something is important not only for the quality of result but also those I may lead. I do not always display my enthusiasm outwardly.

Champion - Enthusiasm is a choice that is imperative if I am going to attribute any resource to a task. The more demonstrative my enthusiasm the more I feel enthusiastic inside and the more energy the task receives.

6) Reaction—Is my reaction my responsibility?

Consumed - People can make you react a certain way and therefore they must accept the responsibility. I never want people to think I am a 'doormat.'

Complacent - Sometimes reacting to another person is inevitable and so it depends on the circumstances.

Competitor - Reaction is never a good thing. It is better not to say anything and just keep going.

Champion - Taking the time to think through a response that builds strength is essential. Avoiding any kind of response is not helpful, especially with those in a team environment, as trust erodes when situations are not confronted.

7) Rest—Is rest important?

Complacent - Rest becomes boring and counterproductive and so I fill my spare time with mindless pursuits.

Consumed - Rest is a luxury that I can afford when things quieten down from my busyness.

Competitor - Cramming my week and then finding space to relax at the weekend or when on holiday feels productive and the right way to go about life.

Champion - Rest is vital to build resilience. It needs to be weaved into the rhythm of the week. Resilience is not built on constant activity. Rest is a place I should be working from not working for.

8) Disappointment—What do you do when you feel disappointment?

Consumed - I avoid disappointment by not setting goals. If something good happens then I will celebrate. However I do not want disappointment in my life. Previous disappointments have taken the wind out of my sails.

Complacent - Disappointment can set me back for a period and even a season of my life, but eventually I get back to the place I was before.

Competitor - I get down when I am disappointed and I am prone to focusing on other areas of my life until the disappointment wears off.

Champion - Disappointment is a perspective and not the deciding factor in my life. I must learn to evaluate moments when I feel disappointed. The moment disappointment happens is the best time to sharpen conviction.

9) Thoughts—Is it important to manage your thoughts?

Consumed - I do not spend much time thinking about the way I think. I do not see the significance.

Complacent - Managing my thought life is very important but I do not have anything in place to do this.

Competitor - Every now and again I have to spend time sorting my thinking out. When my mindset is clearly affecting what I want to do I make sure I do something about it.

Champion - Managing my thoughts needs to be part of my daily rhythm. I actively try to understand what I am unaware of as I know I am not consciously aware of many of the thoughts that are shaping my actions.

10) Exercise—How important do you rate physical exercise?

Consumer - It is great if you are that kind of person but most of the time it is a necessary evil.

Complacent - Being physically in shape is important and I attempt to use the latest methods to achieve fitness. However, this often starts with enthusiasm but dissipates after a short period of time.

Competitor - I have a plan to stay physically fit and try my best to keep to it.

Champion - I have fitness <u>goals</u> because I know growing this area will influence the other capacities in my life. Physical endurance creates endurance mentally, emotionally and spiritually.

PRACTICE V POTENTIAL of the RESILIENT conversation

Based on the answers to the above questions, how many times could you honestly say that your answer was 'champion'?

Consumer: 1-2 times
Complacent: 3-5 times
Competitor: 6-8 times
Champion: 9-10 times

My Overall POTENTIAL: I AM A CHAMPION

MY Overall PRACTICE: I HAVE BEEN A _____

In order for my practice to match my potential I have identified the following three things I can do to unlock the champion in me:

1_____

2_____

3_____

Day 32: The Winning Accountability

Pulling this whole week under the title of 'be stirred and not shaken' enables us to be able to review this conversation quickly. Using the dice in spare moments throughout the day, or in a small group, helps me to focus on the inner conversation of passion.

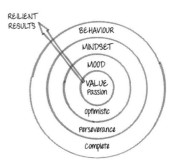

The Winning Dice—**Be stirred and not shaken**

Resilience is a person's inner strength. The only way to develop

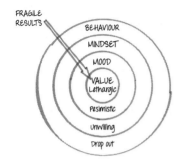

resilience is by persevering regardless through challenging situations.

When you are stirred, you begin to shake the potential that has become settled. When it comes to carbonated drinks the last thing you want to do is shake the bottle. The shaking produces a build up of pressure and when the pressure increases beyond the ability of the container to hold it, it will explode. When we do not learn to handle the pressures and challenges of life correctly, this is what happens to us. The challenges do us harm rather than bring us value.

I hope I have achieved my aim through this conversation, to create a paradigm shift in each one of us so that we realise that every challenge is indeed a gift. It is an opportunity that can produce something of real value. The key is in our response. If we recognise that every shaking can help us to realign our focus to an unshakeable principle then our lives can be more like bottles of freshly squeezed juice. These containers encourage the consumer to shake the bottle well before drinking in order to get the best possible taste. The act of shaking shifts the goodness from the base of the bottle to the rest of the container. This is what challenges can do in your life. They cause the principles in our belief system to produce fruit in our emotional, mental and physical lives.

An unsettling feeling can in fact be the start of a fruitful period. You can run from this and look again for what produces the settled feeling but you will close the door on a new season of results if you do. You have to ask what you want more—a feeling or a new result? Your next steps will prove your genuine desire.

In sharing this principle with others and the community where you work and play we are aiming to create a cultural expectation. There are many times when we do not feel up to doing something. Sometimes people require a word or challenge that shakes them into action. However, with the 'winning conversation' we choose to stir what is in us and choose to be up for it before feeling up to it.

We make a decision that helps our thoughts and feelings to follow the right pattern.

When we stir up enthusiasm, this is a discipline that relies on internal and not external stimulation. We can stir ourselves into action. We can choose to be passionate rather than wait for something or someone to make us feel passionate.

We stir our imaginations to solve problems and find alternative ways of doing things when what we do is shaken. However, every day we can choose to stir up our thinking so that we discipline ourselves to embrace change by choice rather than circumstance.

Similarly, we get old on the inside when we stop seeking new ways of doing things and we become content with what we have already learnt rather than seeking to learn new things. We want adventure, change and new things and so we choose to make that happen rather than wait for it to happen by chance.

Here is a quick review of what is required if PASSION is to have the loudest voice, drowning out LETHARGY.

Step 1: RECALL together

You can choose to stir yourself from the inside-out or be shaken from the outside-in. The two choices reflect WHO you have determined to be.

What does 'being stirred' look like?
You learn to confide in faith, counsel your feelings and consult the facts

You do not allow your circumstances to set your attitude

You are consistent in setting the bar high in all things

You do not need telling to 'step up'

You have an internal desire to do and be better

You are always up for new challenges in order to see greater results

You like to mix things up because freshness is more important than predictability

You exude the freshness of new life

You sense the strength of your core identity in conversation and practice

You are disciplined in all areas of life—mental, physical, emotional as well as spiritual.

What does it mean to be 'shaken'?

You will easily take things the wrong way

You are highly sensitive and defensive

You are insecure regarding change because what you do is your security

You will go underground during difficult times

Your attitude is set for you

You think other things/people are to blame for the way they are

You let feelings lead you

You allow misery to get on the inside

People feel like they are treading on egg shells around you

People cannot guess what mood you are in from day to day

Productivity and effectiveness will be directly linked to how well things are going in your life, not in spite of what is going on

Step 2: REVIEW with others

With people who are committed to developing the winning conversations get together weekly throughout the journey of this book and this week do the following:

i) Share a time when you were shaken? Knowing what you know now, what would you have done differently?

ii) Give an example of someone who has inspired you because they stirred up what was in them and persevered?

iii) Who do you want to model this to in your circle of influence?

iv) How can you help others create assurance in their lives?

v) What were the key limitations that you know are going to be the hardest to overcome? How could the person or group you are talking to help you overcome them?

vi) Do you have any wins to celebrate now? Inspire one another with your stories.

vii) What wins do you want to celebrate one week from now, six months from now and one year from now?

Step 3: REFLECTION to be shared

Now share a reflection with someone in your group or someone else that you are coaching to be a champion in life. Why not take the time with your children, loved one, or friend over coffee to share what you have learnt. Simply sharing this reflection will accomplish much in your life and deepen relationships, enriching them with vulnerability and moments of movement.

Follow our basic structure:

i. What I realised for the first time/again this week is ….. (share the thought)

ii. The change I need to make is …… (share the action point)

iii. Can you help me make it (Invite help and create accountability)

Once you have developed the habit of doing this, why not decide to turn your thoughts into a blog or even take your coaching to another level? There is so much in you and it is directly connected to your commitment to stretch yourself.

Section 6: Be MORE memorable

Day 33: The Winning Conversation makes you MORE memorable

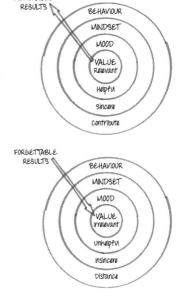

Unlocking your potential is directly linked to helping others unlock theirs. The more meaningful connections a person develops, the more potential is unlocked.

Conversations create connections. The quality and quantity of your conversations with others will directly impact how much potential you unlock in your lifetime. When the voice of relevance is in the board room of belief, a person is able to connect more deeply to others than most people.

The definition of relevance is to be closely connected to the matter at hand.[13]

We are in the information age which means that the challenge to become memorable goes beyond the information you provide and becomes about how your information connects to other people. Never before have we had such an opportunity to connect through border-removing technologies. At the same time, however, loneliness, disconnection and fragmentation continue to grow. The connections on offer do not always lead to meaningful conversations.

13. Oxford Dictionaries. Oxford University Press, n.d. Web. 07 September 2015.

You are designed to be memorable. There is something about you that sets you apart from the majority. This difference becomes obvious when your conversations with others go to a deeper place. While small talk is a great tool, it is merely the gate to a deeper connection. A conversation that is memorable has distinct qualities.

The quality of your outward conversation is due to the quality of your internal conversation. Becoming memorable is simply about keeping a conversation going long enough to reveal the authentic you. The longer your conversation continues the more it should enrich others.

When we are aware of our ordinariness, this becomes the biggest hindrance to our belief that we are memorable in our interaction with other people. However, becoming memorable is not about how interesting we can become but how interested we can be in others.

When I host the MEMORABLE conversation I become:

1) MORE intriguing
The riches of life are unearthed through the value of my conversations

Conversations connect people. They are the currency of opportunity. If you are going to get out of you what is in you then you have to become rich in conversation.

So how do you become rich in conversation? Questions provide answers, therefore the more intrigued we can become by people, the more questions we ask and the more answers we get.

In every conversation imagine you are digging for gold. You know you have struck gold in a conversation when a person talks about what they value most. You will notice how their face changes; their tone alters too when you connect with what they truly value.

Having these conversations is not always comfortable and sometimes it will feel as though you are not uncovering very much. However, if you persevere it will pay off. One trip to the gym will not produce the results you desire but a commitment to the process will do so over time. The more your conversations flow from a genuine desire to know someone, the more your own life is enriched.

Being intrigued by others and then reflecting their value back to them unlocks the door to the real them. In the moment it is almost never obvious which doors or riches are being unlocked though any one conversation. Conversations do not come with a predetermined label stating their significance. No one can anticipate the potential of a conversation. But while you cannot control where a conversation will go, you can position yourself for the best outcomes and enjoy the journey of discovery.

This is the art of building rapport. I have heard a mnemonic and acrostic for RAPPORT: Really All People Prefer Others Reflecting Themselves. The more we reflect others the more people will prefer to talk to us.

2) MORE attuned to how people feel
The right words at the right time make you a 'go to' person

I use an analogy to help me remain aware of the power of conversations.

Every person has their own radio station and I call it 'Soul FM'. A conversation is like a song. There are songs we like and ones we don't. Likewise there are conversations we like and dislike. We all have conversations that reverberate around our souls like a music track on repeat. Some of them we are conscious of and others we have become oblivious to, but they are still playing in the background.

What are the most played tracks on the radio station of your soul? Remember the soul is a source for the mind which informs our decisions. This shows us how important conversations are to the shaping of peoples' lives, including our own.

Like our favourite songs, we are attracted back to positive conversations we have had with others because we like how they made us feel. The winning conversation adds value to people and this is the surest way of keeping a conversation alive and continuous. These conversations have the potential to become the most played tracks in someone else's life and have the power to shape them.

The way to get airplay on Soul FM is to make the conversation entirely about the other person where possible. The champion seeks every opportunity to add value to the person through listening well and seizing opportunities to add relevant truth. The more you do this the more memorable you become and the greater chance you have of being one of the most played 'songs' on 'soul FM.'

The winning conversation will increase the amount of number 1 hits you share on soul FM.

3) MORE aware of converging conversations
If you could follow the significant journey of your words beyond your lifetime, you would decrease the quantity and increase the quality

Every person has a conversation that has truly impacted their life. Take a moment to think of a conversation that has brought you to the place you are today. I encourage you not only to think of a positive example but a negative one too. Both can form what I call a 'momentous conversation.'

So what leads to a momentous conversation? It is the convergence of your internal conversation with an external conversation another person is having with you. A definition of Convergence is 'the concurrence of opinions.'[14] When my self-opinion collides with the opinion given from another person the result can be momentous.

I remember being at a conference as a teenager and hearing a keynote speaker deliver an inspiring message on the power of dreams. There may have been approximately 80-100 young people in the room but it was as if the conversation were just between the speaker and me. His talk converged with an internal conversation I was having about where my life was heading and the reason I was alive. It was my momentous conversation.

A momentous conversation can leave an indelible mark on your understanding of WHO you are. No one person can orchestrate this. This is why two people can sit in a presentation, talk or conversation and one walks away saying 'that was incredible' and the other looks

14. (Definition of converge from the Cambridge Advanced Learner's Dictionary & Thesaurus © Cambridge University Press)

surprised because for them it was forgettable. While no one person can orchestrate a momentous conversation, a champion carries the awareness that they can position themselves to be ready for those special moments. You may never find out that you were part of a momentous conversation but champions have the conversations anyway because they believe in a process and a cause bigger than themselves.

Have you ever gone back to a person and told them how influential and memorable a conversation was that you had with them? The person who spoke to you is often unaware that their conversation had such an impact. Champions expect their conversations to be key moments in peoples' lives even if they never discover how impactful they were.

Many years after my momentous conversation, I was involved with the group who put on that conference I attended as a teenager. Some of the leaders at the time were reminiscing about this very conference and how embarrassing it was. It had had a low turnout and they had brought in a high profile speaker. They spoke as if the whole event had been a failure. I had the pleasure of telling them that what they viewed as a failure was for me the biggest success.

4) MORE focussed on building a platform
When you think your conversations are not taking effect, keep talking!

It is important to remember that a conversation is a continual dialogue between two or more people. It is very difficult, although not impossible, to become memorable to someone during one conversation at one moment in time. The winning conversation is about becoming a continuous source of value to those around us.

It takes time to build the kind of conversation with someone that truly influences who they are becoming. In the world of instant social media, everyone has direct access to a soapbox—a place where opinions can be declared in the hope that someone is going to take notice and 'like' or 'favourite' our statement. People take to the internet as a means of becoming an instant voice that will be heard.

While we have the greatest opportunity in history to be instant, we also have the greatest chance of being forgotten. Memorable conversations come through a commitment to keep a rich conversation alive—one that adds momentous value to someone. The value we add keeps the person open to more and even causes them to seek out the conversation. When you continually demonstrate care and value for someone through conversation you become increasingly relevant to their lives.

5) MORE attentive to others' priorities
Prioritise others and others will prioritise you

With both music and TV shows, we can favourite our preferences and even allow computers to find the programmes it thinks we will like based on our viewing habits. We prioritise what is relevant and relegate what is irrelevant. If we want our conversation to be prioritised by others, we have to make sure that it connects with what they desire.

We bookmark our favourite blog sites, favourite our contacts, have the most valued people on speed-dial. The result of becoming memorable is that you make it into the special place, those areas reserved for the people that matter most to them. A champion does not do this in order to gain a sense of personal value; it is the result of what happens when we commit ourselves to the needs of others.

Being memorable is about creating relevant moments of conversation. One person taps into the need of another and deposits something of value. When high quality conversations take place regularly in your day-to-day life you stand out from the crowd and you become the 'go to' person. People recall your conversation and want to pick it back up again because you learnt how to connect with what they think is important. The more we become aware of what others prioritise, the more memorable we become to them.

6) MORE committed to moments of movement
Our memory favours those who move us

Remembering long lists of numbers and names can be very difficult and yet we have a huge capacity to store an amazing amount of information. Why is it I struggle to remember a number given to me for an office code door thirty minutes ago but I remember a conversation from thirty years ago? It's because a number does not tap into our emotions whereas formative experiences do.

When you create movement in your internal conversation you will start to move people with your external conversations. The more you move people in conversation the more they want to hear your voice. The winning conversation is a rich conversation that adds value to the lives of others.

All this involves cultivating an internal conversation that cannot help spilling out into the conversations we have with others. When I clarify continuously my belief that I am relevant to the people I meet, I unlock an authority to have a conversation that moves them. Moments of movement happen when we focus all our energy and attention on the person and seek to be a lift to their lives. Our conversation is then about revealing a glimpse of their value to themselves. It is about us becoming a mirror that reflects true value back.

People who are antagonistic and hard to converse with are usually that way because they have become hardened through a process of being immersed in negative self-conversation. The way to bring change to this person is to try and help change what they believe about the way they see themselves.

7) MORE authentic
People connect to my authenticity not my 'perfection'

Your personal reality is what is most attractive about you. There is nothing more unattractive than someone trying to be someone they are not. This is usually because they are desperate to feed their internal need for acceptance from the outside-in. Yet the beauty of a person is when they come clean and go real. Relevance is about being real. Once you are real it gives permission to the other person to be the same. You need someone to be real with you in order to create a memorable conversation.

Creating a memorable conversation is not about saying things that are not true, stroking the ego of someone to get what you want. A truly memorable conversation is speaking the truth in a way that will empower someone to be who they can be.

I am an avid watcher of 'reality' TV programmes. The makers of these programmes know what the viewers really want because they have understood what it takes to make a memorable show. They find an ordinary person who has had struggles and weaknesses because they know that something in the human psyche can relate to this and then show how this person steps from obscurity into victory.

Our ability to be authentic and real creates our greatest opportunity for connection. The result of this conversation means you grow in increasing confidence when engaging in conversations because of a belief that you are worthy of having the conversations. You become someone off whom others want to bounce thoughts and ideas. This means that there will be opportunities opened up to you that are not open to others who have avoided or missed the conversations through being irrelevant. Your empathy and compassion for others will increase as you engage with them through listening rather than presenting yourself with the aim of gaining approval.

Day 34: The Winning Voice of Relevance

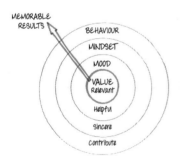

To be a person of Relevance I have to immerse myself in the commands that are going to lead me into the right feelings. The more I immerse myself in the belief that I am relevant the more memorable I will become.

i) I AM committed to inconvenience
My inconvenience is someone else's convenience

My ultimate goals in life are reliant on my being relevant in the immediate moment. Hidden in people are the keys that unlock my future but in order to find them I have to help them unlock their future. Living from the inside-out involves my awareness that the immediate does not take precedence over the ultimate. My inconvenience is someone else's convenience. When I live from a place of relevance I will find that others will help me at their inconvenience which conveniently gets me to where I need to go.

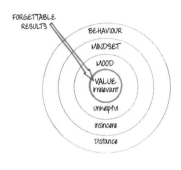

Conversation with myself: How can I practice being inconvenienced today to reinforce this belief?

ii) I AM a source for others
Help others expand to become more expansive

The source of what you need lies in helping others discover what they need. Many people have tried to defy this principle and it costs dearly. A self-centred world is a very small and lonely place to live. We are designed to live expansive and large lives and the route to this is through helping others expand who they are.

Our lives are a treasure chest of experiences, ideas, strengths, talents but we often live with the belief that no one could find this useful. Have you ever thought of selling something and held back because you asked, 'Would anyone really want to buy that?' People sell things every day after pushing past an initial doubt whether anyone would want to buy what they had. They believed what they were selling was of value to someone.

You will be amazed how much value you can add to others.

Conversation with myself: Can I think of a recent conversation where I could have offered my help? Decide to follow that conversation up to ask if you could be of service.

iii) I AM compatible
I become compatible when I become compassionate

Being relevant starts with the belief that there is not a single person with whom I cannot connect. I realise that there are those

271

who are not willing to participate in a conversation and give you a chance. However, that has nothing to do with what you believe. Living inside-out is not about second guessing an outcome. When we do this we talk ourselves out of things. A champion positions themselves for the conversation regardless of what they think the outcome will be. They do this because they believe that no one is beneath the conversation, no one is off limits. They believe deep down that they can connect with anyone and everyone.

Relevance is about connecting deeper than social class, educational background and origin. It is about connecting at the deepest human level. I will show you how to do this later but it has to start with believing in your fundamental compatibility with others.

Conversation with myself: Which conversations have I been avoiding for fear of not being able to add value? Make a move today.

iv) I AM an open book
My authenticity is my appeal

I have a personality defined as choleric; I am therefore driven and wired to achieve. I am always on the look out to help fix other people. However, this is not what people always need. People want the real you. In order to connect with you at a deep level they have to feel like what they see is really what they will get!

When people feel like you are real with them it gives them permission to be real with you. Open the book of your life and you have the greater chance of them opening up to you. Have you noticed that it's when you are most relaxed that you are truly yourself. When you are in this state people feel they can get to the real you. Late in the evening, over a drink, in a relaxed atmosphere, the real you comes out. While you cannot be in that environment all the time, you can maintain the disposition of being real.

Conversation with myself: Think of a current challenge you are willing to share with others. Be real in future conversations by sharing it with an appropriate person.

v) I AM eager to learn
I am a learner before I am a teacher

Teachability is an endearing and attractive trait. There is nothing more frustrating than being locked in a conversation or relationship with someone who is more interested in lecturing you than learning from you. Jigsaw pieces are created to connect both ways (in and out). We too are designed to interconnect. When we find this relationship with people then we have something we can build that strengthens both parties.

Conversation with myself: In my conversations with others today I am going to remember to ask great questions. Based on the conversations I know I am going to have what questions could I ask?

vi) I AM wired to empathise
When I understand then I can be understood

The path to relevance is through trying to put myself in another person's shoes, to see what they see and to feel what they feel. The more I get into the position of the other person, the more my conversation will become memorable.

We can sometimes categorise ourselves as a 'feelings person' or 'not a feelings person.' While certain people have certain strengths, we all have the capacity to put ourselves in the shoes of another and to find our place in helping them get to where they need to go. The voice of relevance causes us to become more empathetic.

Conversation with myself: Think of someone currently experiencing a challenge. Take a moment and put yourself in their shoes. How do you feel? Now communicate that you are thinking of them based on how they must be feeling.

vii) I AM a solution
Listen hard enough and you will hear a problem you can solve

Through my connections I can find the purpose for my existence. The more rich conversations I have the more I will discover the problem that I was born to solve. When I believe that I am a solution I start to cultivate the feelings of being relevant. This starts to create the ideas for solutions and ultimately adds value and becomes memorable to someone because of how I connected to them.

Conversation with myself: From a recent conversation list any challenges that you can recall. Do you see an opportunity to bring a solution?

viii) I AM built to resonate
Only the <u>real</u> me will resonate with others

To resonate means to *produce or be filled with a deep, full, reverberating sound.*[15] Or it can mean to meet with agreement. Every human being is built to resonate. When you hit a point of resonance you know it. It goes deeper than thoughts and feelings; it is deeply spiritual. It is the power of shared belief. The awareness of the winning conversation enables us to communicate in a way that resonates with anyone who is willing to open up to us.

Conversation with myself: When was the last time you felt a resonance with someone? What did the conversation contain that led to this deep connection?

ix) I AM a 'lifter' of people
I am lifted when I lift others

A conversation with someone can either leave you feeling lifted up or weighed down. The conversations we avoid are those that leave us feeling worn out, like someone has tied a weight to our ankle. People remember the extremely good and bad conversations. So in order to become memorable and make it into someone's top list of conversations, you need to work at bringing the 'lift' to people. People return to conversations that left them lifted and feeling bigger.

Conversation with myself: Think of your most memorable conversations with people. How did they bring a lift to your life? How can you do the same to others today?

15. Oxford Dictionaries. Oxford University Press, n.d. Web. 08 September 2015.

x) I AM always leaning in
I am learning when I am leaning

As a leader I look for the posture of people when they are around me because I have learnt that commitment is more important than competence. I can tell in meetings who are the ones who have the commitment to make our goals and objectives work. They are not the ones leaning back in their chairs but those who are leaning into the conversation. Those who lean into a conversation are those I engage with the most. They have the ability to draw more out of me and in turn cause me to draw more out of them. The winning conversation causes people to lean in. Those who lean into me are building a platform; they are more relevant and they become more memorable.

Make the decision to live life at 45 degrees and lean!

Conversation with myself: How can I position myself as a learner today? How does this differ from what I normally do?

Day 35: The Winning Mood of helpfulness

Unlocking the power of WHY creates a helpful mood

My WHY is my PURPOSE. My purpose is the vision of my life. My vision is the future that I choose to have. Vision is potent because it ignites hope inside me. Hope has an unrivalled way of lifting negative mood clouds that drift into the horizons of my thinking. The winning mood is stimulated when I choose to keep clarifying and reminding myself of my vision, my winning purpose. I must follow the pattern of the winning purpose from the inside-out, from the WHO to the WHAT. The power of our WHY is the power of positivity that creates motion in our lives.

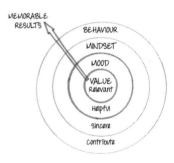

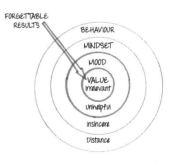

275

I am having the MEMORABLE conversation led by the voice of relevance which means I choose to put myself in a HELPFUL mood.

A helpful mood brings clarity to my voice

If my winning purpose is a message I want to impact others positively, then being in a state of readiness to help others makes my voice louder. When people say 'I have no purpose' and yet could easily list hundreds of needs in the community in which they live, never mind in another location, it highlights a consumer mindset and an outside-in way of living.

While there are needs there are opportunities for the WHY of our lives to get heard. The mood of helpfulness is not about becoming opportunistic, manipulating the person in need so as to get your own way. A helpful mood is the flexible approach of a person who truly values human life.

Helpfulness makes me value conversations more

Conversations can sometimes be mundane when they have no apparent relevance to my current situation. This can produce an insular focus in which I could miss moments of significance. However, when I approach a conversation with another person with a helpful mood then I can always move beyond small talk.

People always have challenges or need solutions to improve their lives. If I am truly seeking to be helpful then my mood will manage my mindset and I will feel a sense of responsibility to leave every conversation having added something of value. A producer seeks every opportunity they can to produce something that adds real value to another person. What adds the greatest value to an individual is a solution to a problem they have. While you may have something of value that you would like to communicate to them, their immediate need takes precedence and if you want to become memorable to them, be helpful.

Helpfulness sown is helpfulness reaped

I need a lot of help when it comes to obtaining the goals I need to reach. Where is this help going to come from? If I can help many on their journey then there will be no shortage of 'help options' for my needs.

This is not a form of 'I scratch your back so you scratch mine.' We are talking about authentic relationships in which we genuinely long to see others do well and succeed in life. Relationships are the currency of life and the more I invest in relationships the more relationships will naturally begin to add value to my life and journey. People remember those who helped them.

So become memorable!

The gift of 'lift'

When I am in a helpful mood, I ask myself when engaging in conversations, 'How can I bring lift to this person right now?' We give lift by either removing something that is weighing them down or by adding something that brings lightness to them.

People may be going through difficult challenges, struggling to keep day-to-day activities going. A helpful mood positions me to ask if there is anything I can do to remove unnecessary weight. Sometimes thirty minutes over a coffee enables you to bring a fresh and positive perspective that brings lightness to a person.

We can all bring lift to people we meet when we step into a helpful mood. This mood alone enables us to sharpen our solution-finding skills which not only makes us memorable but also valuable.

Choose to be aware of your Soul Script

Moods are of course related to feelings and feelings need to be instructed and directed to fall in line behind our beliefs.

Our feelings revolve around three major focus points.

1) How I feel about myself
2) How I feel about others
3) How I feel about the future

Let's see what happens when our soul-script is dominated

by a conversation of irrelevance and when it's dominated by a conversation of relevance.

The Losing Soul Script of Irrelevance:

When IRRELEVANCE leads my conversation I am a CONSUMER and my lack of AUTHORITY leaves me feel an overwhelming sense of being UNAUTHORISED and in an UNHELPFUL mood

'To be unauthorised is not having the right or approval to act.'

The script of the *irrelevant* conversation will shape my perspectives in such a way that I will be *Self-destructive, Me-obsessed* and *Now-focussed.*

Self-destructive statements from an *irrelevant* belief sound like this:

i) I have nothing this person needs
ii) Who am I to add value?
iii) This person has already rejected me so why bother
iv) This conversation will make no difference
v) I have nothing in common with this person

Me-obsessed statements from an *irrelevant* belief sound like this:

i) I will connect with them because they may have something I need
ii) I will connect with them so I can show them what I know
iii) I will connect with them to avoid connecting with others
iv) I will not connect with them because I see no relevance
v) I will not connect with them because of what others may think

Now-focussed statements from an *irellevant* belief sound like this:

i) I do not have time for this conversation
ii) I do not want more connections
iii) I have more than enough people in my life
iv) I do not feel like talking to other people

The Winning Soul Script of Relevance:

When RELEVANCE leads my conversation I am a PRODUCER and have AUTHORITY. I am then in a HELPFUL mood.

'Authority is the permission to do or say something. It is the power to act.'

The script of the relevant conversation will shape my perspective in such a way that I will *Value Myself, Value Others* and *Value the Future.*

i) Value Myself

ii) Value Others

iii) Value The Future

Carrying authority could otherwise be described as 'having the permission to speak out.'

Relevance is about carrying a sense of authority. A friend of mine who is a policeman tells me that there are times when he is not at work and he sees an incident and forgets that he is not at work and yet everything in him is ready to step in. Why is that? Because he lives much of his life in the position of knowing he is a policeman and carries the feeling of authority that comes with it.

If you were a doctor and you were out shopping and someone collapsed near you, you would instinctively respond because you carry a feeling of authority based on the belief, 'I am relevant in this situation and can add value to this person.'

This is why relevance cannot be worked from the outside-in. You can try and become relevant by behavioural change alone and yet sooner or later you will hit the feeling that you can connect with another person in a particular situation. We need to cultivate internal conversations if we are to create an external difference.

Turning up the voice of relevance

Connections bring great personal benefits to our lives. Businesses are built upon connections. Connecting with people who would be advantageous to you is not a sin. If you start from the place of being RELEVANT and INCLUSIVE, you will multiply the benefits to yourself even though your prime motivation is to add value to them.

I can hear the voices in me that are in you, the script that says, 'I could end up wasting a whole lot of time on the wrong people!' The law of relevance runs alongside the law of sowing and reaping. As you value the WHOSOEVER, you will be amazed in time as to WHO sows back into you.

So what does the new script sound like? It flows inside-out and the voice should make the following kinds of statements:

Statements that *value myself* from the valued belief of *relevance* sound like this…

i)   My performance is not key, my motivation is
ii) Helping others grow helps me grow
iii) I am invited to this conversation to listen intently and build value
iv) My relevance is not based on the result of my last conversation whether good, bad or indifferent
v)   I am entrusted with this person's most precious commodity, time.

Statements that *value* others from a *relevance* belief sound like this:

i)   I have a message you need to hear and I commit myself to earning the right to share it
ii) I am about legacy before I am about profit
iii) I am helping all the people this person will go on to help
iv) Results will come but I am committed to simply adding value
v)   The consequences of this conversation will reach into my future either as a result of what is taking place in them or in me.

Statements that *value* my future from the valued belief of *relevance* sound like this:

i)   There is no such thing as a wasted conversation; all people are valuable

ii)   My contribution is based on their need not how I feel

iii) I am part of their journey even if it's just for one step

iv) How I feel in the conversation is of secondary importance

v)   My personal goals will not cloud my genuine motivation to add value.

Conversation with myself: It is important that I create a time of reflection to identify my current soul script and make the necessary decisions to change it. The examples on this page are not exhaustive. I must discover my specific narrative and make choices to change any outside-in statement as I seek to host the winning conversation.

Day 36: The Winning Mindset of Sincerity

High level focus through promoting others selflessly

When I choose the mindset of a champion then I promote others selflessly.

My potential is unlocked through new beliefs that have formed new attitudes. It is not that I could not do it before; it is that I did not have the belief and desire to unlock the activity. Now the voice of relevance is at the conversation table of my life, I feel I have authority and I know I can be relevant in practice.

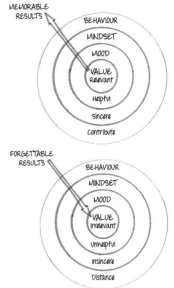

As a winner I believe in promoting others selflessly as this mindset will create future opportunities and unlock my potential.

The winning mindset means that I daily determine to…

1) Promote others through reinforcing value

Reinforcing value in a person reinforces your position in their minds

When I have unlocked a certain belief that I am relevant I know that I can see something in another person that is not obvious to them. In my conversations I resolve to point these things out. My words might turn out to be in accord with those of a long line of people to point this out. They might also converge with a conversation that is going on inside of them (the 'momentous conversation').

2) Promote others through asking great questions
The quality of the question determines the quality of the answer

I am not expecting people to reveal their inmost thoughts without any help. I can ask questions to discover more about the person and the quality of these questions will determine the quality of the answers. When I receive an answer I am trying not only to hear what they say but also how they say it. The way someone answers a question can give me a greater understanding of the person and how the information they have just shared has helped to define who they are.

3) Promote others through quality listening
The longer I listen, the more valuable and memorable I become to someone

When we carry a strong sense of purpose we can be overly eager to share it with the world. There is nothing wrong with the natural desire to pass on what we value but if we want the other person to share our passion we need to understand that this takes time. When I commit myself to connecting with them, over time my cause will start to speak for me. A cause is more than just an idea; it is an inseparable part of everything I am about. Our cause needs to be demonstrated through our actions more than our words. Therefore, if I maintain a posture position of listening, I communicate my cause more effectively than if I gave the person a presentation.

What you are about is best caught not taught. People are more open to catching what we are about when we are positioned as an intense listener. The longer we listen the more we valuable and memorable we become to them. The best connectors are world-class listeners.

4) Promote others by going beyond small talk
'Small talk' exists to lead us to 'big talk'

The words 'I am not into small talk' must never leave my lips again. When there is a true desire to listen and ask great questions, small talk leads to big talk. Small talk is the preparation for a quality conversation. Small talk helps us learn those things that are vital for deepening the conversation. For instance during small talk you can establish the mood of a person and their general circumstances. You can communicate your value towards them by remembering their name, the names of those close to them, asking how those people are and by picking up on any details from a previous conversation. This makes the other person feel that you are not like everyone else; you really do value them.

5) Promote others through unlocking doors
Feel for the key that they are looking for

As I talk to someone I imagine I have a large golden key that feels like it can open a significant door. While talking to them I ask myself, 'What is the door? How can I help this person unlock it using the key that I have?' When you carry a belief that you can do something, you stop asking 'can I help this person?' You start saying, 'I know I have something I can give this person to help them, I just need to locate it.'

Have a think right now of those conversations that helped unlock doors for you. You may be able to recall quite a few conversations where that has happened. There will be many other people who have had pleasant conversations with you but these are not memorable because they did not bring a solution to your world.

Find the key!

6) Promote others through finding the common ground
Every person has a point of engagement if I look hard enough

There are some conversations that take very little time to 'light'. It's like throwing a match on dry firewood doused in petrol. There are other conversations that feel like the wood has been sat in the damp and no flame is going to cause them to ignite. But when I host the winning conversation I know that I am like a jigsaw piece, shaped to connect into them if I keep persevering and find the join. The persistency will pay off. While it may not produce immediate or visible results, you are strengthening the muscle of relevance. You know that every pushback, every act of resistance, strengthens your abilities in this area.

7) Promote others through connecting to WHO they are before WHAT they do
Engage with the identity before the capability of a person

When we are in conversation with a person we naturally think, 'What can this person do for me?' However, if our approach is one of seeking to understand the person we are talking to before what they do then we can connect on a deeper level.

When we compliment people we tend to compliment WHAT they do more than WHO they are. Why is this? It is because a clear statement about WHO the person is to me takes us to a deeper emotional engagement. This deeper level is one at which not everyone feels they can operate. However, the winning conversation empowers the deeper conversation because you carry an authority to communicate on an emotional level based on your development of your own emotional strength.

A simple example is how we address someone. We often ask, 'How are things?' 'How is your day?' The better address is, 'How are you?' The more our conversation can stay on WHO the person is the more we communicate that we care and the more we build a platform with them. Trust is developed through demonstrating care. Trust is the currency that makes life work productively.

8) Promote others through attracting favour
You cannot fight for favour; you have to earn it

There is a difference between trying to become 'flavour of the month' with people and 'attracting favour.' The more I fight for favour with people the more I start to create a perception of the person I think they want me to be. This creates the worst disconnect and irrelevancy. People are perceptive and while sometimes people might buy into our perception for a while, there will soon come a moment when we step out of character and any trust accumulated will be gone.

Favour is about order. As I continue to invest in being a producer for others, I know that others are working for my good without me even being aware of it. When we serve other people we operate on a spiritual level. Selfless service towards other people influences the subconscious of the people we serve. In fact, many times people we have positively impacted are working for our good when even they are not aware of it. Our conversations over time have deposited something in their sub-conscious that has shaped their decisions in our favour. I need to believe that there is a powerful force called favour and that it works for the benefit of those who are selfless.

9) Promote others through the strength of humility
Humility will create the permission to keep a conversation going

We often perceive Mr or Mrs Relevant to be the person who is an extrovert—the 'life and soul of the party.' We see them as people who have the charisma to connect with anyone. However, we must not be duped into thinking that this approach or disposition produces lasting results.

Humility lives in the person who does not need to convince another of their worth in order to strengthen what they believe about themselves. Humility is comfortable with making a conversation all about the other person. The strongest virtue a person can obtain is humility. Humility creates the permission to keep a conversation going.

10) Promote others freely and end up rich
Meaningful relationships are worth their weight in gold

Being rich is more than asset worth; it is about self-worth. True self-worth does not come through the accumulation of good but through the accumulation of meaningful relationships. A relationship grows in meaning when we promote others through the resources and strength that we have.

In summary: the winning conversation is not focussed on WHAT a person can extract from a connection. Putting someone else first is not a 'clever tactic;' it must be genuine otherwise we end up in duplicity. This is harmful and damaging to relationships and does not produce memorable results.

When we genuinely promote others freely we are actually investing in our inner strength. The more we promote others the greater sense of importance we develop. The more that is invested in a person because of who they are, the greater the return in the long run and the greater quality of investment we make in ourselves.

Wealth that is the worth that comes through using all available resources to promote the lives of other people.

Conversation with myself: Which one or two statements do I struggle to believe? Which specific belief must I stay aware of and practice in everything I do today? I must remember that in order to achieve what I want most I must be willing to tackle what I want to do least.

Day 37: The Winning Choices of Contributing Proactively

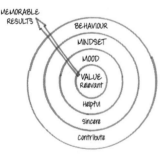

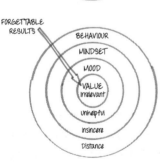

Today we look at some practical ways to develop the winning conversation that will make you MORE memorable. The more you inform the right choices, the more you activate the results.

If you start a conversation with someone for the first time, you will want them to want the conversation to continue. When you do not have any relational credit with them, you have to start creating some in that first conversation. Your ultimate goal is to create an opportunity that allows you to contribute value to them and in turn establish credibility and trust.

Building that platform takes time. It requires you to become an intense listener who knows how to create relevant moments through asking great questions. To create a 'relevant moment' you must learn to shut everything else out of the conversation and focus solely on the person. This gives you the best opportunity for engaging your intuition, soul, mind and body in the conversation. Remember that the quality of your external conversation is determined by the quality of your internal conversation. If your mind is engaging with the distractions around the room, or another line of internal thought, then your focus will be sabotaged and the quality of your external conversation will plummet. We have all been on the receiving end of conversations with people we knew were not present to us. We feel demoted in value because something or someone else is clearly more important.

You need to listen intensely so that you can make statements that create a rapport with the other person. Here are some LISTEN statements that will lead you to make quality observations.

Stay RELEVANT by following this process:

Recall last time
Engage your whole self
Learn key facts
Echo their answers
Value through LISTENING
Avoid over-thinking
Next steps leave them lighter
Talk it back and see solutions

Let's look at these:

Recall *last time*

When someone picks up the last conversation you had with them and remembers what you talked about, you know that you mattered in those moments. You had their attention. Despite their busyness, they remembered you. The pause button was pressed; now 'play' is being pressed. Not only does the conversation carry on; the relational investment is reactivated. This will lead to positive results.

Engage *your whole self*

A conversation is more than just words. While people will rarely be aware of it, there are multiple conversations going on during one conversation. From the way a person stands, to their eye movements and even breathing, many messages are being communicated. A person's body language can put others at ease or on edge. It is futile to work on our words if our body language overrules it with an alternative message.

My relevant behaviour will mean I fully engage my WHOLE self. I become irrelevant when I allow my mind to drift off to something that happened thirty seconds ago, yesterday or something I am anticipating. When I am not in the NOW moment I am out of the game and I cannot produce a memorable conversation. I want my entire being to be focused on the person I am talking to so they feel the maximum value.

Learn *key facts*

Every person has a drawer full of valuables, a place where they put their most important things. As you talk with someone, imagine this drawer with their name on it. As you talk, recognise the things they are passionate about and visualise putting them in the valuables drawer. When you pull these things out of the imaginary drawer in future conversations, you will have their attention because you are valuing what they value. Now you have entered the top 1% of conversations.

There are four P's that help us look for these valuables:

People - those they love and care for

Pleasure - what they do with the precious spare time they have

Possessions - how they express themselves through what they own

Places - where they have been or are going that speaks of who they are.

Echo their answers

The challenge with conversations is that they can become a

multitasking activity if we are not careful. We ask questions or make statements and then rehearse the next lines while the other person is answering. The reality is that it is impossible to multitask. As someone has said, 'to do two things at the same time is to do neither.' We can only focus on one thing at a time which is why it is good to have drummed into our subconscious those patterns that our conversations need to follow. This frees us up to engage wholeheartedly and not be stuck for what to talk about.

The best way to remember what is being said is for us to echo what is being said. When we put another's words in our own voice two things happen. Firstly, we can be corrected should we have heard incorrectly; secondly, we are more likely to remember what we parrot back to ourselves.

I am not advocating a weird kind of repetition of everything people say but the echoing of key facts which help us to remember what has been said. This takes data from short-term to mid-term memory.

Value *through LISTEN*

Here are key statements or questions you can ask that will set you apart from the 99% of other conversations:

LISTEN

'What I **LOVE** about you is...' Examples '...you never give up...you put others first...you bring the best out of me...you are consistent when others are not...'

'I can **IMAGINE** you...' Examples '...turning this story into a book one day...taking this product to market...writing songs from your experience...going for this career...teaching others through your experience.'

'I can **SEE** your strengths are...' Example '...empathising with those in need...motivating those on the periphery of life...breaking down a challenge and coming up with potential solutions...'

'**TELL** me about your challenges...' Example '...at work...

achieving a long term goal…developing that skill to a new level.'

'You **ENCOURAGE** me when you…' Example … 'don't allow your challenges to change your attitude… when you do what you do day-in, day-out…you smile at people all the time even when you are going through challenges…'

'**NEVER** underestimate what… this means/does' … Example … 'your influence through what you do… how you encourage me.'

Avoid over-thinking

You need to keep as much clear thinking space as possible in order to stay in the now moment. Over-thinking how you are coming across and where this conversation could lead takes you out of the now moment. It is easy to switch from a producer who is trying to solve a problem to a consumer who is only concerned with how they are coming across. It is so easy to make the conversation about us; when we do this we become irrelevant.

Next steps *leave them lighter*

Ask yourself the question, 'What is the one thing I can do to help someone walk away with a greater lightness in their step?' It could be a commitment to go away and think of a solution or an offer to follow up the conversation. The old adage of 'a problem shared is a problem halved' has much truth; when you help others with their problems you ignite the law of sowing and reaping; those who sow generously will reap generously.

Talk it back *and see solutions*

When you leave a conversation, the information you have downloaded is in a time-critical phase; you need to talk it back soon in order to put it into the long-term memory box. This discipline may at times feel totally unnecessary. However, the champion lives from the inside-out and is not focussed on WHAT.

Talk it back *and identify solutions*

When you leave a conversation, the information you have

downloaded is in a time-critical phase. You therefore need to talk it back soon in order to put it into the long-term memory box. When you talk it back, you will then be able to identify possible ways in which you can add value to that person. You might get back in touch with them and say something like, 'I was thinking about what we were talking about. Have you thought about X?'

Conversation with myself: Not every conversation will afford you the opportunity to go through the above mnemonic systematically. If you start to adopt the ideas in your conversation habits then over time you will start to reap the results of being memorable to those with whom you interact.

What could you introduce into your conversations today? It may feel insignificant at first but the more you practice these skills the more you will unlock the results.

Day 38: The Winning Evaluation

Benchmark which mindset you have when it comes to the MEMORABLE conversation.

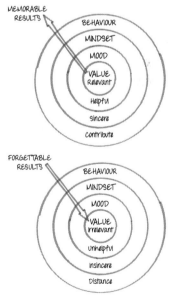

The fruit of my actions will reveal the root of the conversations I host. Today we are looking at ten questions related to specific situations. I encourage you to be brutally honest as to which response most fits your nature. Tally up how many you answered according to which voice and make a decision to go back under the bonnet of your inner conversations to strengthen your foundation as a champion. If you feel frustrated then that is not a bad thing as long as you focus that frustration on making certain you commit to hosting the winning conversation.

1) Strategy: What do you do when you need a strategy in place to go after a goal?

Consumed – The effort needed to gain clarity demotivates me

Complacent – The lack of clarity can cause me to be distant from my purpose and disconnect from those

Competitor – I actively seek clarity in my conversations to find an answer

Champion – I involve myself in helping others with strategy knowing that in turn I will gain the clarity I need.

2) Change—What do you do in the midst of uncomfortable change?

Consumed - I become preoccupied with how I can matter in this new situation

Complacent - I lean back and wait for the dust to settle, not realising that I am disconnecting myself from my opportunity

Competitor - I actively seek the opportunities with a positive attitude and have as many conversations as possible to establish my new position

Champion - I seek to add strength to those who are carrying weight through the transition knowing that as I help the voice of others come through and add value to others so I am building a platform for the future.

3) Ideas—What do I do with a burning idea?

Consumed - Disconnect from facilitating others and focus solely on my idea and how I can make it happen

Complacent - Wait for other ideas to fail and then see if mine fits

Competitor - Persistently flag up my idea, keeping it present at every opportunity even if its connection is not obvious to the current challenges

Champion - Seek to add value to the ideas of others knowing that my ideas require connection points to be a solution to a problem.

4) Ownership—What do I do if I have responsibility for an area but little passion for it?

Consumed - Carry out the tasks to the bare minimum, often neglecting the things that appear of little significance

Complacent - Complete all tasks but have no desire to further the effectiveness of the responsibility

Competitor - Fulfil the responsibility but with one eye on where I want to get to.

Champion - I understand that the only way to be relevant to people is to be wholeheartedly committed to what they are committed to.

5) Big picture—How do I position myself in relation to the future?

Consumed - I lose heart by the distance between myself and my goals so I stop making them to avoid feelings of disappointment

Complacent - I periodically spend quality time looking at the bigger picture of my future and this usually takes place around events such as the turn of the year, birthdays or events that cause me to stop and think bigger

Competitor - I regularly visit the future and keep myself fully available for the opportunity to seize my goal

Champion - I view the time line of my *NOT YET* goal daily in the morning and the evening in order to keep it fresh and alive inside of me. This prepares me to take the daily steps toward its fulfilment.

6) Promotion—How I go about getting promotion?

Consumed - I can easily become disheartened by an apparent lack of progress so I lack presence with people in my current activity

Complacent - I can take my 'foot off the pedal' when there is little progress but then I will be inspired at times to pick up the pace, although this will come from an outside source

Competitor - I will position myself for opportunities that appear to have a direct correlation with where I want to go. My conversations will be based on how the other person can get me to where I need to go

Champion - Promotion finds me as I pursue my goal of helping others feel like they 'matter.' While I have a clear set of goals I make sure that I create a tension between this and a pure desire to help others by listening to them and connecting into them

7) Contentment—How do I stay content?

Consumed - I create a form of contentment that gets me through life but all I do is subdue my goal-setting to avoid disappointment

Complacent - I generally feel content but deep down I know that I am not being stretched and so my contentment is more a satisfaction with what I know than a contentment from being stretched and unlocking my potential

Competitor - I switch between contentment and frustration. When I see obvious wins I get a feeling of satisfaction but I am not sure if that is contentment. I certainly don't feel content when frustrated. I only feel as good as my last win

Champion - My wins lie in me pressing into people and adding value. Therefore my contentment is pretty constant as there are always opportunities to add value. I keep WHAT in my periphery vision and WHO in my line of sight

8) Legacy—What am I doing about legacy?

Consumed - I cannot see the point in building beyond my lifetime because I am not sure I have anything to contribute and because I will not be around to appreciate it

Complacent - I believe in the notion of legacy but I am not right now actively engaged in building something of significance that will outlive me, but one day I will

Competitor - I promote the notion that success lies in our successors and that legacy has to be at the heart of a worthy goal; I will do what I need to achieve first and then I will put my energy into my legacy

Champion – My life is about my legacy. If I build people I am sure to build beyond my lifetime because the seed I sow can become a forest in future generations

9) Preparation—How do I view being prepared?

Consumed - Preparation can be a waste of precious time. I only prepare for events that appear significant for my progress

Complacent - Preparation is seasonal. It is often down to how I feel. Sometimes I go through periods where preparation is enjoyable, even exciting. However, it does come down to how I feel about the task in question and what else is going on in my life at the time

Competitor - Preparation is crucial for the things I prioritise. If I do not prepare for the moments I know are significant, I prepare to fail

Champion - Preparation is a daily and weekly discipline that forms the bedrock of my life. I immerse myself in the principles that keep me in a state of being prepared. I still need specific preparation periods but these are like moving up a gear rather than moving from a standing start

10) Relevant—How do I view being relevant?

Consumed - I am irrelevant. There is nothing inside me that others would want. I do not look above my own lack

Complacent - I am relevant to very few people. Past rejection and lack of self-belief has created a low aspiration in me for wanting to connect. Sometimes the aspiration is snuffed out all together

Competitor - I can be relevant to many but not all, depending on the circumstances

Champion - I am relevant to all. Regardless of who stands before me - whether a homeless person or the Queen of England - I can find points of connection that can create a lasting impression. This is because my focus and commitment is WHO they are

PRACTICE V POTENTIAL in the MEMORABLE conversation:

Based on the answers to the above questions, how many times could you honestly say that your answer was 'champion'?

Consumer: 1-2 times
Complacent: 3-5 times
Competitor: 6-8 times
Champion: 9-10 times

My Overall POTENTIAL: I AM A CHAMPION

MY Overall PRACTICE: I HAVE BEEN A _____

In order for my practice to match my potential, I have identified the following three things I can do to unlock the champion in me:

1_____

2_____

3_____

Day 39: The Winning Accountability

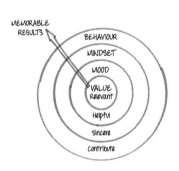

By pulling this whole week under the title of 'building a platform not a soapbox,' we can quickly review this conversation. Utilising the dice in spare moments throughout the day, or in a small group session, we can focus on the inner conversation of relevance.

The Winning Dice—***Building a platform and not a soapbox***

We must never underestimate the strength of our defaults. We are naturally opinionated people who often believe our way is right and want others to subscribe to that opinion. Frustration can set in when we feel our voice falls on deaf ears. However if every opinion was aired and believed, there would be chaos. The way to get your voice heard is not to shout louder. Those who stand on soap boxes are often ignored. People have to build credibility to be heard.

Devote yourself to **building a platform** of the credibility you receive for persistently being fruitful in what you do, even when it does not flow with your opinion.

Even at those times when you feel no one is giving you credit or appreciating all you do, refuse to stand on a soapbox. Focus your energy on building the platform of your credibility by keeping a right attitude and giving your very best. A voice will be heard better when spoken from a bigger platform, so keep building!

Commit to choosing to do the following:

Step 1: RECALL. Sometimes we need a quick review of what a platform builder and soapbox user look like so we can stay on the course of allowing RELEVANCE to have the loudest voice in our lives, in the process drowning out IRRELEVANCE. Here is a description based on what we have looked at this week:

What does a platform builder look like?

They avoid getting caught up in opinion-sharing conversations.
They are consistent in showing up and giving their best
Good reports follow them
They are patient but progressive
They focus energy on solutions rather than problems
They align what they do to the big picture
Their private life matches their public life
They carry humility and an attractive reluctance
Favour follows them
They understand that the process acts to protect them against an inability to handle future pressure
They decrease in self but increase in faith
They are willing to do freely what others require payment for

What does a soapbox builder look like?

They seek to align their opinion to others

Proving themselves in the eyes of others is their goal

Discord follows them

They attach the blame for their disappointment to their surroundings

They seek to elevate themselves by pointing out what others do not do/have

They use flattery to gain access

They ask for promotion

They seek to bypass process in order to get promotion

They are full of themselves and other people are a means to an end

There are always strings attached to what they offer

Step 2: REVIEW with others

Get together weekly with people who are committed to developing the winning conversations and discuss the following:

i) Why are we so prone to pulling out a soapbox and raising our voice?

ii) Why does the process of building a platform seem so unattractive?

iii) Give examples from this past week when you have used a soapbox?

iv) How have you been building your platform this week?

v) What challenge can you set yourself to take your platform building to the next level? (Make sure these challenges are reviewed next time you meet up so that accountability produces results and people are inspired by the stories shared.)

vi) What conversations are your relationships causing you to have?

Step 3: REFLECTION to be shared

Now create a reflection that you can share with someone in your group or someone else that you are coaching to be a champion in life. Why not take the time with your children, loved one, friend over coffee and share what you have learnt? Simply sharing this reflection will accomplish much in your life and deepen relationships, enriching them with vulnerability and moments of movement.

Follow our basic structure:

i) What I realised for the first time/again this week is .... (share the thought)

ii) The change I need to make is...(share the action point)

iii) Can you help me make it...(invite help and create accountability)

Once you have got into the habit of doing this, why not decide to turn your thoughts into a blog or even take your coaching to another level? There is so much in you and it is directly connected to your commitment to stretch yourself.

Section 7: Be MORE influential

Day 40: The Winning Conversation makes you MORE influential

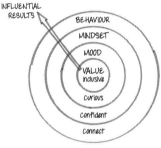

Let me introduce the voice of inclusiveness to your conversation table. A champion allows the voice of inclusiveness to speak over the voice of exclusiveness.

Being inclusive means refusing to exclude any part or section of society.[16]

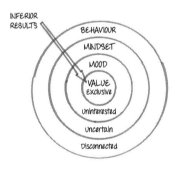

Most people underestimate their ability to influence the lives of others. We are so aware of our ordinariness that we believe the lie that no one would want to be influenced by us. But you are more influential than you realize; there is an influence in you because you are part of an interconnected world. I do not mean a world simply connected through social media but a world connected through human beings working together for the common good. The more synergy an individual discovers with a greater quantity of people, the more exponential their influence can be. Remember, your life is a conversation and it tells a story that is going to inspire, encourage and build the lives of other human beings. It is in your hardwiring to exist for the good of others. Therefore the more connected you

16. inclusive. Oxford Dictionaries. Oxford University Press, n.d. Web. 22 September 2015.

become the more that potential is unlocked.

There is no greater sense of satisfaction than when we know we have contributed to the good of other people. We have to work hard against a default setting that is self-centred and selfish. However, extraordinary good can be accomplished when a person's desire to contribute is connected to more and more people. This is where the voice of inclusiveness comes in.

The potential for your life to count, to matter, to have an impact is far beyond anything you could imagine. The only limitation is a lack of belief and desire. I hope by the end of this conversation you will actively reach beyond the borders of your existing circles of influence. The registered number of people suffering from depression is on an upward trajectory. I believe this is directly linked to the breakdown of community. Despite our level of connectedness through technology, which can continue to break down geographical and social barriers, we are witnessing the fragmentation of society as we become more exclusive in our attitude to others.

People are starving from a lack of acceptance. While technologically we are advancing, socially we are regressing. Many incorrectly believe that moving from interdependence to independence is progress. This has led to individuals buying into subcultures such as gangs and terrorist cells that harness the power of community using objectives that are destructive.

We are wired to rely on one another, to create team, to create community. While it may feel easier to do life alone, we do so to the detriment of our potential and influence. There is **more** INFLUENCE in you than you think. The power of this conversation unleashed in your life is going to astound you!

When I host the INFLUENTIAL conversation I become:

1) MORE interested in connecting the dots
The 'dot' of my life finds its significance when it is connected with others

How much fun are dot-to-dot pictures? I loved them when

I was a boy because there was great satisfaction in seeing how a dispersed and random set of dots could be connected to create a picture using crayons. In recent days I have discovered that you can get *dot-to-dot extreme*—pages with a sea of dots you have to link.

Whether it is a simple or extreme picture, there is never a dot that is wasted. Every dot has a purpose. If a dot is not connected then the overall picture suffers. It is so easy to underestimate the significance of a dot and its importance to the overall picture.

Life is a giant dot-to-dot. While it may seem obvious to us the dots we need to connect, the reality is we only discover the importance of a connection over time and in the light of all the other connections. In this respect we need to take care not to make relational judgments based upon inaccurate and predetermined information.

In order to unleash the power of influence we have to embrace the value of inclusiveness. Our lives are a giant dot-to-dot picture in constant motion. We walk past dots every day—connections that can be part of us outworking the WHY of our lives.

Bringing the voice of inclusiveness to the conversation table of your beliefs will cause you to view people differently. When walking into a room, you will now look at others through an inclusive lens.

Every dot is potentially a key link in our life story. We have to fight to connect with people beyond our comfort zone because when we do we gain traction on our purpose.

2) MORE people focussed
Problems follow people but people are my purpose

We are interconnected and this means that how we interact with one another impacts on ourselves. The central circle shows us that our first priority in every situation, every challenge, is a WHO not a WHAT. Very often in a crisis we ask, 'WHAT do I do?' However the winning conversation reminds us that the answer starts with a WHO. This means that we need to become more about people than about motives, methods and mechanisms. People are answers. Therefore, the larger my circle of inclusion, the more potential answers I will discover in the present and the future.

3) MORE community centric
A healthy life can not be grown without a community

With life moving at a pace we have become a generation of 'snackers', eating on the go—a habit that has further exacerbated the continued breakdown in community. You cannot build a healthy body on a lifestyle of snacks.

All this can translate into our relationship with people. We grab a few minutes with others here and there. This leaves little room for inclusiveness because we do not schedule new connections as 'urgent' or even recognise the need. Therefore when new connections are made they are only given minutes to develop as we continue snacking relationally.

This is not in sync with how are designed. Creation is one big community. When you stop and think about it, a healthy life and living as a community are mutually inclusive. Community happens when people join around a common purpose. Even our bodies are a community of organs that co-exist around a common purpose— keeping us alive!

If I have an assignment for this planet, there has to be a resource for me to achieve that? The resource is community. A community into which a person is born has a profound impact upon their understanding of their identity, purpose, value and future. This can be positive or negative, depending upon the health of the community.

We are who we are today largely because of the environment in which we grew up. While we all carry internal strengths and weaknesses that are the products of our nature, these things are also the result of nurture. While I believe that the WHY of our lives is God determined, how we view our WHY will often be through the bias of our community lens.

The products of a healthy community are strength, resource and wisdom. Wherever you find people who are committed to a common cause, and recognise the importance of interdependence around that cause, you will invariably find these three qualities. They are indispensable if an individual is to fulfil their potential. A healthy community will produce people who are strong emotionally, physically, mentally and morally.

A community is strengthened and grown through the contribution of its constituents. We unlock the power of influence when we commit ourselves to growing our world while growing with others in community. To neglect either will result in living an undernourished existence in which we start to be self-serving rather than serving beyond ourselves, which is HOW we are called to live.

I can confidently say that our growth as people is directly connected to our openness to connect beyond our existing relational matrix.

4) MORE conscious of peoples' needs
True influence is determined by a person's ability to meet the needs of people

One result of increased influence is awareness. When we embrace the conversation of inclusiveness, we engage beyond the familiar. As our engagement increases, our awareness of people and their needs are heightened. Such awareness creates access to untold opportunities. When you carry a genuine desire to get the best out of people, the power of your story can be magnified. The more aware you are of what it is like to live in another person's shoes, the more you become an answer to their questions.

People are drawn to those who are aware how they are wired to help get the best out of them. When you host the voice of inclusiveness at the table of conversation it takes your potential to another level.

5) MORE engaging
The more value I add the more engaging I become

The basis of this book is that life is all about a conversation. A winning conversation improves your ability to engage with yourself and with others. Life is transactional; it is made up of the transaction of conversations through which we ideally add value to others. Trading goods is based upon a conversation. The currency is a conversation between my value and your value. The better I become at these transactions, the more money I make and the greater wealth I accumulate. The same is true relationally. The better I get at engaging with people, the more transactions I make and the more value I accumulate. I have to keep adding value to people in order to be engaging. When I do, the law of sowing and reaping is once again activated.

The more I sow value, the more I reap.

6) MORE aware of blind spots
HOW I present myself speaks louder than WHAT I present

How you communicate with people is critical. This is not simply about the way we speak. We communicate through the way we stand, the way we dress, the way we greet, the way we look at someone when they are talking to us. The inclusive voice will increase our self-awareness in these areas. It will cause us to look at apparently insignificant habits that previously went unnoticed and unchallenged because our goals and assignments demand that we remove all possible barriers to our ability to influence others. It will, in short, make us more aware of our blind spots and give us a greater ability to remove them.

7) MORE aware of the questions people carry
My influence lies in my ability to uncover and unlock the burning question a person carries

Our assignment as human beings is to go in search of questions. Questions make sense of answers and answers make sense of questions. We should be on the constant lookout for people who have question marks hanging over their lives.

Everything I am and will become is to be an answer to someone else's question. People need to know the winning conversation. Once they do, the challenge and responsibility will burn in them to be an answer to those who are about towns, cities and villages with questions.

If I am going to live out my identity, then wherever I am I need to live like an answer. This is not about becoming Mr or Mrs Fix-it. It does not mean being a Know-it-All. It means taking all that you have received so far in life and using that to form an answer.

You are an answer so go practice finding someone who is a question! Inclusiveness is the conviction that I am to include people who have a question, believing that some of these connections will result in unexpected opportunities.

Day 41: The Winning Voice of Inclusiveness

To be an inclusive person I have to believe that:

1) I AM built for discomfort
What I possess without pain is not worth possessing

Possession is the critical step from <u>thinking</u> something is happening to <u>knowing</u> it is happening. When a person believes that what they are planning is happening, their feelings, thoughts and actions are different from just thinking it's going to happen. This is the shift from believing you *are* in the moment to believing you *will be* in the moment.

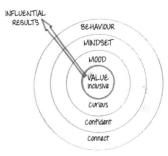

Imagine someone left you a cottage in the country that sits on a quarter of an acre of land. You left the city and took possession of it and now you have been there for many years. Even though it was unfamiliar at the time you have now adjusted to life there. You have got the house looking as you want it and the fenced garden looks idyllic. It is comfortable and familiar.

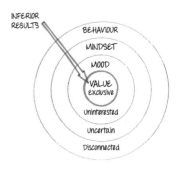

One day, however, you receive notification that the deeds of your house are actually incorrect. Mistakes were made during the transfer of the property. It just so happens that the boundary of your property extends to the next field which is actually four acres of land. The owners who left you the property had plans drawn up to build a mansion there and it all had been paid for. All this means you have to demolish your cottage and stay in a mobile home overseeing the build. What are you going to do?

You would take possession of it, wouldn't you?

In order for you to live in what is planned for the site you are going to have to leave a place of comfort and go into the unfamiliar in order to get there. The problem is we love the cottage of comfort. In fact not only do we love our cottage, we are attached by a bungee rope to it. Even when we want to journey through the unfamiliar to a better future, we keep being pulled back.

We are creatures of comfort. When we find what works we usually stick with it. While this may appear attractive we are essentially allowing the borders of our lives to be permanently defined even though our lives are destined for what is greater than our current reality. Your potential is unlocked as you push out of your borders and into the space you have yet to possess.

The building of your life is directly linked to the building up of other people. The more you grow your circle of concern, the more you step into your expansive future. Get rid of the cottage and go for the dream house. Daily push yourself out of the comfortable and familiar into the uncommon and unfamiliar place; the more you do that, the more dissatisfied you will become with the cottage of comfort.

Yesterday's breakthroughs become today's fences. Keep smashing down those fences.

Conversation with myself: How much do I really want that the opportunity that lies the other side of my discomfort? I decide to claim the 'inheritance' of the opportunity by embracing the feeling of discomfort today.

2) I AM invited

Always make the first move

We have all shied away from making the first move in engaging with other people because of not knowing if we are invited into their world or not. The only way of knowing is by assuming we are invited! Indecision is rooted in fear. The voice of inclusiveness says, 'You are invited, so act like you are!' The voice of inclusiveness says, 'Don't wait to be included. You are the answer to someone's question.'

As with all the conversations, inclusiveness does not happen by chance but by choice. If we wait for our world to grow by itself then the chances are it is likely to shrink before it grows. Inclusiveness goes hand in hand with generosity because it's about being generous with our attention and time. We are driven by a need to engage more than a need to feel accepted.

Decide to be driven by the law of the first move and rest in the knowledge that you are maximising the potential of your connection opportunities.

Conversation with myself: Which conversation am I going to have today that relies on me making the first move? Book it in your diary to remind you.

3) I AM over myself
Move over and let the real you through

It is fear of what others will think about us that stops us engaging with them beyond what is comfortable. Many people carry an inferiority that minimises potential influence in the lives of others. We are prone to overanalyse how we are going to look when reaching out to a person for the first time. Shyness is not humility; it is a barrier that needs to be overcome. The voice of exclusivity tells us that we cannot create new connections and extend our influence because others do not want what we have to offer. When we bring inclusiveness to the table, this changes. The law of self-denial enables us to remove thoughts about ourselves that stand in the way of us connecting with opportunity and with other people.

Conversation with myself: What conversation can I initiate today that will challenge my inferiority?

4) I AM growing through relationships
The power of presence has no substitute

Regularly touching base with people reinforces the belief that your growth comes through people before things and that meeting physically with someone is far more powerful than any other form of connection.

Thanks to technology we can access people in many different ways. Whilst technology provides convenience it comes with a cost. The power of our conversation emanates in its most potent form when people are present.

Conversation with myself: What value I am losing in my relationships through my over-reliance on technology? Who do I need to schedule a face-to-face meeting with?

5) I AM indiscriminate
When I overthink I overlook

When you immerse yourself in this conversation and start to practice it you no longer become intimidated by a room full of strangers. You become indiscriminate. I like to envisage I have a pack of post-it notes and my aim is to get around as many people and talk to them. When I have spoken to them I metaphorically put a yellow post-it note on them. I want to keep going until everyone is walking around with one.

You may think, 'I want to find the right people to speak to'. While that sounds reasonable it is the voice of exclusivity. The story you carry is bigger than you realise and there are characters from unpredictable walks of life that have a critical part to play.

Mentally mark the post-it note of those that connected well in conversation with a big red X. The more people you touch with your story the more connectedness you will enjoy and your world will grow rapidly.

So be indiscriminate and build influence.

Conversation with myself: Which environment have I been avoiding because of intimidation? What opportunities am I surrendering through my exclusive belief?

6) I AM into addition
You are connected when you have added value

Triple AAA is used in many sectors of society to describe the highest possible rating. During the most recent credit crisis we heard of countries having their credit rating reduced from AAA to AA+ and some down to C. It is also a term used in baseball to denote the highest level, class, standard a player can achieve.

When it comes to the quality of being inclusive my belief is that anyone who aspires to be productive and effective in life needs to achieve the AAA rating.

A triple-A connector does three things:

They **APPROACH** people to start a conversation

They **ACCEPT** the person through showing kindness and compassion

They **ADD** value through being an answer even if it is at the cost of inconvenience

In order to win the battle and become inclusive we need to practice **APPROACHING** people that are outside our normal circle of relationships. Something I have done to grow in confidence in this area is to challenge myself on a Friday to make a fresh connection. I challenge myself to introduce myself to someone new, find out what they do and make a positive statement about them that adds value.

Once we have approached someone we need to show we **ACCEPT** them. Everything from our body language, the smile on our face, being positive toward and about them helps communicate that we accept them and value them. Many people have been damaged through rejection and this can sometimes make them seem unapproachable. However, your commitment is to accept, value and affirm them; the more you do this the more you will see the walls come down.

Once we accept a person, we can add them. When I talk about adding someone I am referring to adding them to your regular contact circle, to what I call 'the inclusion zone.' Those with whom I regularly stay in contact and include in my conversations are more likely to be people I can help in the future because I am aware of them and what is happening in their lives.

Conversation with myself: Which connections have I failed to take to triple A status? Based on this principle take time to list connections you have made recently and note which status they currently have?

7) I AM inclusive in crowds
To catch a new type of opportunity I have to fish in different waters

To win in life you need to be inclusive in a crowd. This is like the fisherman who takes his boat out into the ocean and lets down his nets. He does so because he can catch many types of fish, some of which are obviously useful and some not. If you are to grow your world beyond its existing borders, you need to be willing to go into environments where the people are not all your 'type.' This could be community events, networking breakfasts, sporting groups, interest groups or celebration events. The exclusive voice speaks against this approach because it is desperate to limit your influence. However the voice of inclusiveness says you have to do this in order to grow.

Conversation with myself: Where can I go fishing for different fish? How could this grow me?

8) I AM inclusive in small groups
Small environments breed the authenticity that crowds lack

You need to decide who you are taking from the crowd into your core environment. To know someone better you have to remove them from the original environment where you met otherwise there will be no change in their mindset and behaviour. For instance, if you meet someone at a business breakfast, they are in a business mindset. If you invite them to dinner in your home, then you will see them in a very different light. This is how you build a rapport with someone.

Conversation with myself: Who have I connected to that I could invite into a different environment in order to grow the relationship?

9) I AM committed to close moments
Lasting impact lies in the close moment

You need to be inclusive not just in the context of the crowd and the core group but also in a circle of immediate concern where you have one-on-one conversations. The people you include at this level will be those to whom you feel you can add the most value and who will play a part in your own story. You are willing to spend an hour or two with these people either as a one-off after being with them in the crowd environment, or you may meet them on a regular basis.

Your long term legacy lies with those to whom you are committed at this level. These are the people with whom you are going to share close moments, with whom you are going to do high level relationship.

Community is strong and healthy when everyone has a healthy circle of immediate concern and they belong to someone's circle. Being inclusive does not advocate pleasing everyone and becoming everyone's best friend. It advocates breaking new ground through new relationships in which we develop a longevity in which we can add the most value and in the process become increasingly influential.

Conversation with myself: Who must I add value to through intentional close moments?

10) I AM committed to continued concern
Continued concern is continued influence

Through an 'extended concern' list, you can keep in contact with an amazing amount of people if you work it into your daily schedule. You can go from a simple text, email, note or phone call right through to inviting people to events to meet other people in your world. All this goes a long way towards building influence through adding value to people. There is nothing that quite compares to the feeling of having deposited something of worth into the life of another human being. The more you add value to these people the more you will seek to extend your list with new people.

Elvis Presley sung, 'A little less conversation, a little more action please. The voice of inclusiveness sings, 'A little less conversation with the same old people and a little more action involving others.' Whilst the value of this list may not pay off immediately, over time you will reap the benefits.

Conversation with myself: Which ten people can I start off my 'extended concern' list with? Now put the action in your diary so you do not forget.

Day 42: The Winning Mood of Curiosity

Unlocking the power of WHY creates a curious mood

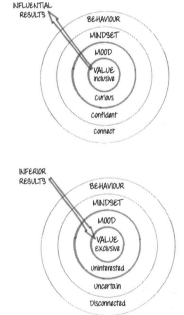

My WHY is my PURPOSE. My purpose is the vision of my life. My vision is the future that I choose to have. The power of vision is that it ignites hope inside of me. The winning mood is stimulated when I choose to keep clarifying and reminding myself of my vision, my winning purpose. I must follow the pattern of the winning purpose from the inside-out, from the WHO to the WHAT. The power of our WHY is the power of positivity that creates motion in our lives.

I am having the INFLUENTIAL conversation led by the voice of inclusiveness which means I choose to put myself in a CURIOUS mood.

314

Curiosity is awareness of the unseen

Beneath the oceans of the world lie hidden knowledge and treasure. This stimulates a curiosity in people which causes them to dive deep to unveil what is hidden. A curious mood longs for those extraordinary opportunities that come when we include more people in our world. A curious mood holds to the belief that every human life is an ocean of discovery.

Whether in the work place, having coffee with someone, or standing in a queue waiting for a bus, I can cultivate that curious mood that comes from a high awareness that there is value in people and I can affirm that value through asking great questions and being a focussed listener. The more I become aware of this unseen greatness, the more intrigued I become and the greater I desire to connect.

My winning purpose is ultimately about people therefore the more I can learn and discover about people the better I become at connecting to the WHO behind the purpose.

Curiosity communicates interest

Every person naturally doubts how interesting they are so when someone takes interest in them that conversation stands out. Too many people underestimate the power of their message and this causes them to settle for a mediocre life. When I step into a curious mood I not only operate from my own potential by being the answer to the questions I meet; I also unlock the potential in the other person and release them from a future of mediocrity to a future of possibility.

The more curious we become about others the more curious they become about us.

Curiosity creates access

What do you lack in order to progress your cause and purpose? The experience, wisdom, provision you need lies inside relationships.

Take a little time to think right now about the positive things you have in life. You will quickly link those to relationships. Relationships are your resource. Therefore you need to resource your relationships.

How valuable is a person's experience? It is *hugely* valuable. Most of the time we can walk past people who carry years of priceless wisdom because we are so focussed on our own lives. We must realise that when we enrich the lives of others by being curious about their experiences, we hugely enrich ourselves. The keys we need in life are walking past us every day.

Think about the experiences of others that have already added incredible value to your life and allow that to create a hunger that causes you to cultivate a mood of curiosity. There is more around you than you think but you have to be curious to find it.

Being focussed is not to the detriment of being aware

Curiosity can give the impression that it is a form of distraction but curiosity follows focus. Being focussed is not about ignoring everyone who has no obvious link to what we are doing; that is exclusivity. We have to manage the tension of staying focussed while remaining sensitive to what is around us. Opportunity does not have to be made, it has to be discerned.

A question I like to ask myself is, 'What is the unique quality in this person that I can value?' While this person may not have a direct link to anything that I am doing, in discerning uniqueness I discover unexpected and invaluable relationships.

Opportunity already exists before you enter a room. Just because you cannot see it does not mean it is not present. You have to discern it through including other people. This has to become part of your daily rhythm if you are going to grow your lives.

I can naturally hold back from connecting with people when I do not feel I have a reason to do so, or when I become concerned if I will be accepted. However, when I believe, I am inclusive and I realise that this is WHO I am and my WHY demands that I connect.

Choose to be aware of your Soul Script

How I feel has a direct impact on the choices I make. While feelings do not and should not rule our actions, they exist for a purpose; they are an integral part of us outworking our beliefs and engaging with the world around us. Feelings need to be instructed and directed to fall in line behind our beliefs. They then become an asset to winning in life.

Our feelings revolve around three major focus points.

1) How I feel about myself
2) How I feel about others
3) How I feel about the future

Let's take a look at how these look in both an outside-in (the exclusivist) and an inside-out (inclusivist) person.

The Losing Soul Script of Exclusiveness:

OUTSIDE-IN

My mood is UNINTERESTED which tells me:

Conversation lead: Exclusive
Conversation flow: Consumer
Soul appetite: Need Acceptance

When EXCLUSIVENESS leads my conversation I am a CONSUMER and my lack of ACCEPTANCE leaves me feeling an overwhelming sense of being UNACCEPTED and in an UNINTERESTED mood.

To be unaccepted means to feel a level of rejection, a sense that we do not satisfy the needs of others

The script of the exclusive conversation will shape our perspectives in such a way that we will be *Self-destructive, Me-obsessed* and *Now-focussed*.

Self-destructive statements from an exclusive belief sound like this:

i)   I am not interesting enough to make new connections

ii) I am not the kind of person who can just start a conversation
iii) I have been rejected before and cannot go through it again
iv) I am better on my own
v) I will look small talking to them

Me-obsessed statements from an *exclusive* belief sound like this:

i) These are not my people
ii) I am too busy to connect to these people
iii) I cannot see how they can help me so I will not connect
iv) I fear rejection and so I will not attempt to connect to them
v) I am here for me today so I will keep myself to myself
vi) I am not a people person

Now-focussed statements from an *exclusive* belief sound like this:

i) I am not a person of influence so why try to connect?
ii) I am happy with the circle of people I have
iii) I do not want to appear needy or have others think I have it together so will wait
iv) I do not trust people and will stay safe keeping myself to myself
v) People will get in the way of my plans for the future

The Winning Soul Script of Inclusiveness:

INSIDE OUT

My mood is CURIOUS which tells me:

Conversation lead: Inclusive
Conversation flow: Producer
Soul appetite: Full of Acceptance

When INCLUSIVENESS leads my conversation I am a PRODUCER and feel ACCEPTANCE because I give it and produce an OPTIMISTIC mood.

'Acceptance is being received as you are. It is when others are willing to see you as a valid connection'

Feeling inclusive comes from the internal conversation that

says 'I am accepted, I am influential and I have it to achieve three things':

i) Value Myself

ii) Value Others

iii) Value the Future

When my appetite for acceptance is filled through immersing myself in life-giving principles I do not approach people with an underlying need to feel like I have a place in the conversation. This means I do not try and figure out how I can present myself in a way that I think the other person wants me to be; I can relax and be the real me. Authenticity is the gateway to connection; people want the real you.

Turning up the voice of inclusiveness

Living your life with an acute awareness that you are wanted because you are an answer will have a profound effect on how the rest of your life unfolds. As you seek to take the value you have and invest it through the acceptance of others your zones of inclusion increase in value and the level of your influence increases too. This is because you are now operating according to the pattern of life's original design, inside-out.

So what does the new script sound like?

It flows inside-out and its voice should make the following kinds of statements:

Statements that *Value Myself* from the valued belief of *inclusiveness* sound like this:

i)   I am wanted because I carry answers people need

ii) My worth is not determined by a person's reaction but an internal choice I make

iii) I am not worth what others think; I am worth more!

iv) I will enjoy the feeling I know I will have when I include others in this now moment

v)   I have a story others want to hear

Statements that *Value Others* from an *inclusive* belief sound like this:

i) They need me to talk to them
ii) There is a question they have that I can help answer
iii) I can make them feel valued by involving them
iv) My conversation is not about how I feel but how they feel
v) They are my 'cause'

Statements that *Value my Future* from the valued belief of *inclusiveness* sound like this:

i) My future lies beyond the boundaries of my familiar relationships
ii) I cannot possess my future without people
iii) The influence I have on those I care about needs me to grow through including others in my world
iv) My purpose lies in helping others find their purpose
v) A conversation I pass up could be the key to unlocking an opportunity

Moment to pause: It is important that I create a time of reflection for me to identify my current soul script and make the necessary decisions to change it. The examples on this page are not exhaustive but I need to use them to discover the specific narrative I carry and make choices to change any outside-in statements as I seek to host the winning conversation.

Day 43: The Winning Mindset of CONFIDENCE

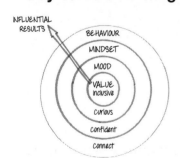

High level focus through presenting myself confidently

When I choose the mindset of a champion then I present myself confidently in conversations with new people.

My abilities are unlocked through new beliefs that have formed new attitudes. It is not that I could not do it before; it's that I did not have the belief and desire to sustain the activity. Now the voice of inclusiveness is at the conversation table of my life, I feel accepted and I know I can be *inclusive* in practice.

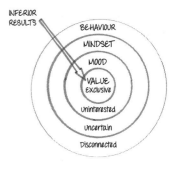

The winning mindset will determine daily to:

1) Present confidently without fear of rejection
Rejection is no indicator of personal value

I have not found one person who enjoys rejection. We are created for connection not rejection. We all want to be accepted. While studying my A levels I worked many hours in my spare time selling double glazing windows and products over the phone. Night after night I would go down endless lists of telephone numbers, phoning people trying to get leads for the salesman to follow up. For every appointment I made, I got paid. One of the companies I worked for was 100% commission so I had to get the leads. There were some evenings when I would make hundreds of phone calls and nothing would come of it. On other evenings I would get three or four. I knew that if I kept the call rate high then the odds of being accepted by people would increase amongst the many calls rejected. The rejection experienced on the phone meant workers would get disheartened and question the merit in the effort, but I knew if I kept going the results would come. The staff turnover in those companies I worked for was extremely high because being rejected more than accepted is hard work. I managed not to allow it to affect me and I enjoyed success.

One reason we stay in the confines of comfort is because we fear the results of stepping outside the boundary of what we know works. What if I start talking to someone and they do not want to know? I am going to look stupid! That makes me feel small. There are many ways that rejection reduces our willingness to try again. How do we push past that?

It is important to accept that rejection is part of life and cannot be fully avoided. The way we do something can make a difference to someone's response and reduce the chances of rejection. However, rejection is ultimately on the menu for anyone undertaking the winning conversation. *Rejection is simply selection.* It results in some being selected to enter my world and some not. When people refuse our overtures, remember this: the rejection of my invitation does not devalue the inviter; it devalues the invitee.

Only when we allow WHO we are to be valued based on WHAT we do will rejection become a problem. If our value flows from WHO we are then WHAT happens to us becomes less significant. Rejection will not be an indicator of my personal value.

I make a determined effort while out for my early morning walks to smile and say 'good morning' to as many people as possible. I get some funny looks, some grunts, and some good responses. However, I am choosing to operate from who I am and reinforce my value of inclusiveness knowing that while my attempt at connecting with people may be rejected, the chances are that over time I will make more connections than most.

Do not allow rejection to produce a fear or trying. Fear shrink-wraps our lives. It restricts our choices and decisions.

2) Present confidently and embrace inconvenience
Anchor your life in the reality of people through new connections

Whilst inconvenience will irritate some personality types more than others, most people do not actively welcome it. We are naturally selfish and so do not like our plans to be disturbed. The voice that drives this philosophy is exclusivity. We wrap our arms around our day and say, 'Everyone else can keep out of my way. This day is mine and I want it to go as planned!' Inconvenience disturbs selfish thinking. Champions are aware of this and recognise the potential value of the inconvenience.

Inconvenience can shape us positively and at times produce greater results than any pre-determined plan we may have. There have been times writing this book when I have tried to keep to a schedule in order to achieve goals I have set. While this has been right, I have underestimated the importance of keeping my structure defined and at the same time flexible. After all, life does not fit neatly into boxes.

My writing flows better when I have had to deal with 'inconvenient' situations that have involved helping others. We must avoid becoming task-obsessed and therefore de-sensitised to people's reality. Everything in life comes down to serving people; it is the currency of life.

3) Present confidently and create an atmosphere of acceptance
When you choose your mindset, it's as powerful as being able to choose your own weather

Never underestimate the power of atmosphere. Have you ever walked into a room and you knew that the people in the room had either fallen out with each other or with you? People's internal conversation creates atmosphere. We create an ambience through lighting; we create an atmosphere through attitude.

There have been times when negative people have left environments I have operated in and it's not until they have gone that you realise the extent to which their internal conversation influenced the atmosphere. The external atmosphere was created by their internal conversation.

The winning mindset creates an irresistible environment through producing an atmosphere of acceptance. Before you walk into an environment put on the mindset that pursues introductions and see how you positively influence the place. You can set the climate of a room though this mindset and becomes the person of influence you desire to be.

4) Present confidently to create new seasons for my life
People define seasons before events

Have you ever voiced your dissatisfaction with the season of the year? Have you ever said, 'I cannot wait till Spring'? What you are expressing is the desire for a new season. Life has seasons.

Some we wish would never end and others we cannot wait to end. Seasons are not determined by events; they are defined by people. The seasons of your life that produce growth lie first in WHO you connect with before WHAT you do. Now you are inclusive you can break out of old seasons because you produce new conversations that create new seasons.

5) Present confidently and reveal what is in me
With new introductions come new questions

When we only have conversations with people who know us we are not adding new perspectives to our world. The best way of getting great answers is asking great questions. Sometimes the best questions come in conversations with new people. Through an initial conversation they will ask questions to which we give answers that surprise even us. This new introduction pulled fresh revelation from us.

6) Present confidently through asking great questions
Great questions have the ability to reveal gold in people

One way to discover who sits at the table of someone's internal conversation is through the quality of their questions. When someone operates with inclusiveness they will improve the art of asking questions because they are practicing what questions elicit good information from people. They will learn to move beyond small talk into deep and meaningful talk.

Have you ever had a one-way conversation with someone where you are desperately trying to get them to say something longer than one sentence? This person has an exclusive voice at the table. Now remember you are a person of influence and they may be open to moving from being closed to being open. It may take some platform-building. However, you might currently be one of those people who struggle to create conversation though asking great questions. The solution is to immerse yourself in this conversation and over time you will develop the skill of asking great questions. Learn what questions can unlock the toughest of conversations.

7) Present confidently and unlock knowledge
Wisdom lies in the unlikeliest of places

The voice of inclusiveness is about making the other person look and sound interesting. One way of doing this is to determine that when you start the conversation you take the role of student while they are the teacher. When you position yourself like this you add significant value to them.

Becoming a student displays strength of character. It tells the other person, 'I want you to be real because I accept you.' Remember, everyone wants to feel wanted.

What is it about becoming a student that gives you a greater level of influence?

Humility - Humility is a foundation stone for personal security. Humility creates an openness that is irresistible. People open up when they feel they are on the same level as you. If we desire a greater openness then we need to create a level playing field.

Trust - When I position myself as a student I am effectively saying, 'I trust you enough to make you my teacher.' In light of this, beware the misconception that says that influence is about how old you are. Age does not determine who teaches. A person's character and cause are what set apart the teachers and instructors amongst us.

8) Present confidently and position myself for promotion
You are your own limit to the opportunity that lies in other people... have the conversation!

Everyone has a form of faith, whether the object of that is fate, luck, the stars or a divine being. This is the belief that there is an external force that influences circumstances I experience. For some this can be a means of excusing themselves from taking personal responsibility.

Successful people are often labelled 'lucky' but most have achieved success by positioning themselves for opportunity. You have heard the saying, 'It is not WHAT you know but WHO you know.' Positioning yourself for opportunity comes through WHO you know. You might then say 'but I don't know the right people?' I would then ask, 'Are you out there trying to meet new people?' You have to be inclusive to win in life so start scheduling your inclusion zones and see how favour follows.

9) Present confidently and go one more conversation than I feel is possible
Believe your conversations are ready to convert into results

In the game of rugby, the idea is that the ball comes out of the 'scrum' and is then passed along a line of players. All the time the whole team is moving towards what is called the 'try line'. Who scores the try is irrelevant because it's a team game.

Your conversation may be a pass to someone else and all you were was a link. However, another time you might be the one who catches the ball and scores. If you are willing to have the conversation for the first time then this may mean you give the winning pass for that person. They may have been in a series of conversations with others and someone may have even referred them to you, but you never know which conversation is the one that demonstrates the greatest result.

Remember you might be:

One conversation away from a key relationship
One action from a result
One encouragement from unlocking potential
One step from a new season

10) Present confidently and enjoy relational 'freedom'
Disciplined choices lead to great outcomes

Every person is created to enjoy freedom. While we may live in a country that has free speech we can often live under a regime of fear that keeps us locked in and stops us from connecting more widely than we feel comfortable. I think the greatest thing that inclusiveness produces is a sense of freedom. You are built for relationships and they fuel your life when you invest in them.

It is time to take a big pair of imaginary scissors and cut off that bungee rope that has you tied to the fixed point of exclusiveness. Most people do not live in such freedom and so may not always respond to your uncommon level of confidence and openness. However, you are a champion and so you are to stand tall and proud in your new self.

Conversation with myself: Which one or two statements do I struggle to believe? Which specific belief must I stay aware of and practice in everything I do today? I must remember that in order to achieve what I want most I must be willing to tackle what I want to do least.

Day 44: The Winning Choice of Connecting wider than you feel comfortable

Today we look at some practical ways to develop the winning conversation that will make you MORE influential in life. The more you inform the right choices, the more you activate the results.

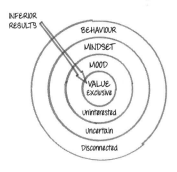

Go in search of questions

I have come to the realisation that if you do not carry any questions you are not thinking or dreaming big enough. If you have everything that you need then it is time to increase your personal challenge and create some need. If our answer is that we have everything then we are either thinking too small or do not have enough clarity on what is going to take us to where we are going.

Your cause should be big enough that it causes you to question, 'How am I going to make this happen?'

The size of the question you carry indicates the size of the person you are. Your question should be causing you to call on the help of other people. This indicates that the problem you are trying to solve is bigger than you but also that you are committed to collaborating in order to achieve the end result.

Once you have the question that is bigger than you, you will want to look for people who are able to contribute towards the cause. The steps to including people in on the cause are simple and yet often undervalued.

Daily learn to **A.S.K**:

Ask *to receive*

We all love to feel needed. Inclusiveness is not only about including new but also familiar people to greater degrees. One way of doing that is being clear on what you need. It is good to review constantly what it is we do need as this causes us to once again focus on our goals.

Seek *to find*

What is in a relationship that can unlock the next level? Have you ever played a computer game where you have had to find keys or items that unlock the next level and you cannot progress until you find them? I am a firm believer that much if not all we need lies in relationships but we either do not have the relationships or the level of relationship to uncover the keys that help us progress to the next level. Think about conversations you could start that could begin a journey of discovery.

Knock *to open doors*

What about starting those conversations? I would say this is one of the most daunting disciplines for people to master. However, having a strategy for a conversation can go a long way to removing our fears because fear is about the unknown. Having a plan helps to create a known path.

When meeting people, learn and practice to **KNOCK**:

Kick-start (Statement-Question)
Name
Occupation and/or obsession
Challenge
Knowledge

Kick-start

Do not just sit and wait for people to come to you. Remember, you are an answer not a question! A great way to start a conversation is to find someone who looks lost. They will be grateful that someone stopped them from drowning in embarrassing unfamiliarity.

Always kick-start your conversation with a statement followed by a question. A statement could be related to the weather, or the place you are in, or anything. People love to give their opinions and you just need to ask about something they value and you will be off to a great start.

Name

A great next step is to say, 'Hi I'm [NAME]. And your name is...?' It is so important that you know someone's name if you are going to discover how you can be an answer to them. When asking for someone's name, often we are thinking of the next question, which then means we are not actually paying attention to the person's name.

When you hear the name, repeat it back to them and include it as often as possible during your conversation. What we repeat, we learn and remember.

Occupation

The key to being an answer to someone is to truly value him or her. Remember that the key to valuing someone is to be more 'interested' than 'interesting'. We may be tempted to fill them in on how great our life is and how wonderful things are at the moment but we are an answer, not a question, looking for an audience.

Try to find out if they enjoy their job or a hobby. We should try to find out who the real person is rather than just rely on our perceptions.

Challenge

Every person has a current challenge, something they are trying to overcome or something they would love to take on. When we try and understand what someone is currently facing, it shows that we are not only interested in them but also interested in helping.

Know

Finally, ask yourself, "What does this person know from their background or experience that could really help me?" This is not a selfish question because we feel valued when we are adding value to others. By asking good questions about what they know you are helping them to know they are valuable.

So, wherever you are, remember there is a power when we learn to ASK!

Day 45: The Winning Evaluation

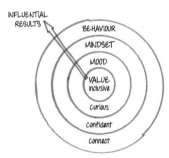

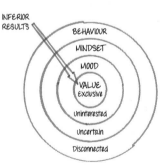

Benchmark which mindset you have when it comes to the INFLUENTIAL conversation.

The fruit of my actions will reveal the root of the conversations I host. Today we are looking at ten questions based on situations we find ourselves in and I encourage you to be brutally honest as to which response most fits your nature. Tally up how many you answered according to which voice and make a decision to go back under the bonnet of your inner conversations to strengthen your foundation as a champion. If you feel frustrated then that is not a bad thing as long as you focus that frustration on making certain your commitment to hosting the winning conversation.

1) Introducing yourself—How do you feel about introducing yourself?

Consumed - I will hold back until I am spoken to as I am not looking for connections. However, I am happy to talk if someone asks the questions.

Complacent - Depending on how I feel and the environment I am in determines how much effort I put into meeting people. If it's an environment where I feel at ease then I have no problem chatting to people.

Competitor - I know I need to make fresh connections and so will be open to the conversations that appear easiest and look like they could be fruitful.

Champion - I choose to enjoy the process even if it does not come naturally. The more I do it the more I see the importance. People need to feel included and that is my job wherever I am.

2) People's Names—What are you like with people's names?

Consumed - I am useless with names so I apologise up front that I am unlikely to remember.

Complacent - I am ad hoc when it comes to remembering. I always have a laugh with people about how bad I am with names. I guess you either have the ability or you do not.

Competitor - I need to try harder with names because I know when people remember mine and the names of those I care about it makes a difference.

Champion - I attempt to remember the names of everyone I meet by using a strategy. The excuse, 'I am not good with names,' is an excuse for not trying. I am always amazed how surprised people are when I remember their names. It is precious to them so it should matter to me.

3) Small talk—Are you good at small talk?

Consumed - I can hold a conversation about the usual things because it polite. However I keep myself to myself.

Complacent - I am good at small talk and keeping a conversation going. I am not very good at understanding or deciding where it could or should go.

Competitor - I can do small talk but I want to get past that to the real issues. After all I want to help people and fix their problems. If they do not want it, that is their problem.

Champion - Small talk is an important tool. It is a way of building a rapport with someone. I am comfortable with small talk but try and ask questions that steer the conversation to bigger talk. It has to feel natural and not forced.

4) Conversations—How do you view conversations?

Consumed - They are important but mainly to get to the point of what needs doing. I don't like wasting words.

Complacent - Relationships need conversations so if I am committed to relationships I have to be committed to conversations. I guess the more I do it the more I will just get better.

Competitor - They are really important and I choose to better myself at conversations, always trying to be more aware of how I come across

Champion - Conversations are everything. If there is one thing in life I should concentrate on it is the conversation I am having with myself that will spill over into my conversations with others

5) Questions—Do you ask meaningful questions in your conversations?

Consumed - I ask the questions that provide the answers for what I need.

Complacent - I will ask questions if I feel like having the conversation and if I think the relationship could go somewhere.

Competitor - I try to get to know someone by asking questions based on the information they offer me.

Champion - I have a set of questions that are like tools. I always try to be ready and armed with questions that can create momentum in a conversation and position myself as someone who could learn something from the person. When I position myself this way I rarely run out of something to say.

6) Acceptance—Does feeling wanted play a part in whether you enter into a conversation or not?

Consumed - I wait for conversations to come to me because I figure people will talk to me if they want to.

Complacent - This is the most important factor because if I do not feel wanted then I cannot enter a conversation.

Competitor - I find it easier speaking to the people who look 'less important' because I figure that they will always want a conversation. However I tend to excuse myself from conversations with more 'important' or 'exuberant' people because I fear I am not important enough. But I will talk with them if they address me.

Champion - I do have to deal with the feeling of needing to be wanted but I do not allow external permission to be the deciding factor. I am an answer and so I will speak to others because it's who I am; that is my choice.

7) Quiet and removed—Is remaining quiet and removed in public ever a good thing?

Consumed - I prefer to observe. I find it interesting to watch people so I am often quiet and removed. Not everyone can be a conversationalist.

Complacent - If I am having a bad day or not feeling like a conversation then I do remove myself from being open to conversations. I just get on with what I have to do.

Competitor - I always think it is important to engage even when I do not feel like it, although there are always exceptions.

Champion - Unless there are genuine reasons why I cannot engage, conversing with people is who I am. The best path to self-help is to help someone else. So I will always challenge any reason why I should not engage in conversation.

8) Learning from others—Is learning something you do through conversations?

Consumed - If I ask then I listen and I will learn. But I always try to figure things out on my own.

Complacent - I am always open to advice and will always listen if it's given. I usually have all that I need but am open to helping someone else if they ask.

Competitor - I am hungry to learn and will learn from people who are further on than me. However most of the time I try and help other people.

Champion - I take the position that I can learn something from anyone. I also find that I learn best when trying to see how I can be an answer to someone else's challenge.

9) Failed conversations—What happens when a conversation goes wrong?

Consumed - This is why I mainly communicate with those I know because I feel at ease talking to them. Most other conversations are small talk.

Complacent - I try not to push conversations with new people because I do not feel it is a major strength of mine. I do not like the embarrassment of when they go wrong.

Competitor - I walk away playing the conversation in my mind time and time again, thinking about what I should have said. I say it doesn't affect me, but it does. If it goes really wrong it can affect my mood and my willingness to engage further. I then get over it the next day so it does not hold me back in the long term.

Champion - Failure is part of progress and I do not believe people think about my mistakes as much I do. I am naturally critical so will try and channel my failure into improving for next time.

10) Confidence—How confident do you feel in conversation?

Consumed - I am comfortable in conversation with those I know but I do not push myself to start them with new people.

Complacent - I lack confidence with new people and so try and wait for the right situations to make themselves obvious.

Competitor - I feel confident with people I know and those who openly engage with me. Some people you just know are open to conversation and so I am confident in those situations.

Champion - Confidence is something that will grow through practice and so I choose to be confident even though at times I do not feel so.

PRACTICE V POTENTIAL of the INFLUENTIAL conversation

Based on the answers to the above questions, how many times can you honestly say that your answer was 'champion'?

Consumer: 1-2 times
Complacent: 3-5 times
Competitor: 6-8 times
Champion: 9-10 times

My Overall POTENTIAL: I AM A CHAMPION

MY Overall PRACTICE: I HAVE BEEN A _____

In order for my practice to match my potential I have identified the following three things I can do to unlock the champion in me:

1_____

2_____

3_____

Day 46: The Winning Accountability

Pulling this whole week under the title of 'be an answer and find a question' enables us to be able to review this conversation quickly. Using the dice in spare moments throughout the day, or in a small group, helps me to focus on the inner conversation of inclusiveness.

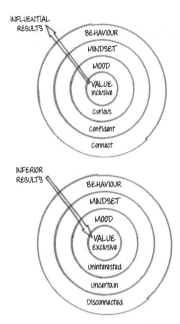

The Winning Dice—*Be an answer and find a question*

When we see someone on their own they are a 'question' and they become our responsibility because we are people called to be an 'answer'. Regardless of how 'irrelevant' I may feel I can always find common ground on which to connect and build a moment to touch their life.

When you include yourself in a conversation with someone else you have an opportunity to build on your mission to help people. Through seeking conversations through new connections you expose yourself to more opportunities to create answers. Be someone who includes themselves whenever a need becomes obvious. While you may not be the direct answer, you can help create options. You can create the anticipation for results and this is how you become influential. Influential people care enough to point to solutions!

We decide to be all about people as they are our greatest resource and have to be our highest priority. The WHO of people always comes before the WHAT of task. Opportunities come from unanswered questions and if people contain our greatest resource then we have to have an incessant drive to discover what is unanswered in people's lives. In doing so people feel valued because it's primarily about what we can do for them and not what they can do for us. People will sit up and take notice of everything I am about if I first centre who I am around what they currently need. A good listener will eventually get a good listen themselves.

'Being an answer' is about initiating, willing to be the last to be heard and elevating the needs of others above our own.

Step 1: RECALL together

Sometimes we need a quick review of what being an answer

and finding a question looks like so we can stay on course to allow INCLUSIVENESS to have the loudest voice, drowning out EXCLUSIVENESS. Here is a description based on what we have looked at this week:

What does 'being an answer' look like?

Being the first to strike up a conversation
Having questions ready that will give you confidence to make conversation
Being among the first to befriend a stranger
Smiling and greeting indiscriminately even when in a crowd
Surveying a room full of people and seeing opportunities to start conversations, especially with strangers
Making a determined effort to learn people's names
Listening intently to the person rather than focussing on the next thing to talk about
Offering possible help when it hasn't been asked for
Anticipating need before need comes looking for you
Being interested rather than interesting
Thinking and planning ahead of meeting new people
Being excited about finding new ways of doing things
Having a healthy discontentment with the way things are

What does 'being a question' look like?

Being comfortable speaking to the same people
Being happy to let someone ask before being asked
Having a lack of confidence and security in how they are perceived in conversation
Being fearful and timid
Standing in closed groups that do not allow new people to join
Promoting in-jokes when those who do not yet belong are present
Allowing jargon to be used when people who are not conversant with it are present
Rarely offering suggestions of how to improve things
Always awaiting instruction

Step 2: REVIEW with others

Get together weekly with people who are committed to developing the winning conversations throughout the journey of this book and this week discuss the following:

i) Can you think of any barriers to conversations that you currently have?

ii) What plan could you put in place to overcome these?

iii) Can you think of significant connections that you have made that would never naturally have taken place?

iv) How do you feel about asking people for help? How do you feel when someone asks you for help?

v) What could you start to do daily that would create a greater experience of being inclusive, therefore driving deeper the conviction inside you?

vi) Based on your winning purpose, how important is immersing yourself in this conversation going to be? What would be the result if you remained at the same level you are now?

Step 3: REFLECTION to be shared

Now create a reflection that you can share with someone in your group or someone else that you are coaching to be a champion in life. Why not take the time with your children, a loved one, a friend over coffee to share what you have learnt. Simply sharing this reflection will accomplish much in your life and deepen relationships, enriching them with vulnerability and moments of movement.

Follow our basic structure:

i) What I realised for the first time/again this week is .... (share the thought)

ii) The change I need to make is .... (share the action point)

iii) Can you help me make it? (invite help and create accountability)

Once you have got into the habit of doing this, why not decide to turn your thoughts into a blog or even take your coaching to another level? There is so much in you and it is directly connected to your commitment to stretch yourself.

Section 8: Be MORE EXPANSIVE

Day 47: The Winning Conversation makes you MORE expansive

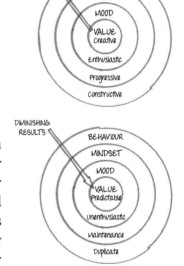

Let me introduce the voice of creativity to your conversation table. The winning conversation empowers the voice of creativity to replace the voice of predictability at the boardroom of belief.

Your future is bigger than you could imagine. During this conversation I want to push you on what you can expect to see achieved through your life. The limits on how expansive your life will be are determined by you and no one else. Immediately some readers will protest that they are limited by where they live, by family traits or experiences they have been through. However, you have control over your decisions and your life **CAN** change if **YOU** want it to!

It all comes down to who is sitting at the table of conversation. The default voice is that of predictability. Predictability convinces us that we can only plan according to what we have experienced. Incremental improvements over long periods of time are fully acceptable when it comes to predictability because most people incrementally improve as their life progresses. They acquire more knowledge and understanding and make more informed choices. Whilst incremental adjustments are fully acceptable, incremental results over prolonged periods of time jar with the spirit of a winner in life. I believe that we are wired for more than incremental improvement; the principles that produce multiplication are available to us too.

We live in a world of possibilities. Especially in western societies, we have more resources and opportunities available to us than ever before. These are also increasingly prevalent within developing countries. During this conversation I want your imaginations to run wild. I want to challenge the boundaries of what you believe is possible. You are more EXPANSIVE than you think and the voice of creativity will help you get there!

When I host the EXPANSIVE conversation I become:

1) MORE focussed
What I focus on I feed and what I feed I grow

On the rowing machine at the gym one day I gained a fresh understanding of focus. I had been rowing for many years but realised that if I focussed on the tightening of my muscles and adjusted my posture even slightly (to make sure the maximum amount of muscles were under the resistance being created) I could burn more calories and improve fitness.

I realised that the 5000m that I was doing on the rowing machine is a series of hundreds of sequences and a single sequence seems insignificant. However hundreds of sequences become extremely significant because they form the total exercise. If a person learns to focus on sequence and its correct procedure, the energy and effort used can produce extraordinary results.

Why do sports champions use coaches? Because they know that the distance between good and great, between being a competitor and a champion, is in the small details and tiny margins. When refinements are made, these changes compound over time and produce extraordinary results. As a result of intense focus, small adjustments make all the difference.

2) MORE desperate
It is only a true desire when it is a desperation

If you were to ask me if I could raise £100,000 by next week to purchase a small house, I would more than likely say no. However, if I knew my child needed a life-saving operation this time next week and it cost £100,000, I would say yes. What is the difference? I am desperate to achieve the goal because of my love for my child. I do not love the house enough to make it happen but I would die for my children and so I would get friends together to work on creative solutions to produce the desired results.

We deliver what is directly linked to our desperation. Creativity is linked to love. We become creative when we love someone or something. When we have a desperate passion for a goal, the level of our commitment hits a persistent high.

3) MORE aware
The 'big' events in life are created by the thousands of 'little' daily choices we make

We make thousands of choices daily. On their own they appear insignificant. However, when grouped together they make all the difference. A cheeseburger, bag of chips and full fat coke on a single day appear harmless. However, repeat this everyday and we will end up hooked up to a heart monitor.

There are events outside of our control but much of our future is in our control. We just need to become aware of what is growing us and diminishing us.

During this conversation we will heighten our awareness of the power of choice and increase our understanding of how the size of our future is determined by the small choices we are willing to commit to daily.

4) MORE empowering
The results of collaboration far exceed the extended effort of working with others

Our ability to live expansively is determined by WHO we engage to help us. Synergy is based on the principle that the sum total of what two people can do working together is greater than combining the individual results of those two people. The voice of creativity questions WHO you are working with in order to accomplish your goals. This conversation will cause you to view relationships differently. There is MORE in your relationships than you realize; they can become a multiplier of results if handled correctly.

5) MORE youthful
The expansiveness of your life will not exceed the expansiveness of your imagination

Creativity is the ability to think freely and to give full reign to the imagination. This is why we are often most creative when we are children. Children are blissfully ignorant of their limits. While this at times can be dangerous, at other times it means that they express themselves expansively. It is said that the older we get, the wiser we get. This is not actually true. The older we get the more experienced we get. However experience does not equal wisdom. Wisdom is applied understanding. To live expansively we must manage the tension of using acquired knowledge and understanding alongside an imagination that is unhindered by experience.

6) MORE moment-conscious
Momentum is never created in a moment but is created from moments

Understanding how you work best is a key to being more expansive. Speed of action multiplied by mass of energy determines the momentum of an object. The greater weight and force I put behind daily decisions will mean that what is hard on day 5 will be almost effortless on day 40. When we are more aware of the power of a moment to create momentum then it changes our approach to that moment. When we are immersed in this conversation we heighten our awareness and produce extraordinary momentum that will get us from where we are to our goals and beyond.

7) MORE deliberate
Results are often unpredictable but they are always the result of being deliberate

It may sound strange but the more things I do on purpose as opposed to without thought the more profound an impact my choices can make and the more expansive my life can become. Being deliberate is about having clarity on WHY you are doing something. The voice of predictability will tell you to put your feet up and just allow life to happen. If you do this you can wave goodbye to your goals. Only when you are determined to let WHO you are happen to WHAT you do, to be more deliberate in your decisions and choices and have a greater awareness of the ultimate impact of the immediate decision, will you be able to accomplish audacious goals.

Day 48: The Winning Voice of Creativity

To be a person of CREATIVITY I have to immerse myself in the commands that are going to lead me into the right mood. The more I immerse myself in the belief that I am creative the more expansive I will become.

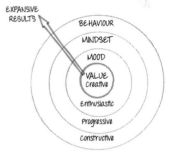

i) I AM positively fearful

Fear has to be present for courage to breathe

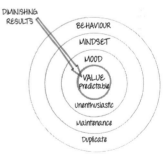

For all I have talked about so far in this book about fear, let me introduce you to positive fear. The best way to differentiate between the two is this: negative fear shrinks your expectations while positive fear helps you set and meet high expectations. Negative fear kills but positive fear keeps alive. Positive fear protects you from poor decisions by heightening awareness of real danger. Negative fear prohibits movement meaning you do not venture out of the ordinary for fear of what might happen.

When my children rode their bikes without stabilisers I gave them clear instructions. As long as they respected those instructions then they would achieve the hugely positive and exhilarating outcome of being free to ride anywhere on two wheels. For this they needed positive fear.

Conversation with myself: What would happen if I did not accomplish my life mission? Taste the regret before it happens and let the fear of missing out feed your certain belief that you will accomplish it.

ii) I AM exclusive when it comes to goals
Focus is a clear choice of what I include and exclude

The winning conversation is inclusive when it comes to people but exclusive when it comes to goals. Once goals have been created the reality of those goals depends upon the exclusive agreement we make with them. The daily space required to accomplish our goals is exclusive and not shared by other goals. If someone offered to trade our goals for another set of goals we would refuse and yet daily we FREELY trade the space required by those goals to achieve goals that are not our own. Life requires much of us and I am not advocating becoming negligent of responsibility. However I firmly believe that if our goals based on our LIFE Map are what we truly desire then the rest of our time, energy and finance has to come under increased scrutiny. Creative ways need to be devised to make sure what needs to get done is accomplished without it diminishing our outcomes.

Conversation with myself: Looking back on the previous week, can I identify what activities prevented me hitting my goals? Were they worthy of the time they were given?

iii) I AM free from the fear of failure
The more I distance myself from failure the greater distance I put between myself and success

How much more would we set out to achieve if we lived unattached to a fear of failure? This fear causes us to shorten our leap and mute our shout. To live expansively is to realise that 'failure' is not only possible but inevitable. This is where our level of certainty needs to be like steel. If the weight of our conviction can be greater than the strength of our fears then we will progress in life.

Sometimes we will not get the outcomes we thought we would. So many times people have made a permanent decision to quit during the temporary feeling of disappointment. However, the voice of creativity welcomes failure as something that can to create momentum for future success.

Conversation with myself: What is the worst that can happen if I fail? What is the worst that can happen if I do not try? Whilst failure is never an aspiration it must always remain a possibility.

iv) I AM certain
My creativity is my certain path to my goal

A piano consists of 7 unique white notes and 5 unique black notes and can produce unique music without limits. Therefore how incredible is the creativity within a human being!

When creativity is at the table it creates not only the path to our goals but also the awareness and certainty needed to get there. Your identity as a creative champion means you can live by choice and not by chance. It is only when I make choices with a definite certainty that my future will be influenced. Without my creative belief I accept the predictability of my nature to do what I have always done and my goals will remain wishful thinking.

Conversation with myself: What predictable habits need to be examined through the lens of my creative nature?

v) I AM what I imagine
Your imagination forms your declaration

We underestimate the power of our words as a key part of our own creative ability. We will daily speak words over our lives that create negative outcomes and yet we still go ahead and say them anyway. We utter words such as, 'I am useless.' We would never declare that to be an aspiration and yet we make it a declaration. The winning conversation increases our self-awareness and makes us acutely aware of our creative ability. *My declaration forms my aspiration*

If you have ever baked you will know that you cannot put the ingredients for carrot cake in a bowl, mix it up and put it in the oven and expect to produce a chocolate cake! You cannot mix red and yellow and expect to get blue. The ingredients that are in the mixing bowl will produce the result regardless of whether you like it or not.

Our beliefs are the mixing bowl that produces our mindset. Our mindset produces our thought life and our thought life informs our life choices. See how important this stage of the conversation is. You need to make sure that your life-giving principles are going to produce the desired results before you start to bake your mind cake!

Conversation with myself: What do I imagine myself doing today? If I am not happy with the answer I need to change what I imagine.

vi) I AM original
I have everything I need to achieve the unique cause for which I am alive

We are able to create paths that make our goals possible because our goals are connected to the raw material of our potential. This means that my goals are not defined by others, including family members. My potential is unique to me. Whether my family members have been successful or unsuccessful, whether they are the kind of people I would want to be or not, the belief that I am unique and original means that my results are my business and not attached to the results of others.

Conversation with myself: What conclusions have I started to make about myself based on my life so far? My ultimate goal has the ultimate say about WHO I am becoming.

vii) I AM a constituent part
A lonely victory is no victory at all

A car engine cannot make progress on its own. The potential of the car is fulfilled when the other parts come together and become interconnected. The universe in which we live is finely balanced and fully interconnected. Each constituent part impacts another. Since you are part of this great harmony, your potential can only be realised when you believe that your life will make sense as you press into others relationally. Therefore understanding WHO you need on the journey is vital but so is how your goals interrelate to the goals of others. You will not get true synergy unless your win is a win for someone else. When your win is a loss for someone else, then the balance is tipped and your potential goals will never be realised.

Conversation with myself: Can I increase the impact of my cause my helping someone else achieve their goals?

viii) I AM designed to blend
I start life as an ingredient but I want to become a blend

Creativity is about blending the thoughts and ideas of many people together to get an expansive and ultimately better result. When I believe this I cannot then declare, 'I am not a people person.' If I am not a people person then I cannot blend. The result of believing I am designed to blend means that I work hard at trying to understand people. I cannot afford to be arrogant and proud believing that I am 'it' and everyone else should revolve around me. I need to believe that when together we create the blend we all get to enjoy the benefits.

Conversation with myself: If my life was a recipe, what relationships need adding for it to taste outstanding to the world around me?

xi) I AM optimistic
Optimism is a discipline not a feeling

People talk about optimism and pessimism like they are a personality trait. But these qualities are based in beliefs not personalities. When your future demands that you stay hopeful, then you become an optimist.

Nelson Mandela had to maintain confidence despite being in prison for 27 years. He said: "I am fundamentally an optimist.

Whether that comes from nature or nurture, I cannot say. Part of being optimistic is keeping one's head pointed toward the sun, one's feet moving forward. There were many dark moments when my faith in humanity was sorely tested but I would not and could not give myself up to despair. That way lay defeat and death."

Creativity is having a childlike optimism that is quick to shake off disappointments and move onto what is next. Winston Churchill said, 'A pessimist sees the difficulty in every opportunity; an optimist sees the opportunity in every difficulty.' All great leaders are optimistic because they carry a certainty of a future yet to be experienced and refuse to accept the world as it is now as what will always be.

Optimism is a discipline not a feeling. It becomes the script of our heart that surfaces under pressure. I love what Ralph Waldo Emerson says: 'Write it on your heart that every day is the best day in the year.'

Our optimism should be based upon the immoveable belief that we will achieve our goal.

Conversation with myself: Which area of my life has pessimism poisoned? What now do I need to be optimistic about?

x) I AM controlled by my future
Maturity is delayed gratification

The fulfilment of lifetime goals belongs to the person who can delay a feeling now for a greater feeling tomorrow.

If I offered you £100 today or £300 next year, which would you take? Would you delay the gratification of having £100 in crisp notes now for the £300 in twelve months time? You might answer that you would take it and then invest it. However, you would find it hard to find any investment where you could get a 300% return without doing anything.

The more you can delay gratification, the more likely it will be that you achieve your goals. Therefore is it vital that enjoy the future definiteness of achieving your goals now to give you the ability to go steady on your journey, not making decisions based on what your feelings demand now. When creativity is at the table you will be able to command a future feeling that fuels present choices.

Conversation with myself: If maturity is delayed gratification then which areas of my life have become immature? In what way do I need to grow up?

Learn to live with a future bias!

Day 49: The Winning Mood of Enthusiasm

Unlocking the power of WHY creates an enthusiastic mood

I am having the EXPANSIVE conversation led by the voice of creativity which means I choose to put myself in an ENTHUSIASTIC mood.

Enthusiasm is about intense enjoyment

Enthusiasm is not a mood you fall into but one in which you actively put yourself into. It is a positive disposition that you choose. When we carry a belief that everything can work for our ultimate good then it is amazing how we can enter a state of enthusiasm in even our toughest circumstances. We do this because we see them as contributing towards our ultimate goal. We can therefore change our outlook by attaching a negative experience or challenge to a positive goal. This gives us an intense enjoyment in life even when the darkest clouds are overhead.

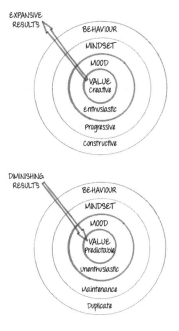

Enthusiasm is about clarifying the WHY

When we lose our WHY we lose our WILL. Have you ever suffered from a lack of will power? It is because we 'delight' in the

351

wrong things. We choose what our soul delights in, what it feeds on. If we embark on a new health and fitness programme and we lose the will to keep going, it will be because we have stopped delighting in the WHY of the programme. When we intensify the image of what we are going for then we unlock creative power in our lives which brings a delight in what is to come rather than what we are missing out on right now.

Enthusiasm is about believing in the mosaic of your life

We default to an unenthusiastic mood when we cannot see how an activity or experience has any purpose or any connection to what drives us. If we know we are lacking enthusiasm then we need to make the choice that our activities now will create another piece of the jigsaw that builds my future. At first an activity or challenge may look alien to our goals. However, in every day and in every situation the voice of creativity can see something positive that can contribute to the overall picture.

Think of a mosaic. A mosaic is created through tiny pieces of stone, glass or pottery that form a pattern or picture. Each piece can be very different in size or shape but it contributes to the whole.

Believe today that each conversation, each challenge and success is a piece being added to the mosaic of your life.

When we tie the smallness of life to the bigness that is inside of us we create positive tension that unlocks our potential.

Choose to be aware of your Soul Script

How I feel has a direct impact on the choices I make. While feelings do not and should not rule our actions, they exist for a purpose; they are an integral part of us outworking our beliefs and engaging with the world around us. Feelings need to be instructed and directed to fall in line behind our beliefs. They then become an asset to you winning in life.

Our feelings revolve around three major focus points.

1) How I feel about myself

2) How I feel about others

3) How I feel about the future

Let's see how these play out in relation to enthusiasm, first in relation to outside-in, then the inside-out.

OUTSIDE-IN

My mood is UNENTHUSIASTIC which tells me:

Conversation lead: Predictable

Conversation flow: Consumer

Soul appetite: Need Achievement

When PREDICTABILITY leads my conversation I am a CONSUMER and my lack of ACHIEVEMENT leaves me feel an overwhelming sense of being an UNDERACHIEVER and in an UNENTHUSIASTIC mood.

To feel like you are an UNDERACHIEVER is to feel unmotivated and lacking excitement about your life.

The script of the predictable conversation will shape our perspectives in such a way that we will be *Self-destructive, Me-obsessed* and *Now-focussed.*

Self destructive statements from a *predictable* belief sound like this:

i) I am subject to the control of my past
ii) I am what my environment says I am
iii) My value is determined by what has control over me
iv) My life does not matter
v) I am hopeless

Me-obsessed statements from a *predictable* belief sound like this:

i) I cannot change even if it is what others need from me
ii) I need others to congratulate me to fill my need for achievement
iii) Other people are there to help me achieve my goals

iv) I will focus on the goals of others once I am confident mine are on track

v) I compare with others to make me feel like I add more value

Now-focussed statements from a *predictable* belief sound like this:

i) My future is determined by chance
ii) My daily decisions are not that significant in the light of the bigger picture
iii) I have plenty of time to work towards my future goals
iv) One day I will feel satisfied that I have achieved.
v) My future looks better when I predict bad results for others

INSIDE-OUT

My mood is ENTHUSIASTIC which tells me:

Conversation lead: Creative
Conversation flow: Producer
Soul appetite: Full of Achievement

When CREATIVITY leads my conversation I am a PRODUCER and feel a sense of ACHIEVEMENT because I give out and produce an ENTHUSIASTIC mood.

Achievement is the result of your desire to accomplish something, to create a positive result that adds real value.

Feeling creative comes from the internal conversation that says, 'I am ambitious and I have to achieve three things:

i) Value Myself
ii) Value Others
iii) Value the Future

When my appetite to feel ambition is filled through immersing myself in life-giving principles I do not need external agents to motivate me. I am filled with possibility even if my circumstances look impossible. I exude optimism because I know there is always a way to achieve a different outcome and I have achieved it already through the potential in me. I just need to actualise it.

I can be ambitious without being reckless and can be calculated in my risk-taking. I am comfortable with steady progress because it allows time to express the answers that my potential says I have already achieved. The voice of creativity says, 'I have created your achievement already. You have passed the exam results. Dream big enough to exhibit the reality of your potential.'

Turning up the voice of creativity

When creativity is at the table of my internal conversation my external conversation has a 'can do' attitude. I will approach everything knowing the result needed is already achieved. I just need to work out how. This level of confidence is exciting and attractive. Great leaders operate with the creative voice at the table. Predictability is not allowed near the table of this person. No problem has determined the outcome because problems create the perception that they have the final word. But creativity has the final word because it can create a path past a problem every time.

So what does the new script sound like? It flows inside out and the voice should make the following kinds of statements:

Statements that *Value my future* from the valued belief of *creativity* sound like this:

i)   My future lies beyond the boundaries of the familiar
ii) My future is only limited by my imagination
iii) The future will not determine my worth but will reveal it
iv) I can stay the course and achieve the goal
v)   My future is not defined by failure

Statements that *Value myself* from the valued belief of *creativity* sound like this:

i)   I can add value through my ability to achieve
ii) I can multiply value in others because I have all the value I need
iii) Even if someone tries to diminish what I do I can create a future feeling that is stronger than the hurt
iv) Who I am is not what I do
v)   My achievements do not define me

Statements that *Value others* from an *creativity* belief sound like this:

i)   I can praise others because I know I add value
ii) I can invest in others because I am an original and I increase as a result
iii) I create better when I make it about us rather than me
iv) I need others so I will place high value on people
v)   There is creative genius in every person

Moment to pause: It is important that I create a time of reflection for me to identify my current soul script and make the necessary decisions to change it. The examples on this page are not exhaustive but are intended to help me discover the specific narrative I carry and make choices to change any outside-in statement as I seek to host the winning conversation.

Day 50: The Winning Progressive Mindset

High level focus through prioritising ruthlessly

When I choose the mindset of a champion, I prioritise what I give time to and I do so *ruthlessly*.

The progressive mindset requires me to determine daily to do the following:

1) Think of different ways of achieving greater levels of effectiveness
There is always another approach!

When the voice of creativity is at the conversation table I never have just one option. I always have a second option. Different options open up when we ask the right questions. The power of creativity is unleashed through the power of great questions like: 'If money were no object what would I do?' 'If someone came from another country and found this problem with no prior knowledge of how others had attempted to solve it, what might they do?' Such questions are signs of the progressive mindset. They can and should create laughter and fun. The presence of laughter and fun produces an atmosphere of expectation. Great ideas are birthed in such an atmosphere.

2) Keep my attitude flexible, like soft clay in the hands of a potter
My ability to adapt determines my ability to grow

A person's ability to adapt and change reveals how much they want to see a desired result. Creativity produces an attitude that is pliable like clay. I become inflexible and unwilling to change when predictability is at the table of conversation in my life. When creativity becomes the driver in my life I will find that I am incompatible with those who are inflexible in nature and unwilling to be open to positive change. Predictability is inflexibility. Clay needs water to stay soft and pliable; our attitude needs the fresh water of creativity to keep our mindset malleable. The results of predictability are themselves predictable; they do not change.

3) Protect the creative space in which expansive possibilities come
The margin for success is created through protecting our margin for creativity

I do not have to just manage the status quo. I can imagine a different result. Are you tired of your job, your standard of living, your opportunities for your children, the unspectacular results for your group or business? Predictability says you can expect the same but creativity says you can imagine a different future, that what you create at the level of desire can be made manifest through your activity. Lasting results are not accomplished overnight but if you commit yourself to the long haul, your creative identity as a champion will see that you get there.

Creative space is protecting time that allows you to imagine and explore the possibilities of 'what could be.' This time will never 'feel' urgent; however, the desire for improved results and outcomes is what causes you to make time. Creative space moves us from 'managing' to 'imagining.' Prioritising ruthlessly protects the essential space to think. The distracting thoughts of immediate pressures can hijack this time and rob us of the permission our minds need to relax and go wild. Free your creativity today through regular slots in your timetable for creative space.

4) Combine desperate determination with strategic planning
My desperation ignites my determination to follow the direction of my plan

Desperation without a plan is dangerous because rash and damaging decisions can be made. However, when I utilise the emotive nature of desperation and harness it to a long-term plan then I have the fuel for the long journey. If I am not desperate about anything then I am not thinking big enough. There is enough wrong with this world for each person to get desperate about one thing. Imagine what could happen if every person harnessed a desperation for transformation with a creative long term plan. You are creative and there is a large space called your destiny which is waiting for you to dream big enough to enter.

5) Embody the change I want to see as I shape a new culture
A change embodied is easier to emulate

Have you ever complained about the attitudes, behaviour or character of other people? To focus entirely on the person who needs to change creates a state of powerlessness. Remember the feeling of power that comes from creativity starts in you. You carry a power to change your environment and every change you want to see has to start with you. The more you intensify the change in your attitude toward the problem or person, the more you embody the change you want them to emulate. The most effective way to change a culture is to embody and exemplify the culture you want them to adopt.

6) Feed my focus in order to frame my goals with clarity
Focus management is more effective than time management.

Prioritising ruthlessly is not about fitting everything in but fitting the right things in. This is why it's more about focus management than time management. The first question I need to ask when prioritising ruthlessly is how much focus time I need to create. Focus time takes into account more than just the amount of time; it also considers the time of the day and the environment. Focus needs the right context because it requires the best of your attention as well as enough time to wrestle with the necessary aspects of your winning goal. Prioritising feeds my focus and the more I feed my focus the greater clarity and intensity I can give to the future I want to bring about. The more creative focus I can create the more expansive my opportunity for results becomes.

7) Create the environment for growth from small beginnings
The quality of your attention to a goal is like the quality of the soil for a seed to grow

I can multiply much from little so will not despise the small. To discount the small is like wanting to grow a forest and discounting the seed. The forest is in the seed. Your potential future is already growing inside you. You just need to believe it and create the right environment to grow it. When seed is placed in good soil and the atmosphere of warmth and water start to work, the miracle of multiplication begins. The formula is as follows:

Right seed + right soil = right results.

The right seed is the belief and certainty of a desire that is in you and the soil is the daily focus and activity that get to work on that desire. As you protect the environment from the weeds of distractions, over time the miracle of multiplication will take place. The voice of creativity never despises the small, because it will view the little though the tunnel of time.

Most positive and significant goals are not the result of one-off events. They are the results of lots of seemingly insignificant choices and activities over a prolonged period of time. Multiplication happens when all these micro-events go in the direction of the one big thing. While it may take some time working out what that one big thing is, you need to start getting the little activities ready to follow it. Over time you will clarify the big thing as you apply focus to all the small things.

8) Carve an original path through obstacles and problems
Problems are stepping stones along your path to fulfilling your potential

Problems are part and parcel of outworking your potential. You are an original and original opportunities usually lie within problems. If you are to reach the territory of your potential, you must first create a path through the undergrowth of obstacles and challenges. The closer you are to an original path, the more problems will be prevalent. However, if it is truly your path you will find that you are built to handle the problems. Do not worry when problems arise; they are opportunities that light up the path to expansive results.

9) Give time to unlearn what is preventing the winning approach
Creativity is a rhythm of positive deconstruction and construction of ideas and methods

Prioritising is about asking great questions that deconstruct practices and patterns of activity in order to construct more relevant and effective approaches. Regardless of age, background or education, you can unlearn what you have been immersed in through the voice of creativity.

What new business idea, song, book, cure for a disease, project, policy is in you that the world is waiting to see? Like a runner running a marathon, you need to get rid of anything that is going to slow you down. Future opportunities are often closed by past and present experiences. What habits, influences, ideas, environments empower the voice of predictability—the voice that tries to convince you that prioritising is a lot of effort for little return? Remember, creativity and predictability are mutually exclusive. The creative voice tells you that ruthless prioritising over time produces winning results. It is time to empower the voice of creativity to break predictable patterns because new results are waiting. While it is too late to change the past, it is never too late to start a new future.

10) Operate from a simple not an overcrowded environment
Overcrowding my life with commitments will kill my potential

In the 21st century we are blessed with so much and cursed with so much. An inability to select carefully what we take on board in our lives will result in creating distance between us and our winning goal. Your potential is like a car that requires a certain type of fuel; you need to fill it correctly if it is to work to its optimum ability.

The voice of creativity needs a simple environment. Think of any successful brand that is currently expanding and you will see a group of people who work extremely hard to keep it simple. Simplicity is not easy but it makes the journey a whole lot more enjoyable. When you know you can create the future you desire, what margin do you need to create in your schedule, finances and energy? When it comes to your LIFE Map, remember your resource to create expansive results is not going to drop out of the sky; it is going to come from how you apply your mind and attitude to what you have.

The way to squeeze creativity out of my life is to over-commit, overwork and overspend. We need to create margin in our lives that allows us to be creative. I do not get creative in expressing my love for my family, wife, community or business when I am simply rushing into the day to day activities in my life. Remember busyness is a form of laziness. It highlights that I am too lazy to stop and think, plan and prepare what needs to change or to spend time on what is essential.

Conversation with myself: Which one or two statements do I struggle to believe? Which specific belief must I stay aware of and practice in everything I do today? I must remember that in order to achieve what I want most I must be willing to tackle what I want to do least.

Day 51: The Winning Choice to Construct Imaginatively

Today we look at some practical ways to look at how you can develop the winning conversation that will make you MORE expansive in life. The more you inform the right choices, the more you activate the results.

It is a myth to believe that the more I do the more results I will see in my life. When the voice of creativity is at the table then the choice I make is to get better not busier. When we buy into

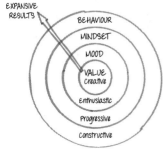

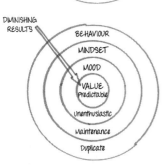

the lie that busy is best then we usually rob resource from other more important areas of our lives, believing it's a loan that one day we can repay. However, time is a currency against which we cannot borrow. For instance, when we take from our family time and invest in our work lives we can never have that time back.

If we are going to win in every area of our lives then we need to learn to construct imaginatively.

The quality of a creative process is determined by the quality of the questions we ask. A question can disturb and frustrate the voice of predictability that tries to perpetuate more of the same in your life. The more we embrace questioning the more airtime we give to the voice of creativity.

To get better we have to become more SKILL-full.

S.K.I.L.L means that I

SHARPEN THE AXE
KILL THE FOXES
INNOVATE WITH OBSTACLES
LEAD THROUGH OTHERS
LEARN FROM THE BEST

SHARPEN THE AXE

A woodcutter knows that his optimum results are not based on effort alone. He has to learn when it is the right time to stop chopping down trees and to sharpen his axe. If he sharpens his axe, less effort is needed to cut through the wood. He has to learn the rhythm of applying effort and sharpening his tool. Getting the right combination and rhythm sets the level of results he will achieve.

The belief that I AM CREATIVE comes when we understand that it's not 100% chopping trees; there have to be strategic pauses in the cutting in order to rest, develop skill and have space to question everything in order to find new ways of doing things and halt any unproductive and inefficient approaches.

During periods of evaluation and rest a helpful question to sharpen our thinking is to ask the question, 'What can produce more results with less effort?'

We can unlock creativity in our rest, development as well as our work lives. All of this will work towards keeping us sharp in living out our lives and pursuing our goals.

KILL THE FOXES

In ancient Biblical wisdom we are told, 'Catch for us the foxes, the little foxes that ruin the vineyards, our vineyards that are in bloom.' Cute little foxes are out to rob from your vineyard. There are lots of little activities in our daily lives that look harmless, just like the foxes. However, in reality they are eating our grapes. In other words, they are stealing the time and energy needed to produce the results we long to see.

What are the little foxes that are robbing our potential?

Procrastination
Distraction
Excuses
Escapism
Laziness
Over-promising
Negativity
Sarcasm
Lying
Poor Body Language
Disorganisation
Bad Manners
Poor comments
Independence
Lateness
Busyness

Identify and kill these foxes!

INNOVATE WITH OBSTACLES

Whenever you're confronted by a major hurdle, ask, 'Is this obstacle supposed to be my mountain to climb?' Just because we are faced with an obstacle does not mean we are supposed to climb it. If it is, then conquer it! The challenge is what will unlock the potential inside you.

Here are three statements that help us see that our obstacles are opportunities for innovation. With each statement there is an expansive question to ask.

i) My limitation is my direction

There are times when obvious limitations seem to deny us progress towards a goal. The person who truly believes that creativity is part of WHO they are enlists the use of their imaginations and resources to create motion in the direction of their goal. They know that limitations lead them to dig deep and mine the creative genius that is only unlocked through challenges.

Question: *Where is my limitation leading me?*

ii) My hindrance is my help

Sometimes a hindrance actually buys us creative time. We will live frustrated lives if we attribute a negative meaning to every challenge we face. I look back and see hindrances that in hindsight were positive because they prevented us moving too quickly in a particular direction and kept us from over-committing to people or projects.

If we let frustration creep in when we experience hindrances we can make poor choices out of desperation. Sometimes a hindrance is simply a 'pause' button being pressed.

I have heard it said that it's important not to make a permanent decision in a temporary situation. Frustration stemming from uncertainty can cause us sometimes to force decisions in order to get a feeling of assurance. However this could potentially create longer term damage.

Question: *In what way could this hindrance be helping me?*

iii) My disadvantage is my advantage

Advantage is about having favour in a certain area or with certain people. Disadvantage is about lacking favour in these areas.

We are naturally prone to identifying what we lack and what others have. This can cause us to want to give up and not pursue our goal. However, our disadvantage is simply an opportunity to focus.

Innovation is about progress. What disadvantage does is prevent us continuing in the wrong direction. For every wrong direction there is a right direction. I need to ask in what way my disadvantage can actually become my advantage. Creativity will always find a way.

Question: *When is my disadvantage my advantage?*

LEAD THROUGH OTHERS

If we are building a legacy that will positively impact the world then the most effective way of doing that is through our investment in others. There are people connected to us who are strategically placed to work through and multiply the results we want to see. It is important that we do not see this as simply using people to get what we want. Our approach has to be to put them first and seek to unlock their potential and uniqueness while giving them opportunity through which to develop.

This can be as simple as giving responsibilities to our children to work with a close team on a community or work project to achieve a shared goal. The sooner we realise that we are a cog in the wheel and not the wheel itself the more we get to play at being ourselves and also have the enjoyment of seeing others flourish. We create opportunity in life through creating opportunity for others. The winning life is all about the right order. If we put others first and we will not be short changed; in fact, we will experience extraordinary increase in the most important areas of life.

So regularly ask, 'Who am I connected to with whom I and they could achieve more?'

LEARN FROM THE BEST

The way we create skilfully is by keeping ourselves in the position of a learner. We must become hungry to learn. Learning is not simply acquiring greater knowledge and understanding to increase skills; it is the environment where we have permission to do things differently. We often carry a subconscious block to trying to do things differently. This comes from a default belief that 'I am predictable.' However, learning from others challenges that belief and causes us to reinforce the belief that I am creative and I can challenge everything I do in order to get better.

The expansive question is, 'Is there someone I can learn from that would cause me to look at what I do differently?'

Day 52: The Winning Evaluation

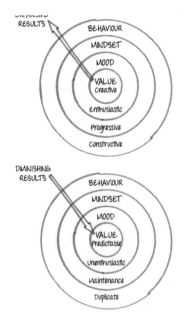

Benchmark which mindset you have when it comes to the EXPANSIVE conversation.

The fruit of my actions will reveal the root of the conversations I host. Today we are looking at ten questions based on situations we find ourselves in and I encourage you to be brutally honest as to which response most fits your nature. Tally up how many you answered according to which voice and make a decision to go back under the bonnet of your inner conversations to strengthen your foundation as a champion. If you feel frustrated then that is not a bad thing as long as you focus that frustration on making certain your commitment to hosting the winning conversation.

1) Frustration—How do you deal with frustration in your life?

Consumed - I allow the frustration to take the wind out of my sails. Frustration feeds a 'why bother attitude'

Complacent - How I feel and the environment I am in dictates how much effort I put into meeting people. If it's an environment in which I feel at ease I have no problem chatting to people; in fact it's a pleasant way to pass away the time

Competitor - I release frustration through quick wins to improve efficiency. I feed off increased busyness to give 'feeling of progress'

Champion - I step back and look at how the change in landscape could steer me onto a more effective path to achieving the goal. I allow the frustration to refocus me and sharpen my priorities

2) Distraction—How do you deal with distraction in your day?

Consumed - Distraction is an innocent trait that has no significant bearing on the future

Complacent - I get frustrated when I realise I have become distracted over a period of time and pressure starts to build because of deadlines and time pressures. I forget about the frustration once the pressure is off and then tend to allow it to happen again

Competitor - Distraction must be managed when it becomes a noticeable pattern

Champion - Distraction is a time terrorist out to kill potential and I am on high alert to prevent it from happening

3) Excuses—How do you view your excuses?

Consumed - Excuses are a personality trait that I have come to accept. They are part of my makeup

Complacent - The excuses I tend to deal with are those that others challenge me about. I live with other excuses because they seem valid to me

Competitor - Dealing with my excuses is important but because I do not seek accountability it is all down to how I feel. I am making some progress though

Champion - My excuses reveal a hidden trait that is eating away at my future. They need exposing and hitting hard. No mercy!

4) Goals—How important are goals to you?

Consumed - Goals make us mechanical and usually set us up to fail. Why waste your life feeling bad about what you haven't achieved?

Complacent - I tend to have points in my year when I am reminded by others how important goals are and when that happens I totally agree. I then tend to run out of steam and return to living in the moment

Competitor - Goals are good because they create tick-lists we can mark on our way to a well ordered life

Champion - When followed intensely, goals cause us continuously to dismantle and reassemble what we do

5) Creativity—How do you view creativity?

Consumed - Creativity is for people of a certain disposition

Complacent - When I have time on my hands I like to think how I can be creative with what I have

Competitor - Creativity is something I do in the extra time I may have when everything else is ordered

Champion - Creativity is the lens through which I view everything; it enables me to form my future piece by piece

6) Scheduling—What do you think about scheduling?

Consumed - I don't waste time on details like scheduling

Complacent - I have control of my schedule for a while but then I tend to just 'go with the flow' and do what feels right to do

Competitor - I get everything that can be done into a neat order. I like to feel in control of my time and that everything gets enough time. I am efficient

Champion - I build my time around a single focus and work hard to simplify. My aim is to do more by doing less, to be effective not just efficient

7) Busyness—Is busyness a good thing?

Consumed - I prefer to stay busy as it helps me keep my focus off deeper issues that surface when I have time on my hands

Complacent - Sometimes it feels good because things are getting done and I do see progress. However at other times I can get overwhelmed and tend to be more reactive than proactive

Competitor - Busyness is what gets my juices flowing. Being 'on the edge' gives me an adrenaline rush. However I do get frustrated that I am not progressing as far as I think I should

Champion - Busyness is a form of laziness. Sometimes life can get full when circumstances happen beyond my control but through planning and focus and building my life around a single focus I make any form of busyness work for me

8) Time—How do you view time?

Consumed - I never have enough of it and I would create another 24 hours in the week if I could

Complacent - I have just come to accept that I only have a certain amount of time to achieve certain tasks and whatever does not get done rolls over to the following day or week. This can mean that pressure mounts but I address that when it happens

Competitor - Time is important and needs to be managed. However, sometimes my desperation to hit goals means I am not in a rhythm and I waste time through lack of order and discipline

Champion - Time is the most precious resource. It is far more precious than money. Therefore I am strict about what I give it to as I will never get it back again

9) Achievement—How do you view achievement?

Consumed - Achievement is looking back at points and highlighting what has been positive and being thankful for it

Complacent - Achievement is for the driven and those who need it. As long as I enjoy life then that is what achievement looks like for me

Competitor - Achievement is about unlocking my potential and is something for which I strive. I have to be careful that I do not attach my self-worth to it

Champions - Achievement has happened because I have the potential. Therefore life is about actualizing what already lies within me

10) Investment—How do you view investment?

Consumed - I do not have enough patience for investment. Life is for living so enjoy the now and let tomorrow take care of itself

Complacent - When possible I try to invest but I tend to allow the demands of now to override any goals into which I am investing. I lose focus and therefore drive

Competitor - I am passionate about investment but can often lack focus about why I am investing. Therefore, deep down I know my levels of investment are not what they should be

Champion - Investment is the pathway to obtaining extraordinary goals. The key is to sharpen the clarity of the goal and stay passionate about the WHY. This helps me to avoid the temptation of trading the ultimate for the immediate.

PRACTICE V POTENTIAL of the EXPANSIVE conversation

Based on the answers to the above questions, how many times could you honestly say that your answer was 'champion'?

Consumer: 1-2 times
Complacent: 3-5 times
Competitor: 6-8 times
Champion: 9-10 times

My Overall POTENTIAL: I AM A CHAMPION

MY Overall PRACTICE: I HAVE BEEN A _____

In order for my practice to match my potential I have identified the following three things I can do to unlock the champion in me:

1_____

2_____

3_____

Day 53: The Winning Accountability

By pulling this whole week under the title of 'multiply and do not subtract', we are able quickly to review this conversation. Utilising the dice in spare moments throughout the day, or in a small group it helps to focus on the inner conversation of relevance.

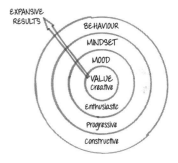

The Winning Dice—*Be a Multiplier and not a subtractor*

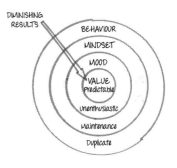

Our attitude which is driven by our values and desires will add, multiply, subtract or divide a community, group or even family. A champion is in the business of building. Our focus should always be on adding and multiplying so as to keep on helping others build bigger lives. A wrong attitude subtracts from a productive and creative environment and a divided belief system can divide a group of people.

The winning conversation creates the expectation that every person **aims to multiply** and demand from themselves **addition at the very least** as they work on the principles that bring multiplication. When a group of people all work hard to bring a lift to what they are doing the level of synergy results in extraordinary wins for the team and a better environment for every individual.

When as a team we are all devoted to one another and a common cause then the result is synergy which has a multiplying effect. Synergy is the belief that the sum total of the potential in two or more people is greater than the sum total of the individual parts.

Creativity is ultimately a belief that moves us from independence to interdependence. At the very least we are creating something for someone. At the very best we are creating something for someone with someone.

We will always get what we have always had unless we try alternative ways of achieving the common goal. Multiplication requires new methods to be discovered to achieve established goals.

There is more in you than you think. You have an expansive life to grow into and this comes as you embrace the stretch created by goals that require an intense focus and a resolute effort every day.

Step 1: RECALL together

Sometimes we need a quick review of what a multiplier not a subtractor looks like so we can stay on course to allow CREATIVITY to have the loudest voice drowning out PREDICTABILITY.

What does a multiplier look like?

- They are a big picture thinker who do not despise the 'little' things because they can see how they can become a lot through creative investment
- They believe their significance is in the bigger picture and not in the single part
- They always look to find a win-win because agreement has an exponential effect on what they do
- They look to find new ways of doing something in order to achieve greater results
- They process challenges with patience and passion
- They embrace challenge in order to bring stretch
- They welcome change because they understand you cannot do what you have always done and expect different results
- They understand that celebrating the success of others is a

win for the team
- They exhibit the principle of giving their first and best to their legacy
- They recognise that multiplication happens through people not tasks
- They seek to understand and learn how to delegate and empower others properly

What does a subtractor look like?

- Their main concern is protecting themselves
- They abdicate responsibility and seek to distance themselves from decisions that have been collectively taken
- They do not push themselves to contribute beyond a predictable point
- They seek personal recognition and promotion and are impatient when asked to simply carry on doing what they have been entrusted with
- They stay within expectations rather than pushing themselves to supersede expectations
- They allow personal issues to get in the way of the team spirit
- They do not deal with relational issues correctly
- They lack an appetite to learn
- They fail to learn from failure
- They respond negatively when challenged on their results
- They do not assume the best of others

Step 2: REVIEW with others

Get together weekly with people who are committed to developing the winning conversations through the journey of this book and ask the following:

i) Looking at the environment I was brought up in, can I identify what has contributed to my philosophy on this conversation?
ii) How do I feel when I am brutally honest about how I am doing with this conversation?
iii) How can I use that feeling to create momentum?

iv) What goals can I put in place to start creating quick wins that will produce a sense of hope that I am winning in the long-term?

v) Are there any relational alignments that need to happen to help me achieve my goals in this conversation?

Step 3: REFLECTION to be shared

Now create a reflection that you can share with someone in your group or someone else that you are coaching to be a champion in life. Why not take the time with your children, loved one, or a friend over coffee, and share what you have learnt. Simply sharing this reflection will accomplish much in your life and deepen relationships, enriching them with vulnerability and moments of movement.

Follow our basic structure:

i) What I realised for the first time/again this week is ... (share the thought)

ii) The change I need to make is ... (share the action point)

iii) Can you help me make it? ... (invite help and create accountability)

Once you have got into the habit of doing this, why not decide to turn your thoughts into a blog or even take your coaching to another level? There is so much in you and it is directly connected to your commitment to stretch yourself.

Section 9: Be MORE valuable

Day 54: The Winning Conversation makes you MORE valuable

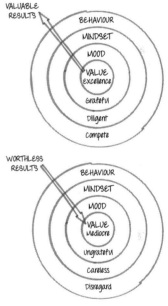

Let me introduce the voice of excellence to your conversation. A champion allows the voice of excellence to speak over the voice of mediocrity.

The definition of excellence is the quality of being outstanding or extremely good.[17]

You are priceless. We need to establish this truth from the outset. The truth is you are invaluable. A champion has an internal knowledge and belief that they are of value and while others may not recognise or verbalise it, it is nonetheless a fact. The potential inside each person is like a diamond—a mineral of enormous value that requires a process to bring it out. While the value you carry may not be clear you have to believe and maintain that you are this diamond. This belief will help you throughout a process that can be challenging and intense.

When I host the VALUABLE conversation I become:

1) MORE aware of my intrinsic value
What I do grows in value when I invest in valuing who I am

---

17. excellence. Oxford Dictionaries. Oxford University Press, n.d. Web. 10 September 2015.

Each of us is tempted to create the perception of value in our lives through external 'sparkle and shine.' We have many options available to us in the western world to create a shiny veneer through the cars we drive, the houses we live in, the clothes we wear and the gadgets we obtain. However this creates a pseudo-value rather than a personal experience of genuine value. Becoming valuable starts with a seed-like belief that 'I am excellent' and is watered over time through a valuable conversation that eventually brings the diamond of our potential out of the rough and into a place of prominence where its value will be obvious to all.

The result of the valuable conversation in your life is that when you walk into any environment your presence alone will add value. Without your presence an environment is poorer and people will notice when you are not there. You will receive comments from others about how your presence adds tremendous value. How this happens will surprise you, as will who says it.

Living with an outside-in approach leaves many feeling worthless when actually they are valued. However, the champion does not rely on the praise of others to establish their personal value. They draw on a consistent source of belief that 'I am excellent and therefore I am valuable.'

We are naturally tempted to compare and contrast WHAT others are doing and accomplishing in order to increase our own experience of value. This causes our self-belief and value to diminish because there will always be others who have an increased appearance of value. This is the poison of comparison. The less we believe we are excellent, the less value we produce. That we are excellent and therefore valuable has to become a solid, unmovable belief.

2) MORE in demand
Demand is created through demonstrating appreciation of an individual's needs

It is part of our nature to want to feel appreciation and value from the world around us. When someone shows us appreciation they become attractive to us. Let me give you an example. Two restaurants can serve the same food at the same price but if one creates an experience through which the customer feels appreciated, they will win every time. Feeling valued taps into our subconscious appetite. We buy into those who move us emotionally.

Value is set by supply and demand. The more demand there is for something and the less supply there is, the higher the value that thing has. If every human being has an internal appetite to feel appreciated and yet we live in a world that is often guilty of not meeting that need, then the more we produce appreciation through what we offer the more valuable we become.

Increasing the value placed upon others results in us being set apart from the majority. The more we value others through appreciation, the more outstanding we become which in turn creates a higher demand for us. Our value to others rapidly increases as the supply elsewhere decreases. To become valuable in the eyes of others you have to make others feel valuable.

3) MORE uncommon in our care
Excellence is to do an common thing in an uncommon way (Booker T. Washington)

If it is true that 'People don't care how much we know until they know how much we care,' then the more we can cultivate 'uncommon care' the more valuable we become to others.

So what would make us uncommon in our care? Surely it's a big act of servitude or heroism? Actually uncommon care is not about one-off acts but the compound effect of lots of little choices that consistently produce that feeling of appreciation and value in the lives of others. Likewise it is often the small unchecked choices that become the obstacle to others experiencing the value and appreciation that will attract them to us.

Over the next few days I aim to encourage you to create a clarity and intensity of desire that you are valuable and that this comes through a persistent and committed journey of valuing others. The results of unlocking this conversation in your life will produce promotions and opportunities you never imagined, as people experience and come into contact with the difference that you carry.

This distinctiveness derives from how you value yourself, the value you place on others and the value you place on your future.

The more value you place on this conversation, the more valuable you will become.

4) MORE commanding
Let your excellence command the attention of others

Some people seek attention; others command it. When I host the valuable conversation, the voice of excellence commands the attention of others without me having to say anything.

Personal excellence produces difference and difference commands attention.

Just as a castle on a hilltop stands above the town below, so your attitude, behaviour and character will command attention.

To many people the statement 'I want more attention' is likely to lead people to the conclusion that I am an 'attention seeker.' But not all attention seeking is negative. If a bomb was ticking and you needed to get everyone to vacate the area, is seeking people's attention wrong if you want to warn them?

A teacher needs to seek the attention of the class in order for pupils to learn. A parent needs to seek the attention of their children in order to create an environment for their growth, protection and development. An actor needs to seek the attention of an audience.

Seeking more attention is not a bad thing in itself. The issue is why we are seeking it.

Your life is an answer to a problem. You make a unique contribution to the world.

What use is this answer, this contribution, if it is hidden?

If you are to become the answer, then you need to stand out from the crowd and command attention.

5) MORE aware of what you sign off
Become a signature of worth

You are unique; an original work of art. Having the winning conversation is about my ability to reject my old signature and adopt my new signature. The old signature is cheap and common but my new signature is excellence.

In everything we do, imagine signing off 'excellence' and it will produce awareness and focus to everything you are and do. If you are not happy to sign off something you do with that signature then you should keep going until you are. Creating an intense belief that 'I am excellent' raises my personal standards and makes me increasingly reluctant to sign off on anything that is below my best.

The voice of excellence says 'you are a signature of worth' but you have to unpack what that looks like in every area of your life.

6) MORE fragrant
Become a fragrance that produces a smile

Have you ever hugged someone who carries a strong fragrance? Later you realise that you are now carrying that on your person. I have hugged someone and been left with the odour of smoke, alcohol and body odour. My reaction is usually a grimace. However, when that fragrance is a quality perfume it produces a smile.

Excellence produces an amazing fragrance that puts smiles on peoples' faces. Mediocrity on the other hand repels people. Every person has the seed of excellence in them. However, they need an inner certainty that they are excellent to break out of the powerful hold mediocrity has on each of us.

Your fragrance is the key to unlocking the doors of opportunity that are available to you. The fragrance that other people carry is also a critical factor. Look for those who are the 'real deal.' You can tell this by their smell. When you leave a person ask, 'What is the fragrance?' If you are left confused, disturbed, uneasy, then maybe you need to be careful how you interact with them. If they leave you wanting to improve and aim higher then the chances are they exude a good fragrance.

7) MORE popular
Excellence is the amplification for your story

Have you ever walked into a shop and needed some assistance but you cannot easily identify who works there? What I do is look for the person who stands out. They usually walk with confidence and carry a look that says, 'You can come to me and ask.' They give off a sense that they are the 'go to' person.

There is a message in you, a story to tell, which will make you the 'go to' person for certain people. The voice of excellence is about sharpening that message and refining that story in your life. A high definition TV is worth more than one with low definition. When the voice of excellence starts being heard, the story you carry and the solution you provide will move from low to high definition. These things become so clear and sharp that people are drawn to the screen of your life, even in a store of a thousand other screens.

Day 55: The Winning Voice of Excellence

To be a person of excellence I have to immerse myself in the belief that…

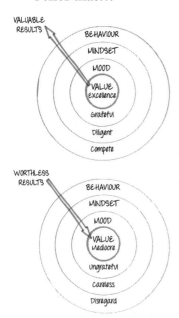

i) I AM not my limits
Limits reflect the size of a task, solutions reflect the size of a person

The champion does not pretend that limits do not exist but views them as temporary barriers that can and will be broken down in order for their personal potential to be displayed. Their limitation becomes their elevation through their perspiration. We can allow limits to define who we are but the champion carries a very clear understanding that limits are purely about my process and have no bearing on my value as a person.

When a champion carries the spirit

of excellence, they know that they can excel beyond any apparent limits that stand in the way of them progressing into all they are. In fact those limits enhance their value. Those who break through limits leave the majority behind and become uncommon people; they start to stand out because they are different. Difference creates value.

Conversation with myself: Which limitation is to become my next elevation?

ii) I AM extraordinary
A lack of distinction will result in extinction

What is ordinariness? The dictionary definition is 'no special or distinctive features.'[18] Ordinary is simply a perspective. I can try something for the first time and it can be an extraordinary experience. However, after trying it regularly it can soon become ordinary. Ordinary is a feeling and not a fact. A champion believes that while their life will project ordinariness to some, this is not a reflection of who they are. They are distinctive and they carry unique difference. They have something in them that sets them apart. The inability to describe our distinctiveness is simply an indication that we are in the early stages of incubating the winning conversation. However our relentless commitment to living the ordinary in an extraordinary way will reveal more of our distinction. Without my belief that I AM excellent, I will lack distinction. When it comes to having an impact on my world, my lack of distinction will lead to my extinction.

Conversation with myself: What is distinctive about me? What do I perceive to be different? Sometimes our distinctiveness is perceived as a negative attribute. However, the winning conversation helps us to celebrate our difference and not hide it.

iii) I AM a success
Success is the pursuit of your legacy before your lifestyle

Success for the champion is about the journey more than a

---

18. ordinary. Oxford Dictionaries. Oxford University Press, n.d. Web. 10 September 2015.

destination. When I carry a belief that I am a success and engage in success as a process there will be no shortage of 'successful' moments.

Before success is a WHAT it is a WHO. Even your biological status as a human being shows that you were successful. Out of all the millions of sperm that raced to the one egg that eventually created you, one made it—you!

However, what I am talking about is even deeper than biology. We are spiritual beings first and foremost. A champion carries the belief that they have already won. Excellence is the spirit of going beyond what is normal in order to work out the success that I am.

A champion carries a difference that sets them apart but they have to embrace the intense and often painful process of bringing the diamond out of the rough if that is to be clearly seen.

Conversation with myself: Does the pattern of the past few months describe my pursuit of a lifestyle or a legacy?

iv) I AM valuable
My value is raised as I raise my value of others

When you invest in others what you yourself want to experience, you will experience true value.

Writing this book I have hit many points of frustration, points when I thought, 'Is this really what I should do?' However, I discovered that the moments when I found it easier to write followed times I had invested what I knew into the lives of others. I realised that teaching and coaching moments created momentum in my writing.

Your potential is unlocked through adding the value of WHO you are and WHAT you carry to others to make them look good and feel good. This has to command everything you are about even when you do not have clarity on WHAT you should be doing in life.

There is something you can do right now to add value, so do it!

Get this in place and you will find that everything else you want will follow you and form around that consistent action.

Conversation with myself: What can I do today to actively demonstrate that I value someone? The value I will experience will create a desire to value people more often.

v) I AM my potential
Results are temporary, my potential is permanent

Being a keen competitor in sports I have experienced the joy of victory and the despair of defeat. The voice of excellence reminds me that my value is not determined from the outside-in. Therefore whether the most recent result is a defeat or a victory, the view I have of myself is measured according to my potential. A champion lives in the appreciation that their potential is not out there somewhere but resides within. Potential is a process that helps me avoid reliance on external results for a sense of wellbeing.

Conversation with myself: What result has dominated my thinking recently and created a lid on my aspiration? This may be a recent failure or success.

vi) I AM a mirror
My behavior reveals my beliefs

My potential is not about looking better than others but reflecting back the value that resides in others. The law of reflection says that more people choose you when you choose to highlight others more.

The most influential people throughout the ages have been those who existed for the benefit of others. They have not sought to be 'glorified;' they have used their position to connect the needs of others to the resource that they have accessed. A champion leverages their influence and value to help others access what they otherwise would struggle to get. They see themselves as managers of what they have been entrusted with and they have an insatiable desire to help others learn how to access the opportunities that life has for them through developing a winning conversation.

The moment being a champion becomes about how I look and

how I can be perceived the pattern changes from inside-out to outside-in. This is a pathway that is sure to end in destruction. It will destroy everything that cannot be bought such as relationships, spirituality, credibility and integrity.

Conversation with myself: Which areas of my life reflect a mediocre belief?

vii) I AM a bar-setter not a bar-settler
We will never rise beyond the bar of our expectations

The world's most influential and successful companies continue to go from strength to strength in a competitive world because they always push to raise the bar even when there is no pressure on them to do so.

The winning conversation requires me to understand where my benchmark is set. It is not set from the outside-in. The champion's drive for personal excellence is always inside-out. A person's default setting is to use the environment and people around them to set the benchmark of expectation. However, the more we host the voice of excellence, the greater our desire to push the bar to another level knowing that our number one competitor is mediocrity.

Conversation with myself: Do my relationships challenge me to raise the bar or settle for where it is? Which relationships have proved a constant downward force on my expectations in life?

viii) I AM responsible for my own sense of value
No one can touch or tamper with your value and promise

You can take a £50 note or a $100 bill, screw it up, spit on it, throw it in the rubbish bin but you will not affect its value. There is a promise attached to that note and what someone does to it does not change that promise.

Your life is like that note. It has a promise attached to it so that whoever interacts with it, value will be deposited.

My worth is set by my personal promise. Your life carries a promise that it will deposit worth into the lives of others.

The voice of excellence demands at all times that I carry a certainty of my intrinsic value and promise. Someone can treat me like rubbish, they can abuse and attack me, but they cannot touch my sense of value and promise. In fact the more someone tries to devalue me, the more potential the voice of excellence has to speak. The voice of excellence speaks louder to the world than the abusive voice of mediocrity.

Command the excellence that is in you to come out!

Conversation with myself: What behaviour has demonstrated that I do believe I am excellent? How can this inspire me to raise the bar in other areas of my life?

ix) I AM the King's speech
Mediocrity is an impediment that hijacks your message

The King's Speech is a film about King George VI who came to the throne in the wake of his brother abdicating. King George, otherwise referred to as Bertie, developed a severe stammer and went on a journey of trying to conquer his speech impediment. The film tells the inspiring story of how a man who was fully aware of his royal position and national responsibility tried to overcome his stutter so that he could speak clearly to his subjects as they faced a great darkness across the Channel.

Excellence is like a language we are able to speak but we must learn to overcome the impediment of mediocrity before we can truly have influence.

Excellence is a language that identifies those who are truly champions.

Let the voice of excellence lead you to place appropriate value on your life, the lives of others and on your future.

Let the voice of excellence produce an excellence of voice. In other words, let the voice of excellence in the conversation that is going on side you produce a voice of excellence in the conversations externally.

The voice of excellence commands an attention to detail

especially in the realm of the words we use and the tone in which they are presented. Words are powerful and as a person of excellence I choose them carefully.

Imagine you are going to propose to your loved one. You have spent all you possibly could on the ring and it is something of true value. However you wrap it up in cheap paper that is greasy and smells of vinegar. You get down on one knee and present the screwed up ball of paper to the person you want to marry. What you are giving is of true value but how you are giving it leaves a lot to be desired! Present it in a velvet box with gold leaf writing instead!

Our words are the ring; our tone of voice is the badly wrapped box.

This is the law of emphasis. Like the king's speech it takes time to get it right but when I do, my voice stands out.

Conversation with myself: Is it possible that my frustration with how others respond to me is down to my mediocre approach toward them? What belief do I need to change in order to improve my approach?

x) I AM care-FULL
The proof of my value is in the care I give

To appreciate means to fully understand and fully recognise the value of someone or something. It also means to increase in value. The champion is someone who takes enormous care to understand their full value and to increase that value in themselves and in others.

When a champion understands how valuable they are they then seek to add that value to their spheres of influence. They utilise all the resources available to them to see this value increased. They are careful not to waste time, energy and focus on the wrong things. They realise that what they do reflects their value to the world around them and so they commit the necessary time to a task in order for it to be done excellently. If they cannot commit the necessary time then they would rather not do it because mediocrity is not an option to a champion.

Like a gardener who carefully prunes the branches that are not producing life, the voice of excellence demands regular reviews of key activities so as to make sure the internal value of WHO we are is represented in WHAT we do. To be care-LESS is the spirit of mediocrity and the voice of excellence cannot tolerate it.

When the internal voice of excellence filters through the conversation of our lives, people feel appreciated. They feel appreciated through the conversations we have, the products we create, the lessons we teach, the businesses we run, the phone calls we answer.

Whether with strangers we meet in distress, a person needing our seat on a bus, we are care-FULL to show appreciate not to depreciate.

Conversation with myself: Which area of my life do I appreciate more now than a year ago? How has that impacted the other areas of my life? Which area needs more appreciation and therefore more care?

Day 56 — The Winning Mood of Gratitude

Unlocking the power of WHY creates a curious mood

I am having the VALUABLE conversation led by the voice of excellence which means I choose to put myself in a mood of GRATITUDE.

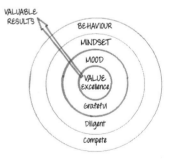

Gratitude unlocks the power of remembrance

Our memories can help fuel our future if we learn to use them correctly. When we access what we are thankful for in the past we tap into an oil well that never runs dry. When we think about the people, the places and the events that we are grateful for it helps remind us of our progress. So many

387

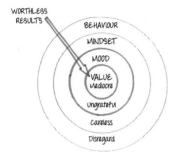

people look back with regret and fail to see the positive things that have got them to where they are. We all need to learn to become grateful for the negative things too. When we do it's like lifting up a gravestone only to discover that there is life underneath.

Everything in our past can play a positive role when we are in a grateful mood.

Gratitude sets us up for every day and for every situation. It is the mood that creates both a smile and a surge of positive emotion. When we are positive we are more productive.

Gratitude clarifies true value

In life we can easily drift from the course we think we are on. We can often drift away from what we truly value and make poor choices based on an incorrect priority system. What we are grateful for reminds us what we desire the most. When I stop to cultivate gratitude, the first place I start is with my wife and children. They are at the centre of my winning purpose. This immediately focuses me on WHY I am alive.

We are bombarded by messages in our media-driven world that promote values often at odds with what we truly believe. Gratitude resets our soul on what is most important.

Gratitude is a platform for possibility

When we cultivate gratitude in our day it's as if we step onto a higher platform that enables us to see further and grasp greater possibilities. Gratitude creates a lift in our soul that influences how we live out the day. Gratitude galvanises our willpower because we have tapped into what truly moves us.

Gratitude is a brilliant teacher

Gratitude makes the best teacher because being thankful automatically causes us to evaluate situations. In the process we learn about ourselves and what is most important in life. Time devoted to being grateful positions us as students of the past, setting us up in turn to apply the lessons needed for the future. When this causes us to express gratitude to other people we also discover what truly motivates them. We find that people long to feel appreciated and when they are we can unlock the best in them.

Choose to be aware of your Soul Script

Let us remind ourselves once again that our feelings revolve around three major focus points.

1) How I feel about myself

2) How I feel about others

3) How I feel about the future

Let's first see what happens when our soul-script is dominated by a conversation of mediocrity and secondly when it's dominated by a conversation of excellence.

The Losing Soul Script of mediocrity:

A champion carries a personal feeling that they are priceless. Unless I carry a belief that unlocks this level of appreciation for WHO I am, I will try and fill or top this appetite up from the outside-in.

My mood will be UNGRATEFUL which tells me:

Conversation lead: Mediocre
Conversation flow: Consumer
Soul appetite: Need Appreciation

When MEDIOCRITY leads my conversation I am a CONSUMER and my lack of APPRECIATION leaves me feeling an overwhelming sense of being UNAPPRECIATED and in an UNGRATEFUL mood.

To be unappreciated means to not be fully understood, recognised or valued.

The script of the *mediocre* conversation will shape our

perspectives in such a way that we will be *Self-destructive, Me-obsessed* and *Now-focussed*.

The old script reflects an 'outside-in' philosophy and prevents you believing you are excellent:

Self-destructive statements from a *mediocre* belief sound like this:

i)   You are deluded about your value
ii) You are not the person say you are
iii) You are the way you have been treated
iv) You are invisible; nobody wants what you have
v)   You are limited and you have to just accept where you are at

Me-obsessed statements from a *mediocre* belief sound like this:

i)   I will improve so I can prove my doubters wrong
ii) I will improve so I can get more value from others
iii) I will improve so I can feel better about myself
iv) I will improve so I can beat the opposition
v)   I will respond to others with the value they show me

Now-focussed statements from a *mediocre* belief sound like this:

i)   I only have to be excellent at what appears important
ii) I perform as good if not better than my friends
iii) There is nothing of value worth fighting for in my future
iv) My future will be more of what I have already experienced
v)   I am happy with what I have now so why change

We are often unaware of the statements that are informing our decisions. These statements are often feelings and so we do not quantify them in words. However hosting the right conversation means describing the feelings we have in terms of statements. Write them out and look at them in front of them. If you are not happy with the descriptions you have then you can change it by changing the belief, the command. Your feelings are subject to your beliefs, so if you are unhappy with your feelings then change your beliefs.

The Winning Soul Script of excellence:

When I carry an innate sense of value and worth regardless of what is going on around me then I can operate from the inside-out.

My mood is GRATEFUL which tells me:

Conversation lead: Excellent
Conversation flow: Producer
Soul appetite: Full of Appreciation

When EXCELLENCE leads my conversation I am a PRODUCER and feel APPRECIATION because I give it and produce a GRATEFUL mood

To be appreciated means to be fully understood, recognised or valued.

Feeling *excellent* comes from the internal conversation that says 'I am appreciated, I am valuable and I have it to achieve three things:'

i) Value Myself
ii) Value Others
iii) Value the Future

Turning up the voice of excellence

Living your life with an acute awareness of your intrinsic worth will have a profound effect on how the rest of your life unfolds. As you seek to take the value you have and invest it through the appreciation of others your value does not decrease but increase. It is like investing in a stock value that is guaranteed to increase. The more you invest the more you will have. This is because you are now operating according to the life's original rhythm.

So what does the new script sound like?

It flows inside-out and the voice should make the following kinds of statements:

Statements that *Value myself* from the valued belief of *excellence* sound like this:

i)   My value is set and is not determined by my performance or position

ii) My contribution is valued by me and not determined by others

iii) I am unique and cannot be replicated

iv) I am original and will appreciate the differences in others and not compare myself with them

v) My difference is my value

Statements that *Value others* from an *excellence* belief sound like this:

i) I will go the extra mile, beyond the standard shown me

ii) My value for others is based on how I would want to be treated not based on what I think they deserve

iii) I will give others beyond what my ordinary informs me

iv) I will place unreasonable demands on myself for the sake of others

v) I believe every person has an intrinsic value and my value increases when I emphasise this

Statements that *Value my future* from the valued belief of *excellence* sound like this:

i) What I do excellently will increase in value exponentially

ii) My excellence today is a step up to the opportunity of tomorrow

iii) My appreciation of others today will create connections money could not buy

iv) My daily improvements will create big shifts in my future

v) An act of excellence in one area of my life today will feed every other area of my life.

Conversation with myself: It is important that I create a time of reflection to identify my current soul script and make the necessary decisions to change it. The examples on this page are not exhaustive. I must discover my specific narrative and make choices to change any outside-in statement as I seek to host the winning conversation.

Day 57: The Winning Mindset of Diligence
High level focus through practicing relentlessly

When I choose the mindset of a champion then I demonstrate diligence through relentless practice.

My potential is unlocked through new beliefs that have formed new attitudes. It is not that I could not do it before it is that I did not have the belief and desire to unlock the activity. Now the voice of *excellence* is at the conversation table of my life, I feel *appreciated* and I know I can be *excellent* in practice.

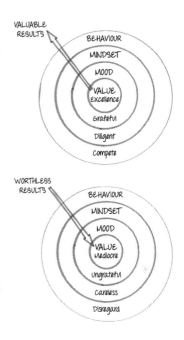

The winning mindset will determine daily to practice the following steps relentlessly:

1) Go one more step than I feel like going
My pain zone is my growth zone

When my feelings are no longer leading my beliefs, I choose to go further than I feel and raise my personal level of expectation. The moment I feel like I have reached the end I know that I have just entered the most critical phase of any activity. This is my growth zone, the place where excellence is demonstrated. I have a heightened awareness of my personal excellence and so I can keep going another step, whether that is another step of generosity, another exercise routine at the gym, another hour at work above my paid time, another conversation when I feel tired. Whatever the activity, I have the mindset that I will be relentless in going another step.

2) Pursue perfection without losing heart
My goal is my chase and not my prize

I know perfection is not attainable in life. However, I can pursue it knowing that the prize is excellence. Greyhound racing provides a good analogy. A fake rabbit is kept just ahead of the dogs and they are never allowed to catch it. Because they desire it, it produces their best efforts. There is nothing wrong with desiring perfection as long as we realise that the joy is in the process. This means moments of failure do not reflect on my self-worth but are simply signposts along the adventure. Failure is an essential part of the mix and reveals information not value.

3) Acquire a new taste for the process
I can learn to do what I least like to do in order to achieve what I have always wanted to achieve.

I am passionate about coffee but I never acquired a taste for it until I was in my late twenties. Now it is my favourite drink. The longer I have journeyed with it the more of a snob I have become. I no longer put up with 'any old coffee.' The reason I love coffee is because of the feeling of satisfaction I get when I drink it. This is of course the effects of the caffeine. I acquired a taste for a drink I never used to like because of the feeling it produced.

The mindset of excellence is to practice a discipline that will produce the most value. While the process or relentless practice may not be appealing, I can acquire a taste for it by my love for what it produces in and for me. At first it may be a struggle but I can acquire it and I will get a kick from what it produces in life.

4) Exceed rather than maintain my best work
Your 'next best' can always be found

There are sweet moments when you produce your best but that can be coupled with the bitter fear of not being able to better it tomorrow. However, excellence is a principle that keeps on giving when you keep on believing. My best work today becomes average tomorrow and because excellence is a voice of WHO I am it will produce a new level of results tomorrow. I must believe this and not allow fear to convince me otherwise. Remember fear is at the root of mediocrity. Shut that voice down and listen to the voice of excellence, you can exceed your best work!

5) Long to learn what I do not yet know
You learn about what you truly love

When you host the voice of excellence you develop an insatiable appetite to learn. Wherever you can get a lesson to improve you pursue it. When I practice I am actually learning and through its process I will uncover what I do not know. This then creates a clear need for me to go and find out what I previously did not know.

Think of something that is valuable to you. How did you acquire it? If it was a car you wanted to know everything about it, including how to maintain its value, how to get the best out of its performance. I guarantee you did your research because you learn about what you value most.

Develop an insatiable appetite for learning new things.

I have recently decided to carry a journal in order to make notes during conversations. I want to communicate to the other person that I can learn from them. I am also speaking to the voice of mediocrity: 'You are not going to get a look in on the conversation around the table of my life. I am excellent and I can choose to love learning, even in frustration.'

6) Love life with the simple wonder of a child
Simplify your life until intrigue has space to move

Have you ever looked at a child and thought, 'Wouldn't it be great to be that age again, having no cares in the world?' It is amazing watching children and how they appreciate the simple things. There is a running joke among parents of young children that you can spend a lot on a present and find that they will usually spend more time playing with the wrapping and the box than the gift!

A child carries intrigue. When we lose intrigue we lose our desire to learn. Intrigue flows from simplicity. I believe the voice of excellence is rooted in simplicity. We lose our appreciation of something when we over-complicate our lives. When we unlock the child inside us and regain a childlike love for the simple things we will start to get new perspective on how to go about living.

Some of the most influential companies now shaping innovation create play areas instead of bland staffrooms. They put slides in place instead of stairs and fake grass instead of carpets. Why? Because the spirit of the child is the key to simplicity and simplicity unlocks excellence.

Live in a less complex world and be excellent!

7) Go frequently beyond the expected norm
Create the response you want to see by planning to do something you don't normally do

People become familiar very quickly with what was new yesterday. Therefore if we want different responses in life, whether from the ones we love or colleagues at work, we need to supersede expectations. When we supersede an expectation we say in effect, 'You were worth doing this for.'

If we want to resonate with someone, we need to practice going beyond the expected norm. When an untidy child chooses to clean their room, or a husband who does not cook makes dinner for his wife, they exceed normal expectations. Do something today that goes beyond the expectations of those around you. Do this inside-out—in other words, because of an innate need to express your value of excellence. You can only do this when you host a valuable conversation. If you host a mediocre conversation then you are waiting for something outside of you to give a reason for doing MORE!

Practice superseding the expectations of those you struggle to serve, whether that is an awkward family member, neighbour or customer. The more you do it, the more in control you feel because you do so from an internal command to value, not from feeling like it.

8) Make an extraordinary and demanding promise
Our quality of life is determined through the promises we choose to keep

I was moved recently when I saw a ceremony where a schoolteacher won an award for an act of selflessness. One of his pupils became ill and he discovered that her kidneys had failed. When he phoned the family to see what he could do, they told him that she had been placed on the waiting list for a kidney donor. Before he realised it he had offered to be tested to see if he was compatible. Sure enough he was. He also made a promise that if he was compatible he would donate his kidney. If at that point he had decided not to keep his promise there would have been no recognition because an intention without action has no value. However, he kept it even though it was uncomfortable to do so. Consequently he was honoured at a national awards ceremony on national TV. That act became a story and that story now adds value wherever it is told. This is the power of excellence.

What extraordinary promises can you make that are uncomfortable to keep? Start today and begin to create momentum.

9) Appreciate those who are unappreciative
Quality is increased by practicing through resistance

When we decide to withhold our appreciation from others because we resent the fact that they have not appreciated us we are living according to the losing conversation. The only person we deny in this situation is ourselves.

True champions focus all they have on producing for others because they carry an intrinsic appreciation that is not derived from what is around them but from within. If we are connected to the life-giving principle of self-value then this underlying current starts to influence and direct our daily choices that in turn shape our destiny.

The moment you start to feel resentment towards someone who does not show appreciation is the moment you realise that your appreciation tank is not full. Keep on appreciating the unappreciative. Remember, inside-out is you choice regardless of what the other person does.

10) Perfect the art of surprising other people
Exceeding expectations communicates my value for others

We love to surprise the ones we love. In these situations we use surprise as a means of communicating value and appreciation. When a person is surprised someone will often ask, 'Did you see the look on their face?' It is this look that causes us deep joy. Practice without purpose is laborious. However, when we keep in mind the surprise that we can create on the faces of those who will get to enjoy what we produce we will always find the reserve to keep on going and not settle for anything less than our best.

Conversation with myself: Which one or two statements are going to be most difficult for me to believe, stay aware of and practice today in everything I do? I must remember that in order to achieve what I want most I must be willing to tackle what I want to do least.

Day 58: The Winning Choices of Competing Differently

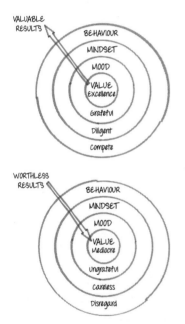

They say actions speak louder than words. This means that our actions and what they produce are part of our external conversation driven by our internal conversation. If we are committed to improving all we do based on an inner drive to express value and appreciation for others then we have to become strong on evaluation. The definition of the word *evaluation* means to 'make a judgement as to the amount, number or value of something.'[19] Unless we evaluate then we cannot measure the fruit that comes from the root of excellence.

You increase your value based upon evaluation. For example:

There are two restaurants you like to visit. They both produce your favourite meal, Spaghetti Bolognese. Restaurant A is consistent and produces the same result every time. This is not a problem because at least you know what you are getting. Restaurant B greets you by saying, 'We cannot wait for you to order Spaghetti Bolognese today. We've tirelessly been working on the ingredients and presentation since we asked how we could make it better the last time you were here.'

19. evaluation. Oxford Dictionaries. Oxford University Press, n.d. Web. 10 September 2015.

While you like both restaurants and both have a good record, which one gets your custom? Which will you champion in conversations?

Restaurant B! They have operated from a belief that they are EXCELLENT which means that they APPRECIATE you so much that they ask you how they can improve your experience with them. This exhibits their desire to improve what they do regardless of what anyone else is doing.

The areas of your life you EVALUATE are the areas you truly value. Here is a simple tool to evaluate what you do:

Expectation *exceeded*
Value *added*
Alternative *approach*
Limits *identified*
Understand *perspectives*
Adjust *immediately*
Teach to *improve*
Explore *imaginatively*

Expectation *exceeded*

Did I exceed expectation? Feedback is priceless. While it is possible to try and anticipate what was in the mind of the other person, there is nothing like hearing direct feedback. Not only does this help them improve but it increases the value that person feels because everyone loves an opportunity to be heard.

Value *added*

Would I have felt valued if I were them? Putting yourself in the position of the other person or someone you love is a great way of challenging our actions. It follows the golden rule to treat others as we would like to be treated.

Alternative *approach*

What or how could I have done it differently? Sometimes we can simply perpetuate the same activity and expect different results. Looking at alternative approaches helps to lift our thinking and keep us fresh in our thought process. It also gives permission to think outside the box.

Limits *identified*

Where were my limits and how could I push past these in future? It is important to be honest and identify limits. No one enjoys looking at limitations but it is vital to identify them to create a way past them now and to form a longer term strategy to overcome them in the future. If there is a financial limit to our action then it might not be something we can immediately rectify but we can use this information to feed our goal-setting.

Understand *perspectives*

What did I understand about the other person and/or myself through this action? Our actions help reveal a lot about ourselves and others and unless we take time to look at this then we do not best inform our future actions. If we are committed to improvement then gaining understanding is vital for building wisdom.

Adjust *immediately*

What would I adjust next time to increase the value of what I communicate? Future plans are good and vital but momentum is about consistent improvements. It is amazing to see the impact of accumulative improvements.

Teach *to improve*

Who could teach me and who could I teach to improve what I do? Learning is about being the pupil and the teacher. Placing ourselves in these two roles multiplies the rate of what we learn. Trending what someone else who is ahead of us does on the journey is vital. Find success and tap into that person's wisdom. Creating a teaching moment where you share what you are learning helps you to focus on what you do from a new angle. It also creates accountability because you have publicly committed to an expected standard.

Explore *imaginatively*

While incremental improvements are essential, it is important to keep approaching your desired result with a blank sheet of paper. Ask yourself, 'If I had no prior knowledge of achieving my objective, how would I go about doing it for the first time?' You cannot truly eradicate all knowledge but you can uncover hidden possibilities. Remember there is MORE in you than you think and there are different ways of drawing out the potential that has been locked up in you. You imagination is a powerful tool; it is like a dog pulling at the leash. Sometimes you have to unhook it and let it burn off some energy!

If we are not growing, we are dying. There is no middle ground. The way we keep any part of our lives growing is to keep investing fresh thought and ideas. This is innovation and we innovate what we truly appreciate.

Day 59: The Winning Evaluation

Benchmark which mindset you have when it comes to the VALUABLE conversation.

The fruit of my actions will reveal the root of the conversations I host. Today we are looking at ten questions based on situations we find ourselves in and I encourage you to be brutally honest as to which response most fits your nature.

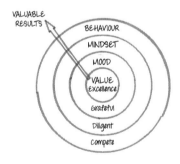

1) Satisfaction—When do you feel a sense of satisfaction in something you do?

Consumed - My satisfaction comes from completion rather than the quality of what has been produced

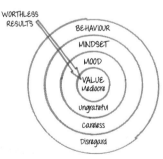

Complacent - Ticking an activity off a to-do list is more important than

how my activity represents and reflects on me

Competitor - I will sign off with 'That'll do' but will make a mental note to do better next time. Any loss in quality will be put down to factors outside of my immediate control

Champion - I will never sign off with the words, 'That'll do'. Whenever this phrase is thought or spoken, I either need to spend more time on it or shouldn't be doing it at all.

2) Perfection - What do you feel about aiming for perfection?

Consumed - Perfection is an unobtainable goal and therefore should never be an aspiration

Complacent - Perfection is an admirable yet unrealistic goal

Competitor - Perfection is a valid goal that produces my personal best

Champion - Perfection requires the narrowing of a goal to a size where all my energy and effort can produce exceptional results - the wider the goal the lower the quality of results.

3) Average—What is your view of an average approach to an activity?

Consumed - Average feels good. The feeling of not standing out is actually one that satisfies

Complacent - The avoidance of the bad is my overriding aspiration rather than the pull of the best

Competitor - Average is a point through which I grow and a baseline from which to work

Champion - Average is an attitude not a result. 'Could I have done better?' The answer is always 'yes'. Average is distasteful and jars against my belief system. It is better not to have done something than to be represented by average

4) Evaluation—What is you feeling toward evaluation?

Consumed - Evaluation involves unnecessary paperwork and creates a negative feeling. Ignorance on the other hand is bliss

Complacent - Evaluation is an aspiration and should always be attempted

Competitor - Evaluation is a deal breaker. Evaluation should be the Siamese twin of the activity

Champion - If there is no evaluation, there should have been no activity. Evaluation expresses value. What you evaluate you appreciate.

5) Comparison—What are my thoughts on comparison? Is it valid?

Consumed - Comparison is a valid activity because it gives me confidence that I'm not doing that badly.

Complacent - Comparison is something I struggle with when I occasionally raise my level of expectation. In fact it is one of the reasons why I revert back to having low aspirations. I do not like how it makes me feel

Competitor - Comparison is something I disapprove of but secretly do when I feel low. While it's not verbalised, it is internalised.

Champion - The only comparison involves how I am doing compared to how I know I can do. All other comparison is poison.

6) Innovation—What are my thoughts about innovation?

Consumed - Innovation is for the entrepreneurs of this world. It's not for me

Complacent - Innovation is an event not a process. It occurs sporadically when I want to achieve something special

Competitor - I wait for a crisis in order to be forced to innovate

Champion - Innovation is a key tool for personal progress. If any part of my life is not innovating, it is dying. Innovation is a discipline that releases fresh life into the day-to-day

7) Mistakes—What do I think when I make mistakes?

403

Consumed - It helps me to remember why I do not attempt to stretch myself too much

Complacent - Mistakes are a part of a life; I just have to pick myself up and move on when I make them

Competitor - Mistakes are a part of life and should be lessons. However, the lessons I learn are generic and not very specific. The potential of the mistake is not fully realised

Champion - Mistakes are diamonds in the rough. My mistakes reveal a lot about me. Evaluating my mistakes may feel painful but they can create a pain-free future

8) Failure—How does failure effect me?

Consumed - My failure becomes my reason for not trying. Raising the bar raises hopes only to be disappointed

Complacent - Failure makes me sad but after a few weeks the feeling wears off and I keep going

Competitor - While failure is not a goal, it is part of life. I brush myself down and press on toward a better outcome with renewed vigour

Champion - Failure becomes a strategic moment that can become as valuable, possibly more valuable, than a successful moment. I decide to use it rather than lose it

9) Feedback—How do I incorporate feedback into my life?

Consumed - What I do is connected to who I am. When someone criticises what I do, regardless of how constructive, it hurts

Complacent - If it is given to me I do listen and take it on board and try to remember the key points for the future

Competitor - I will receive feedback and use it to make me better. I only get defensive when I feel the criticism is given in the wrong spirit. However, I do not actively seek out feedback

Champion - I actively seek feedback because what I do needs to improve and is not connected to my self-worth. I can even use negative criticism given in a wrong way to improve what I do

10) Unappreciated—How do I act towards those who show a distinct lack of appreciation?

Consumed - When no one shows me appreciation it causes me to lose an appetite for trying. I cannot deal with the absence of value this creates in me

Complacent - It does affect me and it causes me to lose momentum. I can get bitter and the wind goes from my sails. However, that feeling will wear off but it does regulate the effort I put into something from that moment on. In fact, if I am honest, the level of appreciation I get sets the level of expectation I place on myself

Competitor - I can shake off a lack of appreciation quickly and I will still compete to do well but will disregard the person who does not appreciate me

Champion - My internal belief of excellence provides the stimulus to value even the unappreciative. I believe that it can have an effect on the person who shows a lack of appreciation even if they do not show it. Sometimes people have become the product of a value-starved upbringing

PRACTICE V POTENTIAL of the VALUABLE conversation

Based on the answers to the above questions, how many times could you honestly say that your answer was 'champion'?

Consumer: 1-2 times
Complacent: 3-5 times
Competitor: 6-8 times
Champion: 9-10 times

My Overall POTENTIAL: I AM A CHAMPION

My Overall PRACTICE: I HAVE BEEN A _____

In order for my practice to match my potential I have identified the following three things I can do to unlock the champion in me:

1_____

2_____

3_____

Day 60: The Winning Accountability

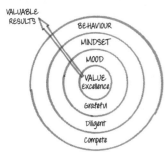

Pulling this whole week under the title of 'uncommon care not unchecked choices' enables us to be able to review this conversation quickly. Using the dice in spare moments throughout the day, or in a small group, helps me to focus on the inner conversation of excellence.

The Winning Dice—*Uncommon care not unchecked choices*

Create a personal culture that says, 'I make it my aim always to be careful and never care-less because I need to increase the value I place on people through my conversations with them in both word and action.' If the saying *'people do not care how much we know until they know how much we care'* is true, and I am all about people, then this is a non-negotiable axiom.

I want to be described as having an **uncommon care** in the transactions of my life. Credibility and reputation take a long time to build but can be pulled down in a moment with an **unchecked choice**. Maintaining an awareness of my 'care levels' is critical so I can make the most of every opportunity. How I maximise the potential of an opportunity is in my care-full handling of it.

Being care-full is about focus on detail. Failing to pay attention and being unfocussed has a wider impact than I will first realise. Constant neglect may not reveal obvious damage at first but its accumulative effect when not dealt with will become significant. The words, 'I couldn't care less,' are off limits. Regardless of how

I feel I **choose to be care-full** with my words because they have immense shaping power. They create my future and potentially shape the future of others.

Excellence is a conversation I have beyond my spoken words; my body language, facial expressions and my response to situations and people all exhibit my true value of self and others. Even when people irritate me and treat me badly, I care-fully take every opportunity to better myself and ask how I can do them good. When I feel forced, I force my feelings to do what is right. I am care-full because what I do impacts the people around me and everything I do reflects on those who back me.

I choose to be uncommonly care-full in my fun so as to be considerate of how others feel. I choose to check my choices to an uncommon standard because I am valuable and others need my potential value to be realised.

This chapter is shorter as it is designed to be more reflective so that key commitments and decisions can be made during a full review of the week.

Step 1: RECALL together

Here is a quick review of what a person with uncommon care and unchecked choices looks like so we can stay on course to allow EXCELLENCE to have the loudest voice, drowning out MEDIOCRITY. Here is a description based on what we have looked at this week:

What does uncommon care look like?

I respond rather than react in a situation in which most people would react
I refuse to allow a 'that will do' attitude to exist
What I do stands out; it becomes 'outstanding'
I show great consideration
I always seek to understand before being understood
I continually seek to do what I always do in new and improved ways

I carry out my commitments on time and beyond the expected standard

I learn to anticipate need rather than wait for a request for help

When I fail, I seek to learn why and use what I find as a lesson to improve

I am friendly in all forms of communication

I sign off well from conversations leaving others with a smile

I smile and am pleasant at all times

I smell good, look good and generally seek to present the very best that I have

What does an unchecked choice look like?

I will generally be disorganised

My desk and area of work will look cluttered

I procrastinate on jobs that need doing

I gravitate towards what I enjoy most but will leave undesirable jobs till last even if they then impact negatively on others

I lack awareness of how I come across

My work displays a lack of care which then communicates a lack of love (spelling mistakes, bad grammar, things thrown together etc...)

I am quick to comment but do not realise how it makes the other person feel

I am hit and miss on following through what I have committed to do

I fail to follow processes that are set in place

My work starts to be picked up by others and I continually lean on others to get things done

I am quick to acknowledge my own rights but will cause the rights of others to be compromised through my poor performance

I neglect to recognise context and talk about sensitive issues in the wrong places in front of the wrong people

I fail to respond to communications within a reasonable amount of time

Step 2: REVIEW with others

Get together weekly with people who are committed to developing the winning conversations throughout the journey of this book and this week discuss the following:

i)   Why is excellence uncommon?

ii) What examples can you think of that demonstrate the potential impact of unchecked choices left unaddressed over prolonged periods of time?

iii) Where could uncommon care potential take a person if it becomes a daily discipline?

iv) What goals could you set to raise the bar on uncommon care in your relationships, finances, health and vocation?

v)   Can you think of a recent situation when uncommon care and/or an unchecked choice created a noticeable result? How did it make you feel?

vi) What relationships inspire me to have uncommon care? Which ones do I have to be aware of that influence me to make unchecked choices? Do I have to make relational re-alignments?

Step 3: REFLECTION to be shared

Now create a reflection that you can share with someone in your group or someone else that you are coaching to be a champion in life. Why not take the time with your children, a loved one, a friend over coffee to share what you have learnt. Simply sharing this reflection will accomplish much in your life and deepen relationships, enriching them with vulnerability and moments of movement.

Follow our basic structure:

i)   What I realised for the first time/again this week is … (share the thought)

ii) The change I need to make is … (share the action point)

iii) Can you help me make it? … (invite help and create accountability)

Once you have got into the habit of doing this, why not decide to turn your thoughts into a blog or even take your coaching to another level? There is so much in you and it is directly connected to your commitment to stretch yourself.

Section 10: The Winning Momentum

Day 61: Winning gears 1

Creating momentum is a vital part of having the winning conversation. Life has ebbs and flows and never runs in a straight line. There are circumstances and seasons in life that we have to navigate. There are times when life feels like a motorway and you can cruise at a consistent speed and there is little to navigate. Then there are times when you leave the motorway either by choice or because you are forced to and you have to learn to navigate winding roads. The key is to know how to work through the gears, accelerating and breaking in the process. The same is true with the winning conversation. There will be times when it feels like you are making little progress but it is important to keep working your way through the gears, breaking and accelerating when necessary.

As we established on day 1, the winning conversation is all about order. We can get frustrated when we try and do the right things in the wrong order. When I take my children out for a bike ride I often forget that I have left my bike in a high gear so I jump on expecting it to be easy for me to get moving. Immediately I have to drop to a lower gear in order to gain momentum and then I can return to the higher gears.

Today I want to help us understand the gears that we need to move through. We will need to remember this every time we feel like we have lost momentum and outworking the winning conversation feels difficult. The chances are we have neglected the lower gears.

Gear 1:   IMMERSE—get in an environment.
Gear 2:   MAP—Make A Plan
Gear 3:   SHARE your plan with a coach

Gear 4: RESOURCE your plan: Rebuild your schedule, budget and energy around your plan

Gear 5: COACH and TEACH others: learn through teaching others. Start with those close to you

Gear 6: BUILD a rhythm to your life that seeks to help others unlock what is in them through your MESSAGE/ PURPOSE.

Gear 1: IMMERSE—get in an environment

Traditionally children have learnt to swim from around the age of 4 or 5 years. However, today more and more people take their children for swimming lessons when they are aged between birth and 6 months. Infants of this age have a 'diving reflex.' When immersed in water they spontaneously hold their breath, slow their heart rate by 20% and reduce blood circulation to the extremities. The top of their lungs is spontaneously sealed off and any water that enters is diverted to the stomach.[20]

When it comes to your life right now, the results that you see are the product of years of experience. Our experiences shape us. The other day my wife commented that since moving to London my accent is changing. I had travelled to London many times when living in the Midlands but it had not affected how I pronounced my words. I had been immersed in the Midlands for so long that day visits or even holidays to another place were not going to change that. However, after we had moved to London, the difference started to show after a few months. Different results are the product of immersion. I am now fully immersed in the new environment.

When teaching my children to swim I had to gradually encourage them to let go of supports which included the side of the pool, floats and touching the floor when they were doing lengths. The only way they could enter the new phase of being classed a 'swimmer' was to immerse themselves.

• 20. Page name: Infant swimming
• Author: Wikipedia contributors. Publisher: Wikipedia, The Free Encyclopedia.Date of last revision: 1 June 2015 08:41 UTC. Date retrieved: 10 September 2015 15:16 UTC Permanent

Immersion creates the awareness you need

The process of immersion produces lasting results. Have you ever wanted to buy a new car and you knew the model and the colour you were looking for? Did you see how all of sudden you noticed those cars in the same model and even colour on the roads? The truth is that all the study into the car created an awareness of what was already there. Immersion created awareness.

The opportunities that will help unlock your potential are all around you. Indeed, you may have walked past them many times a day everyday of your life. However it is an extraordinary belief that helps to see an opportunity no one else sees. That belief comes when we create awareness.

Immersion creates clarity

What is clarity? Clarity is sharpness of image, the quality of certainty. I remember reading the book the One Thing and the author Gary Keller encouraging the reader to read through their 'someday' goal in the morning and last thing at night. I read that and thought, 'Well, as long as I do it more than I do it now, that'll be fine.' However, every day I do not immerse myself in that clarity, I lose sharpness. It is that lack of awareness that is actually slowing me down and working against me. There are some books I have that I read time and time again. When I think, 'But you've read that and you know it,' I challenge that thought because I know it's the degrees of clarity that make the difference between good results and great results.

Immersing yourself in new content that feeds the principles of your belief helps keep the immersion experience fresh and enables new perspectives to bring deeper levels of clarity.

Immersion creates a new predictability

Is there a music album that you have listened to so much that in-between the tracks you start humming or singing the start of the following track? You have immersed yourself in it to the point that the pattern of the album is so marked in your mind that you almost do not need the CD to be playing because it's now playing in you.

Imagine if you could start to decide your predictable patterns? Rather than getting frustrated with what your standard defaults, create a new default through immersion. Immersion creates a pattern that others will know you by. The perception you have of the people in your world is the result of the patterns of behaviour you have observed both consciously and subconsciously. Who they are to you is the result of their patterns.

Think about the regular circumstances you find yourself in and how you respond or deal with those. What are you happy with and what would you want to change?

When we immerse ourselves in the principles that produce new practices, we create new rhythms.

If as an adult you throw yourself into a swimming pool and you are out of your depth you force yourself into a new rhythm, you may start to tread water and so an appropriate action is forced and your breathing regulates accordingly. This is what happens when you immerse yourself in a principle.

What you delight in, you drive deeper

When I was at school the worst sporting activity for me was long distance running. I could not see its value. However, now I am immersed in the principle of excellence which produces an appreciation for whatever brings improvement in my life, I love running. My value of the principle has led to a value of the practice of running.

I immerse myself in certain books that help me stay sharp in the principles that are going to create the right desires and therefore the right priorities and the right practices.

The principles of this book are now a part of my daily immersion. I have to stay aware of what I am naturally unaware of. Find the principles that produce the practices you want to see and immerse yourself in them.

Day 62: Winning Gears 2

Gear 2: MAP- Make A Plan

Assuming that you have been through the process of building your winning purpose, the key to building momentum in your life is how you engage with your life MAP.

If gear one starts with immersion, gear two continues that immersion through taking apart your plan and putting it back together again. The more times you take a car apart and put it back together again the more aware you become when something is not working as it should. You become aware of the significance of each part and its contribution to the overall purpose of the car. The more you engage with your plan the more you are committed to creating new experiences that drive deeper convictions and build greater momentum.

Create tension
More tension is created the more you engage with your goals

The more you expose yourself to the principle and the practice the deeper you drive the belief. The deeper you drive the belief the more fruit it produces in your life.

Whenever you feel like you are wandering or losing focus on where you are going, you need to 'get your life MAP' and 'hold the rope'. Create the tension that comes by clarifying your 'not yet' goal and your 'now' moment.

In order to know what to do and therefore create new experiences a plan is needed. Clarify what you want life to look like thirty years from now and then work backwards by clarifying what you need to do in order to make that a reality.

I have found that reading books like *The One Thing* by Gary Keller, *The Slight Edge* by Jeff Olson, *Seven Habits of Highly Effective People* by Stephen Covey, *Thinking for a Change* and other leadership books by John Maxwell, stimulates my thinking. I encourage you to find the books that help build momentum in your thinking because they create tension.

The winning conversation is about self-empowerment, understanding what you CAN do, what you HAVE now and challenging you to make a choice that you WILL follow through with action.

Conversation with myself: Questions to ask around your Life MAP:

Is there a goal that needs to be increased?
Is there a goal that I never hit but maybe by reducing its difficulty but increasing its frequency can start to build momentum in a certain area of my life?
Why do I have success/failure in this area? What does this reveal about a conversation I internalise?
Do I see the significance behind the goal I do not hit?
How can I build on the goals I have successfully met?

Gear 3: SHARE your plan with a coach

Who you share your plan with is really important. I have discovered time and time again that when a person increases their level of aspiration it creates two reactions. Firstly it will attract new people. Secondly, it will create tension with established relationships. When you raise your level of aspiration it creates questions in the minds of other people such as, 'What are you doing with your life?' Some people will be attracted because your new attitude and behaviour is giving them permission to dream and think bigger. However, the opposite will also happen; some people prefer the ostrich approach which is to bury their head in the sand and believe everything is okay. The reality is that life may be okay for others but your desire for MORE will cause insecurity to rise

There has to be a key voice or voices that are going to champion and challenge your progress. We all carry a 'doubting voice.' This voice questions our ability, our progress and our aspirations. We all have the ability to talk ourselves out of anything that tries to unlock potential. Therefore we need people who can talk us back into a correct perspective.

Sharing a plan also helps to sharpen it. Reading a plan back to yourself is one thing but having to explain it to someone who has not journeyed with it as much as you have is quite another.

Conversation with myself: Is there a different person that I could share my plan with that could bring fresh perspective and new impetus to my journey?

Gear 4: RESOURCE your plan: Rebuild your schedule, budget and energy around your plan:

Every plan needs resourcing. One of the greatest reasons people never follow through with a plan is because they believe they do not have what it takes to make it happen. Your resources are like seeds; they carry all the potential to grow into what your future will demand of you. However, they need to be planted and watered in order to grow into the future resource that will be required.

Your greatest resources are TIME, MONEY and ENERGY. It is really important that they clearly support your life MAP.

Another way of increasing momentum is by increasing investment in an area that we feel would align our lives to our purpose. When writing this book I hit a point where I knew I needed a surge of activity so I invested time and money in a week by the sea. This cost our family time and money but the investment paid dividends.

Conversation with myself: What investment has been lacking or needs to increase to build momentum?

Gear 5: COACH and TEACH others: Learn through teaching others. Start with those close to you:

Actively look for moments when you can talk about the winning conversation. The more you talk about it the more you create your own immersive experience. One of the most powerful challenges is to try and explain the principles to a child.

Albert Einstein reportedly said, 'If you can't explain it to a six-year old, you don't understand it yourself.' When you have to simplify a truth to a childlike level, you will gain a deeper understanding of the truth yourself.

The more people you explain truth to the more you deepen your own awareness of it. Every person carries an internal pleasure when they help another human being understand something new. Helping others understand the principles of the winning conversation will unlock a sense of enjoyment and purpose inside you that will intensify your desire to win in life.

Teaching moments do not have to be prearranged. There are always opportunities to encourage people. I have never heard a person complain about being 'over-encouraged.' When you see someone doing something that is worthy of praise, praise them. When you praise them do it in such a way that it reinforces winning beliefs. Encouragement is the single most powerful tool to create motion in a person's life, regardless of their age. The more you combine that encouragement with a reason, the more motion you create in a certain direction.

Conversation with myself: What teaching moments am I currently missing through lack of commitment or lack of awareness?

Gear 6: BUILD a life that seeks to help others unlock what is in them through your PURPOSE.

The final gear causes us to ask the question, 'How can I incorporate the winning conversation into my daily life?' Regardless of the sphere of life you find yourself in, the winning conversation can become a tool through which your personal development creates greater opportunities for you and other people.

Conversation with myself: Here are some great questions to ask on a regular basis:

How can I use the principles of the winning conversation to build the people who are around me on a daily basis?

How can I attach the principles of the winning conversation to the expectations placed upon me in my work?

How can the winning conversation enable me to go further and higher in the field in which I work?

How can the winning conversation simplify what I do and make what I do more effective?

What conversations can I have that will produce the results that are demanded of me?

I write on a large piece of paper, in no particular order and in random parts of the paper, all the demands that are on me for the coming weeks. I then stand back and view them like pins at a tenpin bowling alley. If I only have two balls to knock as many of these down as possible, how am I going to bowl? Sometimes one answer will unlock all and I get a strike. At other times it will take two. This process helps me to move from what I have to do to what I want to do.

The more I can connect the have-to's to something I really want, the greater the desire I will have and the more effective I will become. This is how we unlock the potential that is inside us.

Day 63: The Winning Awareness 1

It is what I am unaware of in life that is potentially sabotaging my ability to progress and realise my potential. To finish off our 66 day conversation I want to reinforce what I believe to be the attribute of a winner in life and that is awareness. The more self-aware I become, the more opportunity I have to take responsibility and make great choices.

I want to look at five things about which we must remain aware. When outworking the winning conversation there will be times when the only way you can describe how you feel is 'something is not quite right.' When everything appears to be in place but it still does not work, it is what we have become unaware of that is critical.

There are five usual suspects I have discovered that are the reason for this breakdown in my life working the way it should.

i) Soul Hunger
ii) Conversation Clashes
iii) Convincing Conmen
iv) Fear of Feedback
v) Fruitless Fights

i) Soul Hunger

All good parents have said first thing in the morning to their children 'You cannot go out on an empty stomach!' Why do they say that? What is it they know that the children don't? Why don't the children see the importance of eating at the start of the day?

A child by its very nature is not thinking about anything other than now. They have not yet had enough experience of what is feels like to be hungry half way through the morning.

When we do not feed our stomachs properly and at the right times then the quantity of what we eat goes up and the quality of what we eat goes down. The worst time to go shopping is when you are hungry. Subconsciously you are more biased towards food that can be made quickly and in higher quantities. Your buying choice becomes affected negatively. However, if you eat a good meal before you shop you will buy less and consider foods that require more preparation. The more preparation needed for a meal the more likely it is to have less of the ingredients that can be damaging to your health.

An everyday champion is aware of the six subconscious appetites. Every person has a need to:

Feel Affection
Feel Achievement
Feel Authority
Feel Acceptance
Feel Appreciation
Feel Assurance

These appetites need feeding but the question is where are we getting the food from?

There are only two sources for these appetites

1) What is external to us
2) What is in us

WHO is a source. When we have a lack of clarity on the WHO then this source becomes unavailable to us and we switch to our default of seeking to source all these things from other people and the circumstances and situations of life.

Our lives can be compared to a nation. Any nation knows that while importing goods from other countries is an option, it is risky because this source can run out. What happens if war breaks out in that country, or relationships breakdown with them and they cease to be a willing supplier? If a nation can drill deep into its own ground and find what it needs in ample supply then it can have a constant source at all times. This is critical for the prosperity of a nation.

The ability to dig deep inside oneself to draw upon a resource that feeds the feelings of the six appetites is critical to being an everyday champion. As we have discussed, we need to understand what that resource is. For me it is my faith and you need to establish your inner source.

The primary goal for the source

The source is not just so I can be fed but is so that I can be a producer for others. If you turn up to a buffet dinner and you are starving you are less interested in talking to people, making others welcome and letting others get to the table before you. However, if you arrive already satisfied, you can take or leave the food and you can focus on the experience of others.

Can you see how this could influence and affect every area of your life? If the teenager walks into a new school and knows nobody but feeds from an inner source of acceptance, they make better choices in terms of relationships. They do not jump into the first group that shows an interest. When the business man carries an internal sense of having achieved and is not in business to prove he can do something, he is able to be more selective over those he does business with because he is not starving to achieve. When we carry an internal sense of assurance we do not become risk-averse because we are driven by self-preservation. We have a source of assurance that provides the feeling of safety we need to sustain us.

When the new employee has an internal sense of authority based on WHO they are, they do not need to try and become someone they are not in order to be heard. They make positive choices out of a satisfied appetite. They make quality decisions because they are not starving.

Ask the question, 'Why am I doing this…REALLY?'

Our soul is a stomach that needs feeding and we can easily forget this when making decisions. Similarly, we can miss meals without thinking about it but we cannot escape the effects of physical hunger. Our energy levels do not stay the same just because we don't have conscious awareness of that hunger. We will be affected even if we are unaware, which is the most precarious position to be in.

A way to keep us aware is to ask ourselves a question when making choices throughout the day. 'Why am I doing this… REALLY?'

Asking WHY is not natural. We are HOW and WHAT focussed. We get caught up in busyness and often get lost in meaningless activity. This is robbing us of our potential.

There is also huge significance in the '…REALLY?' We are all excellent at pulling the wool over our own eyes, kidding ourselves about WHY we are doing what we are doing. The second part of the question reminds us of this and reveals a quality decision we are about to make or warns us that we are acting out of soul hunger.

Producer Verses Consumer

Your potential is linked to you being a producer of soul snacks for others. A champion wants people to experience their choices and think, 'Wow! That tastes good!' You want them to ask, 'What it different about you?' You do this not so you can look or feel good but so you can help them become all they can be. They become another source of supply for you. Remember there is MORE in you; you are not going to run dry. These are life-giving principles.

Your life is like a river; the greater the volume of water that runs through you, the wider the banks become. You may start as a trickle but every constant trickle becomes a stream and eventually a river and ultimately an ocean.

If the goal is to unlock the potential that is in you then producing for others has always to be the driving force; it has to be the WHY. The moment you become the consumer your supplying days are over and you are in fact at the mercy of your circumstances. That is a scary place to be because we all know how vulnerable we are when that happens.

ii) Conversation Clash

When my subconscious conversation has a different script to the script I am consciously trying to embed in my life I get conversation clash. What I feel becomes at odds with what I think and do. When I try to move in one direction but it feels like the other me is walking in the opposite direction this creates a negative tension. If I stay unaware of this challenge I can start to draw incorrect conclusions such as, 'This is just the way I am so I am going to stop trying,' or, 'I cannot fight any more. I am obviously not shaped to win.'

There are many people who have settled for second best in so many areas of their lives because they were unaware of the conversation clash taking place. It is like Jo trying to turn *LIFE inc* around from his position in the team room. Trying to usurp authority becomes a battle that in the end proved fruitless. I have experienced people who have tried to usurp control without having been given the authority. This is a manifestation of their personal conversation clash. They are unaware that they are working from a distorted reality and think the problem lies in everyone else not in them.

When we have disconnect between what we want to do and what we actually do it becomes like a rowing a boat with one oar; we create motion but do not move in the direction we desire. If you imagine your subconscious mind as one oar of a boat and your conscious mind as the other, you have full control over your direction when you make both work in sync with one another.

In the parable Jo was invited into the boardroom and given authority to change the belief system of the company. He was given both oars and so he turned the boat around.

Creating lasting results in the winning life is a deep process but in the end it produces conversation consistency. Creating a consistent conversation within myself places me in the strongest position to bring about personal change that will unlock the results of my life.

Living with integrity is rowing with both oars, allowing our external conversation to match our internal conversation.

Day 64: The Winning Awareness 2

iii) Convincing Conmen

It is so important that we are honest with ourselves and that we expose our deceitful abilities. We are masters of propaganda. We have an extraordinary ability to manipulate any situation or circumstance and to make ourselves look better than we are.

I look back at times in my life when I thought I was acting out of a right motive only to realise that I had duped myself into believing that to be the case. I was a naive victim of the conman within. It is possible that WHAT we do and even HOW we do it can give the appearance of a right motive when in reality it is the old WHY working towards the ultimate goal of me looking good and feeling good.

Whilst it is possible to create a right perception, the truth comes out in what we produce. For instance, a tree that is feeding from a contaminated source of water will ultimately reflect that in its fruit. It can produce an appearance of fruitfulness but fruit doesn't lie!

The problem is that is our wrong motive does not always look that wrong. I have spoken many times to many people over the years with the sole objective to help them understand truth. And yet more often than not I have left the stage and started to analyse how I was perceived and how I looked. If I felt negatively about it I would seek out compliments and get frustrated when they were not forthcoming. Can you see that my WHY was wrong? I took a noble activity—communicating truth—and made it about me. I should actually have been thinking, 'Did they understand it, regardless of how I looked or felt? Are they now more informed than before? Do they know what to do with the information I gave them?' The conman had struck again.

iv) Fear of Feedback

Becoming defensive reveals a motive. If my true motive is to help someone catch truth then I will seek out feedback that is helpful. However, when it becomes about how I feel about myself, ignorance is bliss. I only open my ears to what strokes my ego.

The biblical figure King Solomon was once faced with the challenge of having to judge which of two women was the mother of a baby boy. In the story we read, "The woman whose son was alive was deeply moved out of love for her son and said to the king, 'Please, my lord, give her the living baby! Don't kill him!' But the other said, 'Neither I nor you shall have him. Cut him in two!'"

How someone acts and what they do or say reveals their true motive and identity.

What Solomon did was to offend peoples' minds by suggesting something totally outrageous in order to reveal the true motivation that lay under the surface. His suggestion of cutting the baby in two actually separated the WHAT of the two women. They both made a plausible case in WHAT they were saying and HOW they were saying it. However, the offensive suggestion made by Solomon drew out the real truth.

The real mother through her willingness to sacrifice possession showed she had the new WHY. The woman who had the old WHY revealed the self-destructive nature of the old WHY. She was willing to allow everyone to suffer.

When our cause in life is to make ourselves look good and feel good it is frightening where that drive can take us.

v) Fruitless Fights

When offended, a winner is able to use this to strengthen the new WHY.

Someone pulls into a parking spot that you were about to use. What do you do? You are well within your rights to let that person know exactly what you think, even to ask him to move so as to let you have the spot. However, your energy is your resource and your inner peace is needed for a much higher calling. You know that to engage in such an offence, regardless of its merits, will absorb much needed emotional and physical energy. The mental space that will be used up thinking about it throughout the day will also cost you. Your WHY is to see that others look good and feel good so you let them have the parking space and calmly go for another spot knowing that the extra time to find a spot costs you less because you have not engaged in negative behaviour. In reality you have gained something positive because that experience has strengthened your inner resolve that you are not here to make yourself look good or feel good, but others—even if they do not appear to deserve it. In fact the more you do it for people like this, the greater the resolve you create.

I encourage you to think back to personal experiences where you have fooled yourself into thinking that your motive was right? It is important to do this because reliving the experience will move you and this means you are more likely to behave differently next time.

Offend the mind and you test the heart

Your heart or spirit contains the coding of life, the commands that produce everything that you see. Picture this: someone offends you. That man is now effectively fishing for something in the river of your heart, something more offensive even than the offence that he uses to make himself look better. But the river has had the rubbish removed and has healthy fish growing and living there. The fisherman can only find what can be used to help him grow—namely, food.

Can you see how the offence creates a reaction that proves where we are with our WHY?

If our WHY is healthy, an offence will only serve to confirm it.

We will not only be able to rise above it but actually use it to feed the offender!

The offender intended to put thoughts in our minds that would harm us.

But in the process he revealed what was in our hearts—a winning conversation that does not depend on outside-in means of gaining self-worth. Hearts that are free from the need for appreciation, affirmation, and acceptance from others are no longer full of rubbish. They are like healthy, unpolluted rivers, devoid of all the clutter and detritus of the person whose life is guided by a losing conversation.

Offence builds internal muscle that unlocks potential

We have all had fights, from light-hearted play fights to those that create relational distance. What is it that causes us to fight? It could be a sense of injustice, deep resentment, isolation or revenge. We allow something that happens to us to get on the inside of us. What is external provokes an internal reaction.

However, there are times when something happens to us and we are able to shake it off. Two people can react very differently to the same set of circumstances. So it cannot be the offence that is the determining factor in the response. It has to be what is inside a person. An internal decision is made by one person to fight while in the other a choice is made to reject the fight.

The size of the fight reflects the size of the person inside me. If I choose to allow a look, a comment or an offence to become my fight, that circumstance actually reveals more about me than the other person. If I choose to fight someone based on the fact their behaviour annoys me, then I am deciding that the energy it takes in engaging in the fight is worthy of such a cause. Do I really want that to be my cause?

What you fight, you become...so pick your fights carefully

I've seen people fight a small offence that has shaped their attitude not only towards the offender but everything else they

427

see. They remain oblivious to it but the fight they have chosen has shaped who they are.

A fight causes a person to engage every aspect of who they are with another person, circumstance or situation. No one ever walks away the same after full engagement in a fight. Why is that? It is because a fight demands engagement with our core being (soul and spirit) and whatever we engage with at that level shapes the lens through which we view the world around us.

Make sure you choose a worthy fight, a good cause.

You were born to fight and born to win!

Day 65: Momentum Killers and Builders

Momentum is easy to lose and can happen subtly because we are unaware of unsuspecting killers. Here is how to identify momentum killers and how to recognise momentum builders.

Momentum Killers

Losing sight of the goal

Hope is a human need. It is like a magnet to a piece of metal. It pulls us through failure and success, difficulty and challenge. The moment success or failure causes us to take our eyes off what we are hopeful for we start to lose momentum. The way to avoid this is to ensure that we spend a few moments at the start and end of our day, or even utilising any waiting time we have during the day, to focus on the goal that inspires hope in us. This creates a lift in the soul that kick-starts the flow of our internal conversation in the right direction, from the inside-out.

Conversation with myself: What can I introduce into my daily rhythm that keeps clarity high on my future goals?

Deciding not to decide

Waiting for perfect conditions is actually a form of fear and is a sign of an outside-in conversation flow. The problem is that it looks like the wise thing to do. Do not get me wrong, I am not advocating reckless decision-making where we ignore the conditions around us. However we can always decide to do something knowing that we will never have the perfect plan because perfection is a perspective anyway. When I decide not to decide and rationalise it as wisdom I actually advocate the belief that what is out there is stronger than my belief to bring change. It is actually a switch from a position of strength to a position of weakness.

Success is not a moment; it is the result of a long process and includes all the lessons that failure has taught me. Not to make decisions is not to allow for failure and the keys those experiences provide for me.

Conversation with myself: Have I dressed up my indecision as wisdom?

Contradictions left unchallenged

By now you should have identified that there are many contradictions inside us. A contradiction is defined as 'a combination of features, ideas or statements that are opposed to each other.' When we go fishing in the sea of our beliefs we have to separate the good from the bad, the healthy from the toxic. Redoubling our efforts just to do more can simply lead to disappointment if we do not understand WHY it is we struggle to break past a certain point. When we have that feeling of being stuck, it is usually a sign that we have an internal contradiction. We have a desire to do one thing but we end up doing what we actually do not really want to do.

This is like pressing fast-forward on the remote only to watch the film go backwards. It does not matter how hard we press it or how close we get to the television, the result will be the same because the remote is wired incorrectly. It needs opening up and the circuit board changing.

Conversation with myself: Is there a contradiction that I am accommodating?

Comfortable goals

Momentum is the about increasing motion and momentum is

created from tension. If we do not have goals that create a tension between the future and now then we will start to slow up. There is a danger in success that we start to believe we can take the foot off the pedal. It is important to celebrate success; it is necessary in order for us to enjoy the journey. However, we should not settle at that point. As soon as you do that you start to lose momentum. Anything not growing is dying. You can die in your success. Get fresh goals that create a fresh stretch and start to build momentum.

Conversation with myself: Can I stretch my goals further to create greater momentum?

Momentum builders

Momentum builders can come in disguise and so I have chosen to concentrate on the untapped potential that lies in some of life's negatives that we can take and use positively to create momentum.

Stress to strength

You will hit period of stress so it is important to realise that stress is an internal prompting to have a conversation with yourself. Our natural reaction with stress is to attribute blame on someone or something. While there will be contributing factors, we must realise that the way we build emotional and mental muscle is by understanding what it is inside us that is creating the stress in our lives. Changing external factors will likely be part of a solution but without self-analysis we do not learn anything about ourselves that can prepare us for greater responsibility and increase our capacity for what we can take on in the future.

When a factory produces a new product it will put it through a stress test. The idea is to understand what can be done to strengthen the product so that it becomes more durable and therefore of higher quality.

Conversation with myself: What strength can I draw from any stress that I am currently feeling?

Struggle to strategy

When we accept that the winning life will be a struggle we will not fall into the trap of self-pity and the belief that the situation is hopeless and there is no sustainable route to move us forwards. The struggle can be turned into a strategy that will increase momentum. A struggle is simply my potential looking for a way out. The greater the struggle, the greater the opportunity will be for your potential to flourish. Your struggle is asking you, 'What can I do differently to grow past this obstacle?'

When you hit the struggle, make sure you make time for a conversation with yourself and then with others that can bring a fresh strategy and a fresh approach.

Conversation with myself: What strategy am I not seeing that my struggle is prompting me to find?

Uncertainty leads to certainty

I have challenged and encouraged you to get a plan for your life. However, we know that life does not always go according to plan. When we do not have a response to uncertainty then it can spread through our thinking and deep into our beliefs eroding the winning conversation we have developed. However, uncertainty is an opportunity to create certainty. Uncertainty is another conversation starter; it asks us once again to get clarity on what we are certain about. Sometimes it highlights that we have not actually built our lives upon principles which are impenetrable. It can reveal that we have an unstable foundation that works fine when the weather of life is good but cannot be relied on when the storms of life hit us.

Uncertainty is a conversation prompt preparing a deeper foundation of convictions that will prepare us for a greater future. We become more convinced of what we believe during uncertain times than in periods of apparent certainty. Purify your convictions when uncertainty comes knocking!

Conversation with myself: What have I become more certain of through recent periods of uncertainty?

Crisis into compassion

One of the most subtle killers of momentum is when we lose our ability to feel for other people. In a consumerist society focussed on 'me, myself and I,' we can lose compassion when everything is going well in life. Our focus can be taken up with the goodness of what we are experiencing and we can become desensitised to the pain around us. However, the winning purpose is about a legacy of significance that exists to serve others and therefore we need to regularly check that our compassion levels are high.

The word compassion comes from a Latin word that means to 'suffer with.' Our ability to 'suffer with' others leads to us becoming people of significance.

When crisis hits us we suddenly become aware of what we have not been feeling. We are reminded of the fragility of life. It is often when we hit crisis that suddenly we are reminded of how others in this situation might also be feeling and also that there are always others worse off than us. When we turn that into true compassion, we enter a powerful place. Compassion often makes us feel weak and helpless but in reality produces clarity and resolve that will serve us in every area of our lives.

Conversation with myself: If I am not currently in crisis myself, is there another person's crisis I can step into that will stir compassion? Is there someone, something or somewhere that can build compassion and therefore momentum in my life?

Failure into future

In failure lies wisdom. Failure is a rich source of knowledge that can help us navigate our way forwards. While we may not be able to identify actual progress we can identify knowledge that can increase progress. What lies in my past failure that can prepare me for my future?

We must never allow failure to get into the boardroom of our belief. Our failure can inform our future but it must not be given the opportunity to predict our future. When we choose to turn failure into future, we can build momentum.

Conversation with myself: What failure have I filed away without using it to build my future?

Day 66: The Enjoyment of Winning

Enjoy winning

Life is to be enjoyed and not endured! If we are simply enduring it this is a clear indication that we are not hosting the winning conversation. The winning conversation is not designed to get you hyped up to live life through gritted teeth, striving for success. It is designed to feed a healthy rhythm that produces increased results over time. This book is not aimed at making you cram more stuff into your schedule; in fact, if you incubate the winning conversation, you will simplify your life. The winning conversation will cause you to work from a place of peace rather than a position of fear and anxiety.

The pace at which the world is moving is constantly increasing. The fast pace is driven largely by the increased desire and expectation for improved lifestyles. When our motivation for progress is unhealthy we can find ourselves operating at an unsustainable pace. We can end up operating from insatiable appetites that are never filled and whose results never ultimately satisfy.

Progress in technology is a two-edged sword. Whilst it creates efficiency through time-saving and improved access to more information, it also takes unhealthy amounts of our attention away from the more important things in life such as family and friends. Our drive to access the plethora of life improvements on offer has created an unhealthy willingness to work more to earn more, often to the detriment of our lives.

Does working harder and longer for a better quality of life achieve that result? Statistics would suggest not as more people suffer loneliness, depression, debt and family breakdown. All these are creating a fragmented society for generations to come. We have become occupied with the wrong priorities—outside-in rather than inside-out.

Winning from a place of rest

People want to go on better holidays to have a well earned

rest from brutal schedules. Their aim is eventually to retire with security and abundance. Ultimately people are working in order to rest! There seems to be something wrong with working harder to make more money to pay for a better rest. Have we not got it the wrong way round? Maybe we would work better and more effectively if we found a place of rest and worked from that! When you discover the life-giving principles of the winning conversation and operate on a 'full stomach' every day, work takes on a different perspective. Rather than joining the 95% who are working in order to achieve rest, you develop the approach of a winner—you work from a position of rest.

When the roots of our lives (the motives and drivers) are fed with the right beliefs, we are in a position to focus on one thing rather than all kinds of activities designed to feed our subconscious appetites.

If you have a computer or a smartphone and you have loads of programmes or apps running, the way to improve the performance of one app is to close down the others that are not adding anything of value to your life. Even if they are out of sight they are still operating in the background.

If you want give your soul a break, then focus on life-giving principles. Install and open this app and close down those that stop you accessing it.

The winning conversation is about regaining a childlike state in your soul—one in which you focus with wonder and passion on what really matters.

Build a winning future for others

The future is exciting and by now your appetite to unlock your potential through unlocking it in others should be insatiable. The future of the community we find ourselves interacting with can become a winning one if we start to believe that we can become a catalyst for others to win. Communities win when the people in those communities win. Every person deserves the opportunity and chance to win.

Is there an environment in which you could start to be a catalyst? A catalyst increases the rate of reaction in an environment without it changing in its substance. This book is a seed that I hope takes root in your life. I hope that the fruit of your life carries the seed of change. I believe your responsibility is to bring the positive change that happens in you into the environments and lives of those you interact with. As you start to sow the seed, who knows what harvest will be reaped!

Be part of the Winning Movement

We are constantly reminded of bad news in the world. Sometimes this can be overwhelming and can leave us feeling helpless. When we choose to do nothing in response it breeds apathy and lethargy. However, while we cannot do everything, we can do something. Together let us create movement in OUR world that will create movement in THE world.

What would happen if this pattern made its way into business, education, families, healthcare, government/political departments and the world of media, arts and entertainment? If you work in one of those areas then why not be a winning conversation representative, someone trained to help others become all they can be.

It is part of my winning purpose to equip an army of coaches who not only work the winning conversation into their everyday lives and environments but also have the opportunity to make a living from coaching. My goal is to help you realise your goal, to do what many view as unthinkable and build a career around a passion.

Conversation with myself: How could I be a part of this winning movement?

What next?

You are at the end of day 66. What is the next step of the winning conversation?

Tomorrow return to Day 1 and keep immersing yourself in the conversation and let's WIN together!

Visit GarethMorgan.TV to access the latest content and for ways you can be part of this winning movement.

Printed in Great Britain
by Amazon.co.uk, Ltd.,
Marston Gate.